In an Iron Glove

In an Iron Glove

AN AUTOBIOGRAPHY BY
CLAIRE MARTIN

Translation by Philip Stratford
Introduction by Patricia Smart

Harvest House
University of
Ottawa Press

University of Ottawa Press gratefully acknowledges the support
extended to its publishing program by the Canada Council and the
University of Ottawa.

We acknowledge the financial support of the Government of Canada
through the Book Publishing Industry Development Program for
this project.

LIBRARY AND ARCHIVES CANADA CATALOGUING IN PUBLICATION

Martin, Claire, 1914–
[Dans un gant de fer. English]
   In an iron glove / Claire Martin ; translated by Philip Stratford ; introduction
by Patricia Smart.

Translation of: Dans un gant de fer.
ISBN-13: 978-0-7766-0612-5
ISBN-10: 0-7766-0612-3

I. Stratford, Philip, 1927–1999. II. Title. III. Title: Dans un gant de fer. English.

PS8511.A84D313 2006   C843'.54   C2005-907012-9

Cover design and typesetting by Laura Brady

ISBN-13: 978-0-7766-0612-5
ISBN-10: 0-7766-0612-3

© University of Ottawa Press, 2006
542, King Edward, Ottawa, Ontario Canada K1N 6N5
press@uottawa.ca   http://www.uopress.uottawa.ca

Harvest House Ltd. was founded in 1959. University of Ottawa
Press bought its assets in 1995. Since then Harvest House has
been a collection of University of Ottawa Press.

Printed and bound in Canada

TABLE OF CONTENTS

Claire Martin

*E*ven though this is the first of her books to be translated, Claire Martin will not need much of an introduction. She is so vivacious, caustic and droll, and her life story is such a shocker, that you will be drawn rapidly into it and will soon be inextricably caught in its quite particular spell.

There are one or two points I would like to make, however. First, every word of this gruelling account is true. By some kind of institutional irony, this autobiography was awarded the Governor-General's Prize *for fiction* in 1966. Unbelievable, parts of it may be; but fiction it is not. The story is told with all the skill and finesse of an accomplished novelist, but Claire Martin has not tampered with the facts. And when you have read it you will appreciate how much more courage it took to tell the truth than to dress it up as fiction.

It was a book that had to be written. From the author's point of view, undoubtedly, as a kind of exorcism, but also from the point of view of the state of evolution and freedom of expression that Quebec society had reached by the mid-sixties. The harsh things that are said in this book had to be said — and could not have been better said than in Claire Martin's incisive and witty way.

Second, as regards the prime villain of the piece, the author's tyrannical father, I want to point out that it is no lapse on my part that his name is never given, that he is never referred to as "Father" but always as "my father," that his house is never called his daughter's home or that his photograph does not appear in this edition. Claire Martin's unforgettable full-length portrait of the man eclipses all need of further illustration; as for her reluctance to name him, the reasons for that will become increasingly clear as you read on in the story.

But, drawing on the translator's privilege of long acquaintance with the work, I would like to add this. It would be a mistake to see him merely as a kind of Dickensian monster. He is that, and Claire Martin never muddies her colours with self-pity or blurs the outline of her portrait with tenuous shadings of compassion towards her subject. But here again it is reality, not fiction, which sets the note. The father is a grotesque, the archetypal *pater tyrannicus*, but he is subjected to such close scrutiny that in the end, though we still think of him as a monster — a comic monster in the second half when some of his fangs are drawn — at another level we become deeply conscious of our own participation in the tyranny of parenthood. We become uncomfortably aware, if we have children, of all the unfairness we daily practise — the threats, humiliations, blows, ridicule and indifference — in short, of our own incipient monstrousness as seen in the unwavering light of a child's sense of justice. But it would be unfair here not to add that *In an Iron Glove* also gives us a piercing view of children's cruelty.

If I were to take up more time than I now feel justified, I would like to trace in detail, through this account of the first twenty years of Claire Martin's life, the characteristics, penchants and experiences that marked her out as a writer. It would be fascinating to analyze the growth of this vocation as defensive lying and tall-tale spinning, as compensation for multiple frustrations, as battle tactics, as dogged contrariness and as sheer zest for invention. But the reader will be able to collect these clues himself as he goes along. And will be able to marvel also, in the end, at the fact that such a crushing childhood could have produced such a talented, gay and vital person.

Claire Martin's memoirs were first published in two volumes, *Dans un gant de fer*, and *La joue droite* by Le Cercle du Livre de France, in 1965 and 1966, respectively. Subsequently, The Ryerson Press published them in English, in one volume, in 1968, under the title, *In An Iron Glove*.

PHILIP STRATFORD

Foreword

When I wrote this book, I thought I was relating a story that was typically French-Canadian, I mean facts that could not have happened elsewhere. Since then I have received a great many letters about it which remind me that mankind is the same all over the world. What I observed, suffered, admired, despised, loved is more or less the same as what my readers' letters tell me, wherever they come from. To be a child or a woman will always be like being destitute or coloured — a hazardous situation. And it seems that mankind is always very eager to point out that whenever anyone is strong enough, male enough, rich enough or white enough to persecute the weak, he will gladly do so. But people like that always have something ridiculous about them. And the weak look on and laugh.

CLAIRE MARTIN

Introduction

A best-selling memoir that recounts the author's childhood in a family dominated by a sadistic and violent father, as well as the dreary and humiliating years of her 1920s convent school education, Claire Martin's *In an Iron Glove* was one of the key works that heralded the arrival of the Quiet Revolution in Quebec. It also has a strong and clear feminist message, and is arguably the first example of what would become an important sub-genre of autobiography in the late twentieth century: memoirs of child abuse. Published in two volumes (Volume 1, *The Left Cheek*, in December 1965 and Volume 2, *The Right Cheek*, in September 1966), it won not only the Governor General's Award but the Prix de la Province de Québec and the Prix France-Québec.

The impact of *In an Iron Glove*, and the considerable controversy the book gave rise to, arose from the artful way in which Martin succeeded in interweaving the strands of her personal story with the collective experience of the Quebec people (and particularly of women) in the years preceding the Quiet Revolution. It was as if Martin's work was exorcizing a past still fresh in the collective memory. Readers and critics responding to the book in reviews, articles, editorials or personal letters to the author all had their own stories to tell and their own opinion as to whether the author was "exaggerating" or telling the truth in her revelations about the sacrosanct institutions of family, education and the Church.

By daring to speak in her own name about the reality of her experience rather than hiding behind a fictional mask, Claire Martin was also breaking a tradition of silence and conformity that extended to literary form. Not only were there almost no autobiographical works in Quebec literature at the time — and none by women — but literary and critical works were still propagating the idea that Quebec was a "matriarchy." Instead, Claire Martin presented her readers with a searing portrait much closer to the real and symbolic power structure of her society: that of a tyrannical father figure who, in an alliance with the clergy, crushes out all expressions of spontaneity or life in the children under his control. As well as being a perceptive observation of a historical period and of a particular society, *In an Iron Glove* — like only the very best of autobiographical writings — is a work of art in which an individual drama achieves universal significance through the power of writing.

LITERARY BEGINNINGS (1957–1965)

When her autobiography was published, Claire Martin was already a well-known writer, the author of a collection of short stories and two novels which had broken new ground in French-Canadian literature by their focus on the psychological complexities of characters living in a secular rather than a Church-dominated society. She would later say that she had consciously embarked on these fictional works as a training ground for the writing of the autobiographical work that she knew would be the most important story she would ever tell.

The name "Claire Martin" was a pen name, a conscious choice to adopt her mother's name rather than the name of her father — Montreuil — with which she had grown up. After the painful years of childhood and adolescence described in her memoir, Claire had worked for a while as a secretary in Quebec before being hired by a radio station. On May 8, 1945, as she recounts in her book, she had the memorable experience in her capacity as a Radio Canada announcer of informing French Canadians across the country of the end of World War II. It was to be one of the last announcements of her radio career, for after her marriage to chemist Roland Faucher in August of the same year she was required by CBC/Radio Canada regulations to resign. When she began to think seriously of writing as a career, she was forty-three, happily married and living in Ottawa, where her husband worked for the federal government. Her first published text, an essay on Colette that won first prize in the annual writing competition of the Société d'étude et de conférences in 1958, displays many of the themes and preoccupations that characterize all of her work, and whose origin in her own life would be revealed in *In an Iron Glove*: love and the obstacles to it, the failure of the couple, the aspirations of women in a male-dominated world, the hypocrisy and pretensions of the upper middle class. As well, the essay contains a description of Colette's use of language that anticipates many of the comments critics would later make about Claire Martin's own elegant literary style.

Over the next eight years Claire Martin became known as one of the most important writers of her generation. Her collection of stories *Avec ou sans amour* (*With or Without Love*), an ironic exploration of a multitude of situations involving personal relationships, won the Cercle du Livre de France prize for 1958 (the first time the prize had been given to a work by a woman). Her first novel, *Doux-Amer* (*Bittersweet*), published in 1960, adds depth to her analysis of love and of the "new woman" through the story of a successful

woman writer, Gabrielle Lubin, who throws aside a safe but pre-
dictable relationship with her adoring editor to marry a self-
obsessed younger man. In her 1962 novel *Quand j'aurai payé ton
visage* (*When I've Paid for Your Beauty*), she explores the conflicts
between sexual passion and selfishness, the need for independence
and the stifling and powerful constraints of bourgeois society.
While all of these works were generally well received by critics,
published in France as well as Quebec and eventually translated
into English, Claire Martin's resolutely modern and non-religious
worldview, as well as her merciless exposure of the hypocrisies of
family and society, were already perceived as a threat by the clerical
establishment, which controlled much of the literary institution in
Quebec. With the publication of *In an Iron Glove*, the murmurs of
disapproval would swell into a loud chorus.

Genesis of the autobiographical project

When it appeared in 1965 — a year of veritable explosion for
Quebec literature that also saw the publication of such other clas-
sics as Hubert Aquin's *Prochain épisode*, Marie-Claire Blais's *A Season
in the Life of Emmanuel* and Jacques Godbout's *Knife on the Table* —
In an Iron Glove was seen, quite correctly, as an eloquent expression
of the mood of the Quiet Revolution. But for Claire Martin the
idea of writing an account of her childhood went back much further
in the past, even (as she reveals in her memoirs) to the age of
twelve, when the trauma of the separation from her beloved grandparents, which her father imposed on his children after the death of
their mother, made her aware of the power of writing:

> All my efforts were trained on remembering every last detail,
> even the minutest, of a period in my life that was as irrevocably

over as if Grandfather and Grandmother had been dead. I began writing down endless notes and in so doing perceived, even then, that my childhood could be told as a story. So much so, in fact, that at the end of this book I could accurately write: *Beauport, 1927–Ottawa, 1966.*

In interviews given after the book's publication, Martin mentions the fact that she had always known that her childhood memories contained "a good story": "I always had the feeling of being surrounded by characters from a novel, very clearly distinguished between the evil and the good. Besides, every time I talked to my husband about my father, he would say 'He belongs in a novel!'"[1] The idea of writing the book as a novel was rejected for a number of reasons, most notably because, as the author notes, her experiences were so melodramatic and "unbelievable" that they would have made a very bad novel. In fact, she claims, the reality of her childhood was *worse* than the image she gives us in her memoir: "Everything couldn't be told, because some things were too enormous, too raw; because there are moments in existence where truth goes beyond what can or should be represented."[2]

The notation at the end of the autobiography ("Ottawa, April 1957–July 1966") alludes to the period of the work's gestation, not its composition. As already mentioned, Martin chose to perfect her narrative skills through her short stories and novels before undertaking her autobiography. But there were other reasons, more social and ideological than personal, that also led to the delay in starting work on *In an Iron Glove*. In a 1979 interview Martin claimed to have put off working on the book because she sensed that in the 1950s the time was not yet ripe for the sort of revelations she was preparing to make:

It was the time for me to write [my memoirs] and I was ready to do it. I'd been preparing myself for years. But I didn't want to publish them before people were ready to accept what I was saying, and in 1959–60 it would have been too early. They would have upset so many people that the book would have gone nowhere.[3]

A final consideration which almost certainly entered into Martin's decision not to publish her book earlier was one almost all writers of autobiography must surely have to take into account: the risk of upsetting or hurting the people one is writing about. While it is logical to assume that Martin began working on her memoirs some time in the summer or fall of 1962, after the publication of *Quand j'aurai payé ton visage* in April and a two-month stay in Paris in May and June of the same year, the first precise documentation indicating that she is working on *In an Iron Glove* is a letter to her sister Françoise dated January 19, 1963, in which she asks for information about their La Chevrotière ancestors. The lapse of time between that letter and the publication of *In an Iron Glove* — almost three years — is much longer than the time spent on any of her previous works. One wonders if it is entirely coincidental that Claire Martin's father — the sadistic and monstrous figure who towers over her childhood and her story — died on December 7, 1965, two days after the book's publication.

AUTOBIOGRAPHY, MEMOIRS, MEMOIR

As the reader may already have noted, the words "autobiography" and "memoir" (or "memoirs") are used more or less interchangeably when referring to *In an Iron Glove*. A word of clarification on terminology may still be in order, however. Is "autobiography" the proper term for this account of the author's childhood and adolescence, which ends when she is in her early twenties? Or would this story, which situates the author's experience very precisely in the context of women's lives in early twentieth-century Quebec, be more accurately characterized as the author's "memoirs"? There are reasons to argue for both of these generic categories, whose meanings have shifted over the centuries and are still evolving.

The word "memoirs" is the more ancient of the two, having been used since the sixteenth century (always in the plural) to designate "a written account a person makes of events he or she participated in or witnessed" (*Le Nouveau Petit Robert*, 1995). The word "autobiography" doesn't make its appearance until the nineteenth century, during the romantic period, when first-person writings focusing more on the life of individual authors began to emerge. Specialists of autobiographical writings usually maintain this distinction. Philippe Lejeune, for example, defines autobiography as "a retrospective account in prose made by a person of his or her own existence, stressing his/her individual life and, in particular, the history of his/her personality"[4]; while in memoirs, "the author functions as a witness: although the point of view is personal, the object of discourse goes beyond the individual; it is the story of the social and historical groups to which the author belongs."[5] In the late twentieth century, the word "memoir" (in the singular) became the term most commonly used in English, but not in French, to describe the now familiar examples of autobiographical writing which deal with a relatively brief period or a particular aspect of an author's life. "Memoir" is also a more "democratic" term than the other two, as the authors of traditional memoirs and autobiographies have tended to come from the ranks of the rich, the famous or the powerful.

In an Iron Glove fits into all of the above categories. It contains all of the traits present in traditional accounts of childhood and adolescence (a sub-category of autobiography): the genealogy of the author's ancestors, the portrait of the family, the various learning experiences of the protagonist, her attitude to religion, her discovery of sexuality, her friendships, her first loves. But this story of the author's slow growth towards inner and outer freedom is unimaginable without the critical perspective she provides on the institutions that imprison her: the family, the convent school and the larger society that upholds these institutions. Claire's reactions to the violence and sadism that surround her — from her initial terror and astonishment to the various survival strategies she devises — give the story its narrative and emotional power. But far from suggesting that her situation is unique, Martin insists on the representative value of her experience, inscribing her own story in that of her era: ". . . it mustn't be thought that I was the only one persecuted. Almost all of us were, each in turn, and each for her own particular reasons"; "Many of us who went through the system complain that our minds were left uncultivated. And what about the heart, then, what about the heart? The very word brought on a blush. Of shame. And of anger, too, often enough."

According to theoreticians of women's autobiography, this sort of fusion between the categories of autobiography and memoir is typical of the personal narratives of many women, whose sense of identity is often more "relational" than that of men, and who tend to describe their own lives through the prism of the important "others" who have played a role in their development. As critic Françoise Kaye notes, such a sense of "intersubjectivity" is central to the narrative structure of *In an Iron Glove*:

> The "I" isn't absent from [Claire Martin's] memoirs, but it has fused in some sense with a collectivity. Claire's story is also that of her sisters, whom we see and hear less often than the narrator, but who have, nonetheless, as much importance in the story as she has.[6]

LITERARY AND CULTURAL INFLUENCES

An avid reader all her life (she made her first attempt at reading *Don Quixote* at the age of five, when she discovered it among her grand-father's books), Claire Martin insists on the fact that all writing, even when it is autobiographical, finds its source in other writing: "All books come from other books. In order to write you have to read a great deal."[7] *In an Iron Glove* is rich in cultural references gleaned from a long familiarity with the Bible and the works of classical antiquity (a legacy of the otherwise mediocre education she describes in detail in her book), as well as with French literature and history. The titles of the two volumes, *The Left Cheek* and *The Right Cheek*, with their evocation of Christ's message of submission, are an ironic commentary on the supposedly Christian upbringing she received at home and in school. Claire's uncontrollable curls, which cause her so much anguish in her years at the convent, are compared to those of the Old Testament figure Absalom, a rebel whose escape is foiled when his hair is caught in the branches of an oak tree: "In height, breadth and thickness of mane, Absalom didn't hold a candle to me." When she sees one of her fellow students daring to appear in class with her hair cut in a boyish, flapper-type bob, she experiences "an extraordinary sensation, a sort of rapture, a confused joy, as if I had seen, as it is said in the Bible, my enemies reduced to serve me as a footstool." Allusions to French literature and to European culture, especially of the seventeenth and eighteenth centuries, are equally present. Claire emerges from her first confession "as proud as Artaban" (the heroine of *Cleopatra*, a seventeenth century novel by the now forgotten La Calprenède); a nun who has excessive "crushes" on various pupils is compared to Ninon de Lenclos (a seventeenth-century Paris libertine famous for her elegant salon); and another of the nuns has a facial expression that reminds the author of "a Hapsburg pout."

Among the twentieth-century authors Claire Martin has read and reread throughout her life, and who have certainly influenced her writing, are Colette, Gide and Proust, all masters of the first-person narrative. She has attested to her lifelong love of biographies and of the correspondences, private diaries and autobiographical works of authors like Julien Green, George Sand and Gide. As interesting to her as literary works are the lives of writers, in particular those of women writers like Colette, George Sand and the Quebec writer Laure Conan, who have had to overcome immense obstacles in order to succeed in a male-dominated literary world.

Literary aspects: the shape of the narrative

Although, as we shall see later in more detail, the impact of Claire Martin's book was indissociable from the scandalous nature of its revelations about her life and about Quebec society, and although the author herself insisted on the absolute accuracy of her story, *In an Iron Glove* is also a work of art, in which reality is transposed and endowed with coherence and meaning, very much a product of the unique literary vision of its author. Claire Martin is a master story-teller, and she tells her story with humour, even in its most painful moments; with great tenderness when she is evoking the people she loves and who loved her; and with unforgettable power when she is presenting scenes of physical and mental cruelty. And her style — limpid, precise and flowing like the classical French stylists she admires — was far from usual in the Quebec literary landscape of the period. *In an Iron Glove* is an important literary work because through her own story Claire Martin succeeds in speaking to her readers about themselves.

The overall structure of the work is chronological, with the first volume treating the childhood and the second the adolescent years of the author. Volume 1 covers the period from Claire's birth (on April 18, 1914) to the death of her mother, a month before her daughter's thirteenth birthday. Volume 2 continues the story until Claire is twenty, ending with the marriage of her sister Françoise, the first concrete sign that escape from the father's house is possible. Among the thematic dimensions that also structure the work is the epic struggle between Claire and her father, which is almost the stuff of fairy tale: the father a gigantic, menacing and yet ridiculous tyrant, towering over a small, innocent daughter with an "irrepressible giggle" whose only weapons are her intelligence, her craftiness and the knowledge of love she has acquired through long stays with her adored maternal grandparents. In the first volume, although Claire's independence of mind and stubborn stoicism give her strength to survive the blows inflicted on her, the power of the father remains unchallenged. The volume ends with a heart-rending account of her mother's death, made all the more unbearable by the fact that the father forbids his seven children any expression of emotion. In the second volume, although the cruelty and persecution at home and school continue, Claire evolves towards moral and intellectual independence. Now cut off from all those whose love has sustained her, she goes through a long period of dryness and bitterness from which she gradually emerges thanks to the solidarity of the Montreuil sisters and brothers, more and more effectively united against their father as they grow towards adulthood. The final words of the book — "He went on talking, but nobody listened." — are a mirror image of those that ended the first volume, and demonstrate the reversal of power that has taken place between the tyrant and his victims.

Another important literary dimension of *In an Iron Glove* is the overarching theme of love (and its absence). Present in all of Claire Martin's work, the preoccupation with love colours not only each moment of Claire's personal struggle, but also the book's devastating critique of French-Canadian society and its ideological and religious underpinnings. "In those days, it was pretty difficult to love in this country. It either made people laugh, or set their teeth on edge," says the narrator. This embarrassment about love, especially its corporal manifestations, is a symptom of the Jansenist mentality which pervaded traditional Catholicism, especially in Quebec, and which Martin characterizes with precision: ". . . no body, no heart, and none of the words that name them." Claire observes it and suffers from it not only in the hypocrisy of her father, an exemplary Catholic who beats his wife and children, but in the petty and rule-driven Catholicism of her paternal grandparents and in the values and behaviour of the nuns, who hate and fear the body, and who exercise their authority over their pupils through a variety of sadistic tortures. "When I look back on all those wretched years, I realize that the thing that was lacking in our convents was kindness," she observes. When she does encounter love and goodness in the convent, the little girl is overwhelmed with astonishment and gratitude: "It was the first time in that institution that I had encountered a truly human feeling, the presence of a real heart. I was enraptured. A fervent gratitude drove me on in my work, since it was all I had to offer"; "Was what had just happened really possible? Were there really sisters who could understand a little girl's heart, her preferences, her need of reciprocity? I wouldn't have believed it." Worn out by her sufferings and by the coldness that surrounds her, she enters into a state of emotional paralysis where she too is incapable of love: "I was almost incapable of feeling any more pain. I was nothing more than a bunch of nerveless scars." By showing the effects on one child of the spiritual and ideological climate of traditional Quebec, Martin goes far beyond simply providing a satiric portrait of her society. Her memoirs are, above all else, an appeal for love and a testimony to its healing powers.

NARRATOR AND PROTAGONIST

Autobiographies that recount a painful childhood represent by their very existence a reversal of the power structure under which the author formerly suffered, and in that sense they may often constitute an act of revenge. By writing, the author takes control over the persons and situations that oppressed her and represents them as she chooses. The opening paragraphs of Claire Martin's memoir dramatically demonstrate this reversal of power, with the author now speaking as an autonomous adult and her father in old age reduced to the status of a "wrinkled little creature . . . completely deprived now of the cruel strength that had once been both his pride and his master." While the first sentence of the book — "I have forgiven everything" — informs the reader that the author has gone beyond anger and the desire for revenge to a state of serenity, in which her overwhelming feeling for her aged father is pity, there is a major shift in tone at the end of this passage on the healing effects of time. The narrator states that she must now "put aside that pity" and "tell things as they were."

Some early critics of *In an Iron Glove*, commenting on what they considered to be the unnecessarily cruel portraits of the author's father and of the nuns who taught her, were skeptical of the author's claim of forgiveness. But a look at the contrasting portraits of Claire the protagonist (the little girl whose experiences constitute the "plot" of the book) and Claire the narrator (the mature woman who is telling the story) highlights some of the factors that make *In an Iron Glove* a work of art suffused with wisdom and serenity. In almost every sentence or paragraph, thanks to the ironic smile of the narrator, the terrifying past of the child is redeemed by a present in which reign good sense, intelligence and justice.

For the reader, the main focus of attention is on the experiences, thoughts and emotions of the author's younger self, brought to life with all of Claire Martin's talent as a novelist. Rarely has there been such a precise literary evocation of the terror of a child literally petrified by the power of an adult bent on humiliating her as in this passage where Claire must explain to one of the nuns after mass why she didn't go to communion: "My hands were moist and the blood hammered in my ears. . . . I couldn't utter a word. . . . I didn't have the courage either to tell the truth or to lie. Just enough to keep on standing there, a little outside myself, feeling the way you do just before you faint. Only one thought: *It can't last forever, there's nothing to do but wait.*" Sometimes the humour of the text comes from the naïveté of the little girl, incapable of figuring out what she has done wrong when her father or the nuns begin to rage at her; but this innocence also has a tragic resonance at times (as in the moving scene where, during confession, a horrified young Claire hears the priest enumerate a list of sexual perversions whose existence she could never have dreamed of). While the narrator sometimes smiles at the naïveté of the little girl she was and even judges her on occasion, she never expresses pity for her; and as a result the reader also, rather than feeling sorry for the little girl, is filled with admiration for her rebellious spirit.

As well as mediating the story of her younger self, the narrator is present in the text as the spokesperson for the author at the moment of writing. Her serenity and *joie de vivre* are evident, not just in the humorous way she speaks of her past, but in her comments about her present situation: "Life was to keep its promises quite differently, and far beyond what I was then asking of it." The writing of her memoir is a healing process, in that it allows her to reexamine her past and often to see it in a new light: to feel compassion for her father as she remembers how his children gradually became leagued against him, or to discover that there actually were some nuns who were capable of kindness.

Finally, many of the reflections of the narrator serve to universalize her own experiences, especially as far as the psychology of children is concerned ("A child doesn't just hunger after tenderness, caresses and presents, but justice"). Her comments on Quebec society, particularly on the educational system and on the situation of women, make her book an important document of social history. For example, she dares to admit that she was fascist and antisemitic at the age of twenty-five, and then proceeds to analyze in depth this mentality as the product of an education system that made students incapable of thinking for themselves: "Headed straight for eternity, face to face with God, no one else around, a little object in transit, I really didn't need to know anything, all I needed was to be a regular little bigot." Reflecting on the fate of her own mother and of other women within this system, and on the ferocious resistance to admitting women to Quebec universities in the 1920s, she observes: "We had no right to knowledge, either general or specialized. But yearly maternities, sleepless nights and dreary days, nursing children, washing, cooking, finished off with eclampsia or puerperal fever — no objection to that. Feminine vocation."

CRITICAL REACTION

In an Iron Glove was very favourably reviewed by most critics, who recognized not only the literary merits of the book, but the importance of its shocking portrait of the collective past. Gilles Marcotte, writing in *La Presse*, calls it "a true and a terrible book. Without any ornaments other than her style — as precise and colourful as in her novels — and with remarkable accuracy, Claire Martin takes us inside a world where the most naked cruelty is exercised without any restraint."[8] Jean-Éthier Blais notes in *Le Devoir* that the memoirs reveal the source of the ferocious need for love present in Claire Martin's novels, and admires the powerful portrait of the

xxviii • IN AN IRON GLOVE

education she received: "They are anecdotes of convent school, but Claire Martin tells them so well, with such a transcendence of hate and such inexpressible love, that they are little masterpieces. . . ."[9]

Critical enthusiasm was far from unanimous, however. Many of the literary critics writing in newspapers and periodicals at the time were members of the clergy or of religious orders, clearly unhappy with and even threatened by the book's exposé of the Church and the educational system. While almost none challenged the accuracy of Claire Martin's portrait of the past, they objected to what they claimed was her tone of "scorn," "condescension" and "coldness" and took issue with her claim of having forgiven her tormentors. Some were shocked by the author's lack of respect for the figure of the father. *Le Soleil*'s Clément Lockquell (a teaching brother) described the book as a "settling of accounts [in which] the father's hatred is surpassed by the literary vengeance of his daughter. . . . This is not a literary character but a real person she is executing."[10] The revelations about convent school life also gave rise to contro-versy. An editorial by Fernande Saint-Martin in *Châtelaine*, accusing Martin of "resentment (even if she claims to have gone beyond it) [. . .] We don't want to challenge the fact that the author really experienced all these things. But she enjoys wallowing in it too much,"[11] gave rise to several months of letters to the editor (March–September 1966) in which women passionately took sides (mostly in favour of Claire Martin's book) and spoke of their own convent school experiences. Several of these letters end with the vow that these women will not allow their daughters to suffer the same humiliations: "I will never send my children to boarding school"; "I suffered so much in boarding school as a child. Please, mothers, I beg of you, don't send your daughters to the nuns for their education. We have suffered so much from their bigotry."

Whether for or against the book, all commentators were united in recognizing the importance of the documentary aspect of *In an*

Iron Glove. Many joined their voices to that of Claire Martin in call-ing for honesty in confronting the past and for reform in the present. Poet Jean-Guy Pilon, writing in *Liberté*, expressed regret that "no document as powerful as this was presented to the Parent Commission"[12] (the commission of inquiry which led to the major educational reforms of the 1960s). Alain Pontaut's observations in *La Presse* give a good sense of the feeling of outrage against injustice Martin's book had awakened in her readers:

> This experience is not unique: in how many villages, in how many homes . . . It is therefore communicable. It includes the experience of many other women, other sisters, and considers it a duty to plead for them, to speak the truth, to denounce on their behalf the reasons for their devastated childhoods, their mutilated intelligence, their traumatized senses, their destroyed lives. Destroyed — and this is the worst of it — in the name of a religion of love.[13]

"It was in order to be capable of writing this book that I became a writer"

Shortly after the first volume of her memoirs appeared in print, Claire Martin confided in an interview that she was afraid that once the book was finished she would have nothing further to say as a writer. "When you come right down to it, I think I could have written only that and nothing more. I almost believe that it was in order to be capable of writing this book that I became a writer. There are even moments when it seems to me that once I've finished these memoirs my source of inspiration will have dried up."[14] On the whole, this premonition turned out to be accurate, for, with the exception of one novel — *Les Morts* (*The Dead*), published in 1970 and adapted for the theatre by Yvette Brind'Amour in 1972 — a full thirty years would elapse before she would return to the writing of fiction.

The years after the publication of *In an Iron Glove* were studded with literary awards for the book: the Prix de la Province de Québec (1966), the Prix France-Québec, shared with *A Season in the Life of Emmanuel* by Marie-Claire Blais (1966), and the Governor General's Award (1967). Philip Stratford's excellent English translation of the memoirs (reproduced in the present volume) was published by The Ryerson Press in November 1968, and well received by English-language critics. Jack Warwick noted that "Philip Stratford's version of *Dans un gant de fer* is a very good one; it reads like English and it reads almost like Claire Martin, which is no mean feat for an author whose brio is so intimately bound to the syntax and idiom of her own language."[15] In 1975, a two-volume edition of Stratford's translation was published by Harvest House.

In 1972, Claire and her husband Roland, by then retired, moved to the south of France, where they lived until 1982, at which time they returned to Quebec City. During their very happy years in France, Claire's only writing activity was a number of translations, including novels by Margaret Laurence (*The Stone Angel*) and Robertson Davies (*The Manticore* and *World of Wonders*). Roland Faucher died in 1986. In 1995 Claire Martin returned to writing, with a number of short stories published first in small periodicals and later in a much praised collection *Toute la vie* (1999). Since then, she has published four short novels: *L'Amour impuni* (2000), *La Brigande* (2001), *Il s'appelait Thomas* (2003) and *L'inconnu parle encore* (2004). In 2001 she became a Companion of the Order of Canada, and in 2005 a critical edition of her autobiography appeared in the prestigious collection "Bibliothèque du Nouveau Monde" — the first critical edition in the twenty-five year history of the collection to be devoted to a work by a living author.

In 2003, the periodical *Voix et images: littérature québécoise* devoted an issue to Claire Martin's work. In an interview contained in the issue, she looks back on the years since her return to Quebec and emphasizes the happiness of her life: ". . . I live my widowhood in a calm and peaceful fashion. I am a happy woman. If you have a disposition for happiness, I think you carry it with you throughout your life."[16] A few years earlier she had confided to a journalist in another interview that she hoped "to keep going at least until I'm 100."[17] At the time of this writing, in the fall of 2005, she is 91 and still the witty, contented and generous woman she has always been. Her next book is due to appear in the spring of 2006.

PATRICIA SMART

NOTES

1. Letter to Sabine Tamm, 16 February 1989 (Centre de civilisation canadienne-française, University of Ottawa). Except for the quotations from Philip Stratford's translation of *In an Iron Glove*, all of the French-language citations in the Introduction were translated by the author.
2. Alain Pontaut, "Claire Martin et l'exorcisme d'une adolescence," *La Presse*, 10 September 1966.
3. Françoise Iqbal and Gilles Dorion, "Claire Martin: une interview," *Canadian Literature* 80–83 (1979), p. 76.
4. *Le Pacte autobiographique* (Paris, Seuil, 1975), p. 14.
5. *L'Autobiographie en France* (Paris, Armand Colin, 1971), p. 15.
6. "Claire Martin ou le «je» aboli," *Incidences* (May–December 1980), p. 49.
7. André Ricard, "Entretien avec Claire Martin," *Voix et images*, Fall 2003, p. 19.
8. "*Dans un gant de fer* ou l'histoire d'un combat," *La Presse*, 24 December 1965.
9. "*Dans un gant de fer* de Claire Martin," *Le Devoir*, 30 December 1965.

10. "Un livre de Claire Martin: *Dans un gant de fer*," *Le Soleil*, 8 January 1966.

11. "On ne peut prêter aux autres ses souvenirs d'enfance," *Châtelaine*, February 1966.

12. "*Dans un gant de fer*," *Liberté*, January–February 1966, pp. 68–69.

13. "L'enfant devant les monstres," *La Presse*, 17 September 1966.

14. Jean-Guy Pilon, "Portraits d'écrivains," Fonds Claire-Martin, Library and Archives Canada.

15. Jack Warwick, "Translating Brilliance," *Canadian Literature*, Fall 1969, p. 82.

16. André Ricard, "Entretien avec Claire Martin," p. 15.

17. Robert Chartrand, "Et pourquoi pas le bonheur? Claire Martin," *Le Devoir*, 8 April 2000.

VOLUME 1

The Left Cheek

I have forgiven everything. Yet when I was twenty if someone had told me that I would forgive, and easily at that, I would have been really incensed. I clung to my hatred. Not a day went by that I didn't take it out and give it a good shake. Not to get rid of it. To make sure that it was still as fresh as ever. To hear the clanking of those old chains again. To convince myself I must never reach the point I am at now. But hatred and rancour are such useless things that even a daily airing won't save them from the worms. Of all commonplaces, the commonest is, I suppose, that time is the greatest healer.

Time — time for me and for *him*. During those last years he was defenceless, frail, pitiful, at the mercy of others as much as any child. It is too difficult to refuse a child forgiveness. He had lost all trace of violence and tyranny, even the memory of them, and he would have been very surprised to learn that we hadn't always loved him. He departed this life like a good father, content with himself and content with his offspring. All's well that ends well. The time when I couldn't imagine his passing except as preceded by dramatic recriminations now seems very distant. Recriminations? And who was there to blame? Surely not that wrinkled little creature, shrivelled to half his size, trembling, stripped of everything that makes a man — sight, hearing, muscle and understanding? Surely not that poor creature completely deprived now of the cruel strength that had once been both his pride and his master? At the last he inspired nothing but gentleness in us, that same gentleness that at the other end of his ninety years he must have inspired in his mother, as if the relationship between us had been reversed. I had always known he would live to he very old, built the way he was like a stone wall, but I had not foreseen that this longevity would leave time for pity to come.

When you have truly forgiven someone, when you have done it after long thought and not simply because you have forgotten — and blessed with a pitiless memory, I have forgotten nothing — when you have brought yourself to it without watering down your pardon with moral considerations, by which I mean that you pardon your father not as your father but as any human being who has offended you, when you have done all that, which is what I mean by truly forgiving someone, then you feel an inner peace that nothing can match.

At first thought the idea of forgiveness must seem to conflict with my decision to tell the story of my childhood. But the two things have nothing in common. No, my father really belongs here in these pages for he was one of those characters people speak of as being "right out of a book."

And now, if I want to tell things as they were, I must put aside that pity that came to me like a late visitor who rings at the door in the middle of the night, someone for whom you must set up a bed and make room, and who will be there to reckon with in the morning.

*   *   *

I don't know how old I was when I realized that in the house where I was born happiness would never be my lot. But I can say for certain that it wasn't very old. One day I discovered that everything was a mess and that I had actually known it all along, that I belonged to the species "child-martyr," and that the house was full of them. From then on I watched my childhood pass by with a sharp, unwavering eye, struck by a sense of the anomaly and monstrousness of it all.

Sometimes when I talk about this book I am writing, people say: "It's just folklore. You're making it up. Memory doesn't enter into it. One doesn't remember one's early childhood so precisely." With a twinge of envy I conclude that my critical friends had happy childhoods. A happy childhood leaves few memories. It is an even tide that carries along a host of little things: a day in the country, a favourite toy, a birthday party. But when every hour brings fresh cause to fear that today's miseries will be greater and more numerous than yesterday's, why then one's awareness sharpens and becomes horribly precocious. And, as a consequence, memory does too.

Hope grows just as keen. "When I'm big. . . ." But those tomorrows seem so far off and childhood seems so long that I often wondered where I should ever find the strength to wait.

Yet we were always told that these were the best years of our lives and we were just too stupid to appreciate our happiness. That was a familiar air, and we had the sense not to take it too seriously. Stupid we may have been, but not to the point of giving up hope that life had something better to offer. A child's hope, though its fulfillment may seem infinitely distant, and though he may find it impossible to put into words, that kind of hope is not just precocious, it is impregnable.

At any rate, we had no right to any opinion whatsoever. Those were the best years of our lives, and that settled it, once and for all.

The cruellest punishments were just part of our happiness. Spare the rod and spoil the child, and children should be brought up by an iron hand in a velvet glove. As far as that was concerned, an iron glove was slipped on over the iron hand, nor was the rod spared. No velvet anywhere: *Get up, get a move on, kneel, turn the left cheek, the right. Two iron blows. Shut up, you're happy.*

*   *   *

I was born on the 18th of April 1914, of a marriage between a tiger and a dove. You may think two tigers would have made a more dangerous pair. I wouldn't like to say. All I know is that I wish the dove had married into her own kind.

At twenty-three Mother was still single, and I imagine that they were beginning to worry about her in the family. Several young men from Montreal had proposed to her on her frequent visits to that city to stay with her cousin Antoinette Lafontaine, but she didn't wish to leave Quebec where her parents lived. At least that's what my uncle told me. It seems plausible and corresponds very well to the kind of girl she most certainly was.

I know the women of that generation all too well. In them, timidity, apprehension, the inability to face life, a fear of the world and of the hereafter reached a pinnacle. In earlier days, women, or city women at least, still breathed a little of that fresh air that circulated before the Victorian era. Grandmother, her sisters and sisters-in-law, though quite estranged from the spirit of Voltaire, were much more daring than Mother ever was. Their own grandmothers, to judge by the anecdotes I heard about them, were even more so. At the other end of the scale, my generation began to throw off the yoke. My poor mother and her contemporaries lived through what was really the most suffocating stage of the feminine adventure.

That adventure was, I believe, more painful here in Quebec than elsewhere, for despite our remoteness we were at the intersection of every reactionary trend going, situated right in the middle of the most heavily trampled crossroads in the history of bigotry. I spoke of the Victorian era. We all know what the world owes to Victoria. We were extremely well placed to get full weight of it. Add to that the "Puritan way of life" of the Americans, and the far from negligible influence of clerics from Brittany and elsewhere sent our way by a wave of French anticlericalism, immigrants who arrived firmly resolved to fight anything that might ever force them to move on again. And there you have us, true Quebec stock, and especially our women, starved for oxygen and parked in a place where romance had no scope whatsoever.

Mother was an intelligent woman. That didn't prevent her from being chronically terrified by all the bugaboos of the age or from accepting them as perfectly justified. I can see her setting the trap that life was to spring under her own feet. I see her cherishing her parents with a love more childlike than daughterly. I see her having very little disposition for the turmoils of passion, and totally unconvinced that the pursuit of earthly happiness is a legitimate goal. And I see her, too, quite persuaded that no woman has the right to escape the task that heaven requires of her devotion. The sacrificed woman was never so common as in those days. Almost every family, for example, had its "unmarried daughter" who stayed to take care of a feeble old mother or a bunch of orphaned young nephews and was taken quite for granted.

My father was a widower. His first wife, a poor girl named Laura, had died at the age of twenty-two leaving a little boy, Gérard. The child fell sick. A Jesuit priest, who also happened to be mother's confessor, was given the job of finding a mother for the child and a wife for the father. Nothing is more certain than that mother saw all this — the prospect of living close to her family, the sick child, the recommendation of her confessor — as so many signs from Providence. To make a long story short, my father was accepted.

I have often heard the story that on the eve of the wedding one of poor Laura's relatives came to see Grandmother to beg her to refuse my father while there was still time. This sort of move always comes too late to be effective. In 1908 it must have been even more difficult than today to break off a marriage the day before the ceremony. It was solemnized and the newlyweds set off on their honeymoon. They were back the next day without anyone ever knowing why, and Mother, it was said, "had a face like death."

I have no trouble imagining their life together before I was born. The principle of invariability plays a great part in such situations. I know for a fact, for instance, that Mother already knew what to expect by the time my eldest sister was born after ten months of marriage, that by then she had already been cruelly beaten, and that my father was already doing everything in his power to prevent her from seeing Grandmother and Grandfather.

After six years, the tiger and the dove had four little ones of whom I was the youngest.

*   *   *

My earliest memory, when I was two years old, is a charming one. Very vague but charming. And that's a blessing. Had I remembered a little less, the second memory would have replaced the first, and that would have been a sad beginning indeed.

I have always had kinky hair. And to this day, that head of hair has always been an affliction. It earned me persecutions from the convent nuns, the envy of straight-haired schoolmates and the scorn of the hairdresser. To untangle it when it had that cloudy consistency that hair has before it is first cut was no mean task. So I haven't forgotten the bathroom, its cool green walls, the tall stool, myself upon it, and Grandmother singing to make me think it didn't hurt. I even remember the song she sang, for she still sang the same one combing my hair out several years later when I had reached the age of true memory, the kind that stores and learns.

> When I was young, my granny used to say,
> Everything was better than it is today.

That was the verse.

We used to play at Simon says. . . .

That was the refrain.

The song finished — I've forgotten the exact words — by suggesting: *When your grandfather found me, he didn't have far to look.* She sang this, as was the fashion in those days, in a muted voice. Naturally, I thought the song was about Grandfather and herself. You don't have to be very old to see when a man and a woman love each other. Children sense that immediately by the peace they live in. It was too good to last.

The long visit we made at Grandfather's was due to my parents' separation. One day, Mother couldn't stand it any longer and left with the four children she had at the time. I have heard the story of this, the one exploit in my Mother's wedded life, at least twenty times from her brother, my uncle. He and my grandfather had gone to see my father's boss — luckily the Minister was one of their friends — they had begged him to send the tiger away somewhere for a few days so Mother and we little ones could escape in peace. The Minister was not one to do things by halves: my father was sent to Hudson Bay for six months. No sooner had he gone out the door than off we went, all five of us, the whole platoon with full kit and kaboodle. Perhaps the metaphor is a bit too military. We were more like passenger pigeons. Mother wrote a little letter to break things off, and Grandfather kept us for the next two years.

I should say here that Grandfather was Mother's stepfather. My real maternal grandfather, Joseph Martin, died when Mother was still a girl. Her own name, Martin, was the one I took as soon as I had a pretext for choosing a pseudonym, which was when I became a radio announcer. Joseph Martin was a brilliant young lawyer who had begun to have bright hopes of a political career. He wrote a *Municipal Code for the Province of Quebec* which does not, however, entitle me to say that I owe my taste for literature to him. He had not made his wife happy. At his death his affairs were in bad shape and Grandmother had to give piano lessons to eke out her meagre budget.

*   *   *

I have been curious enough to hunt up a few details about this grandfather Martin, for since his son had no children I am the last Martin in the line, so to speak. At all events the name seems fated not to be passed on in any very regular fashion if we may judge by this pretty pearl from the pen of a certain Father Le Jeune: "The name of the Martins was not perpetuated by the male line, but only by the Plains of Abraham." I find this genealogy hard to understand, but I can clearly see that I am here, and all other Martins with me, by some strange stroke of fate.[1]

Wherever he came from, Joseph Martin joined forces with a great many other French Canadians in 1885. That was the year Louis Riel was executed. My grandfather was one of those who, subsequent to these events, noisily quit the Conservatives. When Sir John A. Macdonald was burnt in effigy at Quebec, he uttered some "historic words" which have been preserved for posterity: "I am breaking with my party, with the party of Sir John, that slave to a handful of Orangemen." Then he ran in the election of 1887 against the Minister of Militia, Sir Adolphe Caron, who was re-elected by a narrow margin. After these events and the bishops' decision to side with the English, Joseph Martin gave up all religious practice, which caused grave misunderstandings between him and my pious grandmother. He died on April 20th, 1896, three days before Wilfrid Laurier's triumph against those same bishops who had campaigned against him. Martin was forty-one years old and he died too soon from any point of view.

For that matter, the Riel affair caused great agitation all through my mother's side of the family and it was never spoken of without considerable reticence. Now we are beginning to see much more clearly what an upheaval it caused. Traditionally Conservative families looked on with horror as certain of their members passed over to the new party. Pious young men, scandalized by the treachery of the clergy, became what was called, behind one's hand, "Voltairians," and some of them, already liberal-minded, became "free-thinkers." None of these words was used freely, and in the same connection I remember the hesitant and mysterious terms that Mother used when speaking about her cousin's husband. This man, Alfred Pelland, had taken care of Louis Riel's orphaned son until the boy reached maturity.

I don't know how far the Riel affair had influenced Alfred Pelland, but I do know that he "wasn't pious" either, to use the euphemism that Mother did when she spoke of him. At any rate, he couldn't have belonged to a submissive party. With the help of two comrades, Honoré Mercier and Paul de Martigny, he tried to blow up the Nelson monument in Montreal, which caused a certain stir in the Queen's Empire. He died suddenly without having had time (the maternal vocabulary comes back to me) to come to terms with himself or receive the solace of our Holy Mother the Church — an omission that his wife never got over.

* * *

After two years of widowhood, Grandmother met a young pharmacist, François Chavigny de la Chevrotière. (Grandmother's maiden
name was Oliérie Douaire de Bondy — with such double-barrelled
names they were predestined to get along.) They married for love,
which didn't much please the Martin family. It appears that in 1898
love was not a sentiment that was very highly thought of in this land
of Quebec. "Oliérie," my great-aunt Martin said one day, "had no
reason to remarry, for we could have helped her financially."

Any commentary I could add to this declaration would detract
from its pure beauty, so I will make none.

Grandfather de la Chevrotière's family was very different from
the Martins. Politics and law, which so often go together in this
country, had attracted neither my grandfather nor his father, who
was a land surveyor, and you have to go back to the generation
before that to find the notary. The family had lived since 1672 on
the ancestral domain of Deschambault, and Grandfather was the
first eldest son to leave the family *manoir* for a career in the city.

I have the history of this family and can't resist the pleasure of
telling a little of it. The first Canadian to bear the name came from
Créancey in Champagne in 1641. He had married Eléonore de
Grandmaison, who at nineteen was already starting on her second
marriage and who later on was to marry twice again. I have always
found the story of Eléonore with all those widowhoods and remar-
riages a little too overfurnished and romantic to be edifying. M.
Pierre-Georges Roy wonders, "What gave M. de Chavigny the idea
of coming to New France?" And he quickly embarks on all kinds of
pious hypotheses: that M. de Chavigny was related to Madame de la
Peltrie who came here with Mère Marie de l'Incarnation; that he
had read the *Jesuit Relations*. But when one considers that this same

M. de Chavigny returned to France to die alone, "abandoning everything he possessed in this country," that his wife took a third husband, Sieur de Beaulieu, who was later on assassinated by one of his servants, that she then took a fourth, M. de la Tesserie, less than five months after the murder of M. de Beaulieu — why, one begins to wonder if in fact M. de Chavigny in his own day might not have had very good reasons for his self-imposed exile.

Whatever the case may be, he left six children in New France and one of his daughters, Marguerite, married Thomas Douaire de Bondy. That meant that even if Grandfather was not my grandfather, it so happened that thanks to this relationship he was at least my cousin I don't know how many times removed, and that delighted me. This distant cousin is the only grandfather I acknowledge and the only man I have loved with a deep filial affection.

I can remember a photograph or a portrait, I'm not sure which, of his father, André-Hospice-Télesphore, the land surveyor, which always hung in my grandfather's house. He had died suddenly while working far away from Deschambault. They brought his body back to the *manoir* one December night, and years afterwards Grandfather still spoke of this event with great sadness. Nonetheless, knowing his sense of irony, I imagine that he would not have been able to recall without laughter the obituary notice written at the time by a certain Abbé Thibeaudeau. It might have been titled "An Exercise in the Commonplace," and on these grounds I think a quotation is justified:

We learn with the most heartfelt grief of the death of T.-C. de la Chevrotière, Esq., Surveyor, late of Deschambault, who departed this life on the 6th inst. in the county of Peterborough while surveying for the government. This death, whose circumstances were as surprising as they were unexpected, has thrown not only his family but the whole of the parish of Deschambault into deep mourning, for he counted none but friends among us.

He had been absent three weeks in the line of duty and he was just about to put the finishing touches to his task and prepare to return home to his dear ones, when, last Monday evening after a heavy day's work in the woods, at a distance of two miles from any human habitation, he was struck down by an indigestion which carried him from life to death in less than a quarter of an hour. He died surrounded by some of the men who had helped him in his work and who had been summoned to his tent by the last pangs of his agony. They brought him what succour they could, but to no avail.

Alas! how true it is to say that death does not choose his victims. He often strikes so suddenly and in such strange ways that those who witness his cruel blows are left totally dismayed. And such was the tragic end of M. de la Chevrotière. Nonetheless, and this should be a consolation to his friends and family, Almighty Providence could not have called home a soul better prepared to face such precipitous circumstances.

A model father, an honest citizen, a highly respected and respectable man, a sincere and fervent Christian, M. de la Chevrotière passed through this world doing good. As head of his family he brought up his children with all the kindness, prudence and severity that duty prescribes. Throughout his entire life he provided them with an example of the most ardent Faith and the most perfect love of God. As a citizen he was in contact with the best society; held in great esteem in his parish, he was one who called no man his enemy; well known in Quebec where he had numerous friends, the news of his death was learnt with the most profound regret.

With that pretty anacoluthon I will stop, long before Abbé Thibeaudeau — who continues the exercise for several more pages and closes, true to form, with a Latin quotation from the Bible: *Paratus sum et non sum turbatus.*

While I am on the subject of my ancestors I would like to mention the little I know about Grandmother's family. Her mother was Adeline Franchère, of the same family as Gabriel Franchère who was a fur-trader in the West, one of the founders of Astoria at the mouth of the Columbia River, who described his experiences in *An Account of a Voyage to the North-West Coast of Septentrional America in the Years 1810, 12, 13 and 14.* If I remember rightly, Grandmother had a copy of this book in her library. But what ever happened to all my grandparents' books?

On the Douaire de Bondy side of the family, the first of this name was the Thomas who married Marguerite de Chavigny. He had come from St-Germain d'Auxerre. He drowned near the Île d'Orléans in July 1667, and this is how the *Jesuit Journal* records the event on July 19 and 22:

July 19. Sire de Bondy, drunk, drowned near the Île d'Orléans.

July 22. Bondy's body found and buried like a dog over by our mill.

Indeed, to encourage abstinence in our ancestors no better way had been found than to refuse them Christian burial if they died in a state of drunkenness. Apparently boredom — which must have been dreadful in this young country to judge by the amount of it that is still on tap here after three centuries — could sometimes be stronger than fear. I note in passing an odd dislike of dogs on the part of this charitable Jesuit.

Grandmother's father, Agapit Douaire de Bondy, was a doctor in

Sorel. He came from Lavaltrie where he is buried next to his wife. The story of his death, which Grandmother often told, used to terrify me. One bitterly cold day he was on his way home after having finished his daily rounds. The church square was frozen over like a skating rink. The horses took fright, turned too short and upset the sleigh. Doctor Bondy's head violently struck the ice but he was able to right the sleigh and go on. Except that — and this is the part of the story that sent a shiver up my spine — on entering the house he said: "Send someone for the priest and the notary. I have just killed myself." He had time to dictate his will and receive the last rites, then he died. This story left me dumbfounded, and I kept asking Grandmother to tell it over again.

"And he really said that, Grandmother 'I have just killed myself'?"

"Yes, he said that. He had fractured his skull and he knew it."

I came close to believing that I was descended from a prophet.

I also loved to be told the story of the Papal Zouave,[2] an even more mysterious and tragic tale. It was about one of Grandmother's brothers, Agapit again, for this name was passed on in the Bondy family from one generation to the next just as the name François is found over and over in Grandfather de la Chevrotière's family tree. In 1868 — he must have been one of the eldest of the family for Grandmother was only six or seven at the time — he went over to defend Pius IX, like quite a few other French Canadians, and like most of them, I believe, he never had a chance to fight. Safe and sound and ready to return home, he went out alone on his last day abroad. The next morning, at dawn, his body was found with a dagger planted in his back. He had dragged himself as far as the courtyard of the house or barracks where he was staying.

"Why did they kill him, Grandmother?"

"I don't know. Those were troubled times. Maybe he was mistaken for someone else, or maybe someone wanted to rob him."

"Perhaps it was a jealous husband — " Grandfather suggested with a little laugh — it was more than fifty years since the man had died.

But the story of the jealous husband didn't seem very romantic to me. I preferred the other. To be assassinated by mistake, in place of someone else, we would never know who, opened up such a range of possibilities it made my head spin. The one idea that never occurred to me was that he had quite simply been taken for exactly what he was, a Zouave. For two or three days at a stretch I would hunt up new solutions and try them out on Grandmother.

"Don't tell me! You're not still thinking about him?"

But I was, and I still do think of him sometimes. In the Cathedral in Montreal, on the left hand side as you go in, his name is engraved along with all the other Zouaves: *A. Bondy.* Strange irony of fate. His death, like that of his forefather Thomas, probably had the same root cause: boredom.

My, how I loved those Bondys, all of them, even the ones I had never seen. That they were related to Grandmother was enough. During the long visits I paid her as a child, one of my favourite pastimes was to find their photos in the family album: Great-Aunt Eloïse, so slender and beautiful, and her husband, Doctor de Pontbriand (whose second marriage was to the grandmother of my friend Jean Filiatrault the novelist). Great-Aunt Marie-Louise whom I was particularly fond of and who was godmother at my confirmation, and her children, our Paulet cousins. Great-Uncle Ovide, the musician, who lived in the States.

Sometimes, going through the mail, Grandmother would exclaim: "Well now, here's your Aunt Marie-Louise coming next week."

I would quickly telephone Grandfather to tell him the news. It wasn't hard to telephone, even for a toddler. First there was the telephone lady you gave your number to, and then the number was never more than three digits long. So I found it hard to resist the temptation to telephone at the slightest provocation.

When some great event happened in Quebec, Aunt Marie-Louise would arrive with her whole family, including her sister Eloïse whose delicate health didn't permit much travelling. Grandmother got out her fanciest table linen, drew up menus, went to the florist's. Since in my father's house we never invited a solitary soul, all these preparations, especially the trip to the florist's, filled me with delight.

For that matter, I lived in an almost continuous state of delight at my grandparents'. A state which was always menaced — but in early childhood threats to happiness are easily ignored. Next week is another world and the time to leave is unimaginably remote. Besides, I always secretly nourished the marvellous illusion that something would eventually happen to keep me there forever, and no one would ever be able to come and take me away.

In fact, far from granting me this wish, life held the opposite in store for me. One day we were to be brutally and hatefully separated. All we could do then was write one another: "We'll be together again, we'll never part," but we were never to see each other again. Several nights a year I still dream that I pass, by chance, before a door that is carefully pushed open a crack. Someone calls me in a low voice. I enter and am taken into their arms. They hug and kiss me and tell me that all this while they have been living there in hiding, waiting for me to get out of my prison, waiting for chance to lead me past their door. Our love has not changed, and when I awaken it always takes me a long time to realize that I have been dreaming.

*   *   *

Though Grandmother was pious, she was no prude. She loved to laugh for she was pretty, intelligent and cultivated, three things that make women gay. The letters she wrote me after we were forbidden to see each other were delightful, full of humour. Yet at the time she had few enough reasons for gaiety. Another thing I liked particularly about her was that she didn't believe there was any conflict between intellectual accomplishment and manual skill. It was always maintained in my father's family that cerebral persons (this should be said with the mouth screwed up, very superior) never knew how to do anything with their hands. But I have since verified, beginning with what I knew of Grandmother, that it is these people and not the others who make the neatest darns, cook the best dishes and sew a sleeve so that it hangs properly. Grandmother could talk about anything and do anything humanly possible for two human hands to do. For example, when her son married and she was unable to turn up a tailor whose qualities would rise to the occasion of stitching the nuptial garment, she made the suit herself.

"It was so well made," my uncle often told me, "that I wore it till it was threadbare."

Grandfather was always attentive to her, tender and full of admiration. He was gay too, and never at a loss for a witty remark. He never missed a chance to be generous either. His business was prosperous, and yet he left very little. It's not difficult to imagine where his savings went. We loved each other, he and I, with a love like no other, a true passion. It has marked me for life. No one has ever been able to win me over unless he was one of the same breed.

When we arrived at my grandparents' I was only a few weeks old, so I always remained their baby no matter how many grandchildren came after, and I enjoyed all the privileges that entails; saying this I think especially of all those happy interludes, all those sunny holidays that I was the only one of the children to know.

* * *

At the end of two years my father had had enough of the bachelor life. So he went and cooked up a reconciliation with Mother's confessor — still the same Jesuit — who arrived at my grandparents' loaded with vows and promises on my father's behalf. For his own part he came heavily armed with threats. To listen to him, a woman separated from her husband was responsible for all the sins solitude might lead him into, and that was the only thing that counted. It was enough to terrify the poor woman, all the more so because my father had taken the trouble to write on several occasions to let her know that "he had all the women he needed." Then there were his promises: she would not be beaten again, would have everything she wanted, could see her parents often.

So we left. And a cruel parting it must have been, for I know that Grandmother didn't put much stock in all those fine promises.

To shelter the family my father had bought a large house, well-proportioned but perfectly glacial in winter. The site he chose was a suburb very little frequented in summer and deserted the rest of the year. The building had been put up in the middle of a vast uncleared lot, doubtless to house some schizoid or fugitive from justice. Just what we needed. There was no road to it. To get there you had to take the little shoreline railroad that connected Quebec to La Malbaie. From the house to what one could scarcely call the station — only a platform and a mean shed that stank of urine — there was a muddy path. The closest neighbours lived a quarter of an hour's walk away, more or less. At least they weren't within call. You could have yelled "Help!" and it wouldn't have carried very far. The trap had been sprung and it was to hold us for more than twenty years.

I don't remember anything about the move, but my elder brother and sisters often used to talk about a little sailboat that the previous owner had left in the attic. They put it in a nearby stream and one night the current carried it away. How I dreamt of that sailboat on those interminably long days of my toyless childhood! It made me furious that I couldn't actually remember it, and I couldn't understand how the others could. So Mother explained what memory was, and in the course of our conversation we discovered that while I hadn't forgotten the bathroom where Grandmother used to do my hair when I was two, my sister Dine remembered the kitchen of another house we had left when she was the same age. In both cases the walls were green. Is there some link between the colour green and a child's memory? Who knows?

Besides the sailboat, there were four or five huge cardboard boxes in the attic containing monstrous mortuary wreaths of mauve and violet cloth flowers. Mme Gagnon who had sold us the house was supposed to have someone come and pick them up. It was strictly forbidden even so much as to peek into those boxes. However, the flowers pulled out so easily and they made such pretty bouquets that it was no mean temptation. Mme Gagnon, who seemed to have left our shores never to return — I can hardly blame her — never did reclaim her goods, so finally Mother, tired of scolding us, sent the wreaths on to the widow. I can imagine her surprise on receiving this package seven or eight years later. It would be fun to add that during this time she had remarried, but I really can't say.

My parents had come together again in June. In July, Mother became pregnant with her fifth child. What can have been the state of mind of that poor woman, so gentle and frail, when she found herself on her way to producing yet another little misery, a part of whose life, as she well knew, would be abominable.

At all events, she made them solid. And this one had occasion to prove it before he was out of diapers.

If only adults would stop to meditate a little, as they go along, on the phenomenon of a child's memory — how exact it is, how early it starts to stock up impressions — perhaps they would behave quite differently for fear of being ashamed one day before this other adult that the child will become. But would he listen to a prompting that might make him forgo the pleasure of anger? My father? Never.

It is as though it all happened yesterday. Mother takes the baby upstairs to put him to bed. My father follows her up. A few seconds later we hear cries and terrifying noises. The baby tumbles down the staircase right to the bottom, followed by Mother who, not being bundled up like her son, takes longer about it. A great deal more. Interminably. We children huddled together in the kitchen not daring to stir. Very young we learned, I don't know how, but we did, that in circumstances like this you had to pretend to see nothing and hear nothing, that you mustn't cry or call out. But all tyrants suffer from a common weakness in system: they cannot prevent those they tyrannize over from thinking. I was three and a half. That's pretty small to choose hatred and scorn.

That evening my father's brother who was, as chance would have it, a practised ear, nose and throat specialist, came to take care of Mother. Her face — I can see it — was black. Her nose was broken and enormous. My uncle looked grim. He knew his big brother, and the story that Mother chose to tell, out of kindness and fear, didn't fool him.

*   *   *

It was the first time I had seen this uncle. I rarely saw him afterwards, and then almost exclusively when I needed free medical treatment — twice for otitis, at five and eleven, and once for an eye examination when I was nineteen. (I don't count those rare meetings at his own mother's house; there he kept as silent as we did.)

I knew him so little that when he came to the convent to treat me at the time of my second otitis, I didn't dare call him uncle. I could see that this man looked like the one who had cared for me before, but I wasn't absolutely sure. Besides, my father was there and said nothing, my uncle didn't say anything either and the nun in attendance was mute too. But my childhood is full of experiences like this, grownups who never speak and children who don't dare ask questions.

Still I liked this uncle a lot. He looked like my father in features and colouring, but something difficult to define made the two brothers totally different and proved again what an imperfect mask the body is for the inner truth. My uncle was my father over again but civilized, drawn in pastels, dusted over with decency. He spoke rarely, but well and gently, and carried himself with an aristocratic air. I thought of him as a kind of *seigneur* and would gladly have exchanged him, though I knew him so slightly, for the author of my days. But we had next to nothing to do with him, for neither he nor his family were our kind of people. We were the good kind, they the bad. They saw people, went out, had guests, had things to say beyond pious platitudes. They came terribly close to living a happy and normal life. Not our kind of thing at all.

Basically, my father didn't detest his brother. But this brother led — like everyone else for that matter, absolutely everyone else — a life that my father did not approve of. My father was the only one in the whole universe who led the kind of life that my father approved of.

I will never forget the long, patient interrogations he put me through when I was going to his brother for treatment, especially at the time of the second otitis. Had I been aware of anything wicked? Had they offered me something to drink? Or had they taken something to drink in front of me? Yes, my aunt and I had had a glass of lemonade.

"But — what about wine? Hadn't there been just one little glass?"

No, not a drop. But wasn't I liar enough to cover up anyway? Well then, hadn't there been any subversive conversation? Hadn't there been suggestions that — about — which tended to — ? Of course there had been nothing of the kind, and even if I had been told the most shocking things imaginable, I would have been very careful not to repeat them. Mouth clamped shut, hiding behind a doltish mask that would have discouraged the saints, that's the way we grew up.

Yet it was not terror that made us suffer most. Primarily it was boredom. Everything was forbidden: to run, to shout, to stray even the slightest distance away from the house. We had no toys. The first ones that Grandfather and Grandmother had ventured to send us brought down endless reproaches on Mother's head. Why hadn't this money been used to buy clothes for us? So you should have seen us unwrapping our Christmas presents: slippers, gloves, trousers, stockings, shoes. When we had finished opening the parcels, my father always flew into a rage because there were papers and ribbons on the floor. There was a rush to tidy everything up. That was relatively easy, because we never put up a Christmas tree at home. The presents were laid out on armchairs in the living room. By eight o'clock in the morning everything was back to normal. It was just another day like the others when laughter was forbidden.

The least laugh, for that matter, might have dire consequences. My father never took laughter for anything but a symptom of lewdness. And we had all been suspected of dirty-mindedness from the cradle up. Though we laughed very seldom, it was still too much, if you consider the dangers it exposed us to. One Sunday morning — I must have been about three and a half for my elder brother, who is two years older than me, was still not going to mass and the rule was that everyone went from the age of six on — this Sunday my brother and I were left at home with my father while Mother and my sisters were at mass. The baby was sleeping upstairs. We were sitting on the bottom step of the stairs. My father was working in his study. I have no idea what André and I were talking about, but I remember distinctly that he said "that individual." It was a new word for me and it seemed so comical that I collapsed in uncontrollable laughter. I have since noticed that this word often tickles children's sense of the ridiculous. André tried to get me to be quiet but it seems that even in those days my laughing fits had already reached catastrophic proportions.

Anyway, it was too late almost before I had begun. In less time than it takes to tell, we were seized and led off, one to the study, the other to the dining room. No matter how small one is, one comes through an adventure like this with a very good idea, that can later be used in history studies, of what the inquisition must have been like, and by this I don't mean any simple asking of questions. For the interrogation my father began with the standard tricks: your brother has told me everything; and to him: your sister has told me everything. As far as I was concerned I hadn't the foggiest idea what kind of confession was expected. I had to feel my way.

I didn't begin to see the light until the interrogation, punctuated with slaps, became really very precise. Then I guessed that the time had come to talk, so I told him that André had said "that individual." My story wasn't a great success. It earned me a double punishment. (At least that's what my father called it for we, the punished, could never see much distinction between the single and the double.) The first was for having done what I knew very well I had done, for it was out of the question that I hadn't; the second was for having lied about it. What punishment? Always the same. It began with openhanded blows which immediately became very heavy, then, getting into the swing of it, blows with the closed fist, and if he got really swinging he would finish off with kicks that sent us skidding from one room to the next all through the downstairs. When you think that he was six feet tall, weighed two hundred and thirty pounds, and was still known throughout the whole of Anticosti for the Paul Bunyanesque feats he had accomplished there in his youth at the start of his career as a civil engineer, why it's a wonder he didn't kill one of us. It makes me think that he must have held back a little, that he didn't give himself up wholeheartedly to the full pleasure of it, and from this distance I find that a trifle melancholy.

When I was small I confess I often wished an accident of that kind would happen. I used to look at my brothers and sisters and wonder which one of them I would have the least trouble sacrificing if I had a choice. I loved them all dearly. Therefore, it would have to be myself. But to give up being present at his punishment? Never. I saw myself giving evidence before a judge, no longer afraid of anything, crushing the accused under the full weight of my testimony. I dreamt of it.

Scenes of this kind happened at the drop of a hat. I can't understand why, because it seems to me that we weren't sexually more advanced than we should have been. But his suspicions were certainly not underdeveloped, and they fell on everyone regardless of age or sex. When Margot was born I was five years old. She was put into my room as soon as she was weaned. (At that time there were no rooms on the top floor, they were only to be added later on.) Margot woke up at dawn every morning, soaked to the skin in the best tradition, and bringing the house down with her cries. Mother would get up, come in and change her, and naturally would not be able to go to sleep again before it was time to get up. That bothered me. So one morning I decided to do a good deed. As soon as Margot gave her first squeak, I jumped out of bed, took off the wet diaper and, not knowing how to put on a clean one, settled for covering her bottom copiously with talcum powder. Alas! good deeds didn't pay at home. I knew that, but I must have forgotten it. I had scarcely got back into bed when my father came bursting in. He went straight to Margot's crib and lifted the covers.

"Aha! I thought so!" he shouted.

There's no need to go on, this story ends the same way as the previous one. But by now I was big enough to want to explain myself to Mother. So when my father had left for work, I told her what I had been trying to do. She took me on her knee and offered me this extraordinary piece of advice:

"When your father is at home don't ever do anything. Just do nothing at all."

"You mean stay off by myself in my own little corner?"

"Yes."

"You know, Mother, I don't like him. I wish he'd die."

She put her work-worn little hand over my mouth and explained that I must never wish for anyone's death, least of all my father's, that it was a wicked thought, and besides, it was quite useless.

I don't know if I knew what death was, but the word was familiar enough, as it is for all children who grow up in wartime. As for the war, of course all we knew of it came from the papers, but it seems to me that it was discussed endlessly. All I knew was that it was a very noisy business. In an illustrated almanac I had found a cartoon that showed a mother trying to calm her howling baby, saying: "Hush, child, listen to the bombs."

I also knew that it was going to end soon and I imagined that day would bring great jubilation, even to our house. One evening — I can still see myself clearly, standing near the front door — my father came home and said:

"The war is over."

That was all. We ate our supper in lugubrious silence as usual. (But fate was to make amends when, in 1945, I had the opportunity of speaking those same words over Radio-Canada. Besides, I find that it has richly compensated me for everything!)

* * *

Naturally, meals were the most painful part of the day. I can't remember a single one that didn't end in some kind of scene or other. Though we tried our best not to speak, not to raise our heads, it was to no avail. The scene seemed to spring up out of nothing. Perhaps it was our fear that engendered it. Perhaps my father, feeling the full effect of his power, seeing us all trembling around him, couldn't resist the pleasure of verifying that "it" was still in good working order. All of a sudden shouts burst out, knives flew, the baby, not yet broken in to the household routine though that would come soon enough, began to cry.

My place at table was beside Mother. If I was the one under fire she would stroke my knee under the tablecloth as long as the attack lasted. It didn't matter then what happened, I felt myself melt with love.

My father's fads helped considerably to make meals odious. What horrors he made us swallow! All his life he was infatuated with naturist nutritional theories. He subscribed to all the journals and magazines which promised, as a reward for following impossible diets, long life (that was for him) free from medical attention (that was for us). As far as I can see, the adepts of such cults experience an irrepressible desire to eat what other people throw away. Since most people usually die before they reach a hundred, it follows that what they discard must necessarily contain that little something that makes a centenarian. Such logic seemed irrefutable. So our diet followed the latest treatises of the most fashionable charlatans, and we were likely, for example, to find ourselves one morning sitting down to a breakfast of slices of unpeeled orange powdered with unrefined brown sugar, almost black, and tasting horrible, that my father had sent direct from Barbados in wooden barrels at great expense. When we had apples, we were expected to eat the skin and the seeds and that little piece that was called in my natural science textbook: *the corneous partition of the carpellary loculi*. There at least was a term

I was quick to recognize — I had spent so many days already in my short life with a corneous partition stuck halfway down my gullet. All we were allowed to leave on the plate was the stem.

"The skin and the core contain the most nutritious elements in the apple."

Out of respect for this principle, and in the name of longevity, scarcely a day went by that we didn't risk choking to death. Any kind of skin was good. If we never went so far as to eat our egg shells, it was only because no naturist had yet recommended it. We also consumed endless quantities of porridge made with the whole grain. Coarse wheat gruel, of spermatic aspect, sprinkled with black sugar was enough to disgust any human being with the idea of eating, and even of living, if that was the price to pay. When we were bigger we were allowed coffee sugared with buckwheat honey and other fantasies of the same ilk — bulk ilk, of course. Ah, well! We were all en route to our respective centennials and, whether we were sick or not, the doctor never darkened our door except when mother was in labour.

*   *   *

For me those times were holidays. As soon as mother's pregnancy began to tire her, which happened quite early, for she was of a delicate constitution and worked far beyond her strength, she would put all my little possessions into a box, all my last year's Christmas presents, and send me to my grandparents.

I remember the house perfectly, rue Saint-Jean, number 151 now that the street numbers have been changed. Even though they left the house the year I was ten, I could draw its exact floor plan, complete with all the windows, doors and cupboards.

Behind the house there was a gloomy courtyard where Grandmother persistently tried to grow flowers. A handful of zinnias pushed up feebly in the shade of some big trees. All the cats in the neighbourhood used the courtyard as a hangout for their implacable rivalries and strident lovemaking. One night an old tom pursued by his young challenger tried to sneak off at the end of the fight by diving into the house through an open window. The quarrel would probably have finished up on the kitchen floor under the calculating eye of the tabby, who looked as if she just happened to be there by mere chance, if Grandfather hadn't chased all three of them out by slashing at them with a bath towel. They left great tufts of hair behind and a spattering of blood.

At the far end of the courtyard were some mysterious sheds that my grandparents never used and where I was forbidden to set foot. Apparently you could still see some old box stalls in there and over them the names of the horses in silver letters. Two little redheaded neighbourhood boys had told me.

"Oh, Grandmother, I'd so like to see that! They say they're old stables that must have belonged to millionaires!"

"And what if they weren't as interesting as you think they are? Why go in then? Anyway, it's certainly very dirty and dangerous."

I wasn't convinced. Not until one of the redheads fell off a pile of old packing crates and came out screaming like a stuck pig. So I never did see the silver lettered names of the millionaires' horses.

In the house, marvel of marvels, I had a room all to myself, a room that was ready waiting for me from one year's end to the next, a room where no one ever came with threatening words and fists.

Every morning when I got up I found on my bedside table a present that Grandfather had put there when I was asleep: some lollipops, or a chocolate bar or candied fruit. Grandmother had asked me, once and for all, not to touch them before breakfast, "Just to please me." Hard as it was, I always obeyed her because I always found this such an incredibly wonderful reason to obey. Diana, the maid, whom I called "Dear-Anna-who-I-love-with-all-my-heart," gave me my breakfast. Nothing but good things to eat, no peels, no black sugar that smelled like jute. Then I had my bath in a bathroom that was never chilly, in water that was always warm and perfumed. Nobody in this house played the Spartan. Diana dressed me and brushed my hair with gentle hands, and then I would go and join Grandmother in her little sewing room where every morning she busied herself making clothes for one or another of her grandchildren, and for me when I was there. How painstaking she was! Never content with anything less than perfection, she would tolerate around her neither cheap material, nor heavy pins, neither needle nor thread that wasn't fine; nothing ugly, nothing rough, never cotton when silk was needed; never any of those things that people usually excuse by calling them "quite good enough."

She would start by pinning a pattern of rustling tissue paper on me. Its tickle put me into a state of happy numbness. The fitting went on and on — it makes me sleepy just to think of it. Lift your arm. Turn around. I obeyed in a dream, just by habit. Then I would watch her cut the cloth, her lips tightly closed on a dozen pins, and little by little I would wake up again. While she put in the basting I began to lose patience — until the next fitting, not long after, would cast that delicious numbness over me again. I could hear the gentle whirring of the sewing machine. I would soon have my new dress!

When I was big enough to know my colours, Grandmother let me open her treasure box. I mean the button box. Like all women of her stamp, she knew that a handsome garment deserves fine buttons. Some of them had been bought in Paris. Ah! how those little Parisian button shops make me think of you, my dear! They were irreplaceable and had a box of their own. I was allowed to look at them, but not touch them. Mother-of-pearl, bone, crystal, ivory — I learnt that only genuine materials are of any real worth, and that a button in true mother-of-pearl is better than one in gilt. An even easier lesson was learning to count and tell the colours.

"Find me eight little buttons the size of a five-cent piece — "

In those days we had the very small ones. If I remember them, it is because Grandfather used to fill my piggy-bank with them. Otherwise I wouldn't have known anything about them, for my father never gave us a cent. (I will never forget blushing with shame the day that Marguerite, who must have been eight at the time, proudly displayed a poor little ten-cent piece to my sneering friends, quite obviously the first one she had ever had.)

I left my bank at my grandparents' when I went back to my father's house. It waited for me there on the dressing table, like my dolls, my set of blocks, and my picture books waiting in the cupboard. Only once did I ever take a doll back to my father's with me. He gave it to Margot (this must have been several years later than the point I have reached in my story, for she was then two or three years old.) He didn't even say a word about it to me, and I never tried that again. When I complained to Mother about it, "You must learn to be generous," she said.

"He's the one who gave it to her," I replied.

A few days later I overheard her telling this to Grandmother who had come to see us.

"That child worries me," she concluded, "she doesn't like her father."

Grandmother answered in English. Ah! those observations in English! People still do that. But they never fool children. Children know very well that their good looks or intelligence are being discussed, or that parents are admitting that they are right, though it isn't decent to say so openly, or that dark designs are being fomented against them — for example, that they should be sent to bed — and that anything that doesn't fall into these categories is about sex.

When Mother and Grandmother talked together, I would lie on the sofa pretending to be asleep. It was a way I had discovered of intercepting what they said about my father. As the years went by, the reasons for grievance multiplied constantly, and who could Mother have confided in if not her own mother?

I remember another of those confidential conversations which brings me back to where I left off. The set of blocks I mentioned had the letters of the alphabet stamped on them. When I had learnt them by heart, Grandmother taught me how to form simple words. "Mama" first, naturally. Then she wanted me to go on to "Papa."

"No, I don't want to write 'Papa.' I want to write 'Grand-papa.'"

Mother didn't like that at all. When she began to discuss the advisability of cutting out the long visits I used to spend with my grandparents, I began to squirm on the sofa. Then I burst into tears, sobbing that I would rather die. I must have convinced them, for until Mother died I went back there several times.

However, these visits did little to make my life easier under my father's roof. Whenever I came back I was closely watched. The least flick of an eyelash brought on slaps and scolding. I had, it seemed, developed insufferable manners.

But above all, I must have been frightfully gloomy, for leaving my paradise for our family atmosphere seemed to me exactly like falling into the seventh circle of hell. Those first nights when I found myself back in my icy bed, I couldn't help sobbing, which put me in the category of someone "whining for nothing."

"I'll give you something to whine about."

It was like a kind of vaccination. I have already said that we all developed, very young, a prudent impassivity, but nonetheless we sometimes did cry occasionally. It was our one resource by way of consolation. Of course, I am not speaking about tears that came from punishment. The standing rule was to shed them promptly. Otherwise we would have run risks beyond our endurance. No, I am talking about what might be called intimate or personal tears. No question of that. Swallow them.

*   *   *

Sometimes, when Mother's state of health was really bad, my holidays would stretch out to several months, even seven or eight, and in the end my father would begin to worry. As he never refrained from speaking against our maternal grandparents in front of us, he naturally believed they did the same on their side, in which he was completely mistaken. So, in full agreement with the rest of his family, he would decide to remove me from their pernicious influence. By means of an imperious telephone call I would be invited to spend a few days with my paternal grandparents. And off I would go, my tail between my legs.

I hated that house. All I ever found there was coldness, an incapacity to love or to make oneself loved, and instant sarcasm the moment someone showed the least sign of heart. Moreover, my father came to make a little visit every day at noon. As soon as I arrived, without fail I would be subjected to a host of treacherous questions among which, because of my tender years, I had considerable difficulty navigating. Sometimes these questions seemed quite innocuous.

"What do you have for supper at your grandmother de la Chevrotière's?" my aunt would ask. No matter what I answered, the kitchen floor immediately began to heave under my feet.

"At supper?"

Wave my antennae as I might, I could never make out what they were criticizing, whether it was too much or too little, too heavy or not substantial enough. Truth to tell, I had never really noticed whether what I was given for dinner was different from what we had for lunch, so I would fumble around, looking unintelligent. Then, instead of naming a dish I had really eaten one evening, I would try to guess one that wouldn't get Grandmother into trouble. It was a waste of time.

"For supper? Did you hear that Mother?"

My paternal grandmother would shrug her massive shoulders. She had no particular opinion on the vespertine nutrition of young brats, furthermore, she had long ago abandoned all control of whatever current of thought reigned in the house. (She was a good person, and my only reproach is that she didn't know how to bring up her eldest son. Anger can be corrected. I know that, for at birth I received a good share of the paternal heritage. But not only had she failed to discipline him, she also required us to think him gentle. On her deathbed she almost cursed me because she heard me say, "He's in a fury today." All he had done was beat one of my sisters to the point of splitting her lip and bruising her face all over. But I was the one that was cursed. Logic was scarcely a strong point with adults in my youth. If we appealed to it we were called "reasoners." As far as they were concerned, that beautiful word "reason" could only be abusive.)

When the supper menu was settled, the questions sidled over to other subjects. And when they became too difficult, I would take refuge in stupidity. I knew nothing, had seen nothing, understood nothing, had heard nothing.

The thing that wounded me most was their unkind remarks about my clothes. Since it was Grandmother who had given them all to me, they were ugly, they didn't suit me, they were impractical, their colours were unbecoming.

"Your hair ribbon is terribly faded. How could your grandmother put a thing like that on you?"

In fact, the ribbon was new, which was perfectly easy to see, but, horror of horrors, it was rose-coloured, a very discreet pink.

"I'm going to dye it for you."

During the preparation for this procedure, I slyly made off with the dye and in one bold stroke emptied it down the sink. Then, after the storm this raised had subsided, I crept off without a sound, collected all my little things together, and escaped by the back door. Grandmother lived close by and I knew the way. The only trouble was that from the back garden I had to reach the street and had to pass in front of the window of the little sitting room. My aunt and her mother, when they were not busy dyeing my ribbons, mounted permanent guard there. Not a single passer-by escaped their notice. I was no exception. I answered their imperative signs to me by sticking out an indignant tongue. Grandmother, warned by telephone, was waiting for me at the top of the front steps with a stern face. I was well scolded and deprived of dessert. I would gladly have reconciled myself to never eating dessert again in my life, if only I could have stayed there forever.

This adventure didn't leave me with any great guilt complex. It seems that I ought to have nursed a deep one. When my father remarried fourteen years later, this was the first thing my aunt told my stepmother about me. Just to show her what I was capable of, even at such a tender age — a warning as to what might be expected of me.

It was ordained, however, that visits with my paternal grandparents should never last very long. The second only lasted four days. The day after I arrived I began to feel sick. The next day, a Sunday, I was really feeling miserable. But just the same I had to go to church. I have never been able to understand why, when I was small, children who felt sick on Sunday were always suspected of wanting to skip mass. Adults must have surmised that we, too, found it all extremely boring.

We hadn't been there ten minutes when I fainted. It was the first time. It came on slowly and I had time to think I was dying. I didn't dare sit down because — as I explained to Grandmother later, which later still became a favourite subject for Grandfather's teasing — it was a "kneeling bit" of the ceremony. Ah! those famous kneeling bits — they were to be the end of me more than once. I had to be taken out and back to my paternal grandparents' house where I dragged around in a lamentable state all the rest of the day.

"You'll be all right," they kept on saying.

On the strength of that opinion there was never any question of putting me to bed. I would go at the regular hour.

The next day I came down with a good otitis. My ear ran like a tap, and the pillowcase I had slept on was ruined. My uncle was called to my bedside and was mainly told about the pillowcase, "really a total loss." This went on so long he finally lost patience and told them that he was going to look after my ear first. Then I was wrapped in a blanket and taken back to my father's house. When I was better I went to Grandmother's to convalesce.

*   *   *

That was in the fall of 1919. I had had my fifth birthday that April. It was about the same time that Grandfather was stricken with diabetes. I discovered this one day when I was passing the candies around. When he refused and I insisted, he explained why he couldn't eat any more sweet things. Never eat chocolates again? Or candied fruit? Or cake? That seemed such a horrible fate that I started to cry. And then there was something else, something I couldn't have put into words, but which upset me terribly. Never eat any more candies? Couldn't this disease be cured then? I had already known for a long time what anguish was, but I had never felt it for such a reason before. Discovering that the person I loved was threatened, I discovered, at the same moment, what love was. When we are little we love without thinking about it, and love, for us, is chiefly the love that others bear us. That day I felt an independent emotion, a feeling that drove me to say, "I love you," and to throw my arms around him. All this ended, as you can imagine, in general tears.

When I look back, I realize that this climate of love was much more important to me than all the little treats, though it would be wrong to minimize their importance. A piece of chocolate at that age is something. But you must be able to eat it without a knot in your throat. Yes, it was that climate that I adored in a house where there was no shame in speaking from the heart, in weeping freely if what one was saying was sad, or bubbling over if it was gay. Over at my paternal grandparents' house, the most distant allusion to feelings in any way connected with the heart, even the purest, brought on embarrassed grimacing. One can judge this by the attitude adopted whenever the body somehow entered the picture. Young newlyweds holding hands gave rise to, "Really, they look so stupid!" Physical love was sheer buffoonery, and dirty at that. Procreation alone could save and excuse this abomination. Consequently, couples without children were frowned upon. They weren't doing their duty, for "doing one's duty" never in any circumstance meant doing a job well, or being good, or just, or courageous. No, the expression had no other meaning than to beget children. This had to be done according to the only known procedure, as damnable and humiliating as that was for the poor woman. The union of bodies, the union of those "rags" as the retreat preachers used to call them, what an atrocious necessity it was!

It has always remained a great mystery to me that all those pious people could still say "God created man in his own image, in the image of God created he him." Everything leads us to believe that they should have considered such a man well made. A body made by God is no mean thing! Or is it? Well, to start with we had better get rid of the buttocks, or if a lady, the breasts. As for sexual parts, better not speak about them, positively unmentionable. While we're at it, it wouldn't be a bad idea to do away with the skin, the word itself is revolting enough. Only then do we begin to have a work that God doesn't have to blush to acknowledge. The whole thing was obviously undertaken without consulting right-minded people. And that's why they are now obliged to improve on the work of the creator with the help of flattening corsets and loose clothes. What a shame!

It would have been better for me had I got used to this state of mind right from the start — no body, no heart, and none of the words that name them — for that's the mentality I encountered everywhere until the end of my adolescence. The only exception was the one I have already mentioned. It was an important one. So much so that, at that time, the exception was my rule. Very soon I was to miss it grievously.

*　　*　　*

I had known my letters for some time, and the sounds. I had begun by learning to say them, then to read them. By now I knew how to write them not too badly. When my otitis was better, I really learned to read. Grandmother was very anxious to teach me herself. We often talked about it together, the two of us. Especially after I received that set of blocks with all the letters stamped on them — even the ones that you never used, like W for instance. I have never met such a good teacher. The lessons were so much fun that I followed her around all day long with my ABC book in my hand. I understood everything she explained to me and, since then, I have so often understood so little of what people have tried to teach me that, in all humility, I can give the credit not to my own intelligence but to hers.

I know nothing about the methods used today to teach youngsters to read and write. Perhaps I am very old fashioned, but I will never be able to believe in their effectiveness. I have seen the results too often.

"If you take great care to understand what you are studying, you will never forget it," Grandmother used to say, for she was a long way from thinking of the brain as some kind of photographic apparatus.

It was too beautiful a promise. But it was I, not she, who failed to keep it.

When I knew how to read well enough to puzzle out the newspaper (at first it was newspapers much more than books that stirred my curiosity), I noticed that certain words changed their spelling all the time: *parlait, parlais, parlaient*. In very clear terms she told me what a verb was, why it changed this way, and that I would learn all about that when the time came. How incredible! And what a mystery! When, at the age of seven, I left the pronoun behind and, turning the page, read: "A verb is a word which describes an action or the state of the subject," I had the feeling that I had reached the end of my studies. Could they possibly find anything more difficult to teach than this word that changed constantly according to whether it referred to me or to others. Some ten years later, when I was cleaning out the schoolbook cupboard, I found my first little grammar, all pencilled over. On the page I refer to, there were a dozen verbs written in the margin: *courir, manger, coudre*, et cetera. Underneath, this sententious conclusion: "That's verbs."

Then Grandmother wanted to move on to numbers. Addition. Nothing doing. I only wanted to know how to read. Anything else seemed a waste of time. Long afterwards she told me laughingly, which makes me think she was not too fond of numbers herself, that I kept on interrupting her to ask: "How do you spell *seven? plus? equals?*" I took to numbers very gingerly, and never really more than nibbled at them until, at the convent, I noticed that at the end of the month a good mark in arithmetic was just as important as a good mark in French.

The first book I read was *Don Quixote*. A little crazy, but that's a fact. Grandfather kept a skeleton library in the back room of the drug store. As soon as I knew how to mouth words, I took down the lowest book and carried it off to my corner to read. I understood strictly nothing for the simple reason, first of all that *Don Quixote* at my age, well — but also because I read too slowly to remember when I had reached the bottom of the page what had been at the top. But what did that matter? With the same flushed cheeks that reading always gave me until I was grown up, I kept on reading. Grandmother and Grandfather read every day. I wouldn't have been caught not doing likewise.

Besides that, I was already driven by an irresistible urge to do everything my father disliked. I was always hearing him insult Mother about her books and the time she wasted reading. (Though God knows books weren't numerous in that house. Perhaps a hundred insignificant things that Mother read over and over rather than be completely cut off.) That would have been enough to awaken my appetite, even if I hadn't already had a hunger of my own. At all events, it sharpened it considerably.

I must have been turning several pages at a time in my *Don Quixote*, for one afternoon I came to the end — of my first difficulties and my first delights. When I put the book back on the shelf Grandfather said, chuckling:

"Was it interesting, Ti-Claire?"

"Ye — es — "

Then Grandmother bought me *La semaine de Suzette* and everything went better from then on.

In that back room in my grandfather's store I knew an immense happiness, but one that was never perfect because it was always menaced by the possibility of having to return to my father's house. That back room! I close my eyes and I see it. First the scales, the flasks and the mortars of the little dispensary where Grandfather prepared his mysterious prescriptions. Beyond that a large room, a bit dark, a bit austere.

I step in.

On the left there is a staircase blocked off since the time the pharmacist (not Grandfather but someone before him) lived upstairs. At the back, a work table. On the right, a sofa where I have my afternoon nap. Above the sofa Grandfather has fixed a little hook in the ceiling. When I wake up there is always a candy swinging on the end of a string tied to the hook. I stretch up my arm, and each time Grandfather laughs himself silly, as though he had just thought up this good trick he is playing on me for the hundredth time.

Because of my otitis, and because Mother was expecting Marguerite, I spent the Christmas holidays with my grandparents. I will never forget that Christmas, the only one I ever spent in happiness, laughter, and peace. Grandmother had a Christmas tree set up in one corner of the dining room. The living room was all decorated in red and green bells and branches of mistletoe under which the three of us never tired of catching and kissing each other. For breakfast we had grapefruit, a rare treat in those days. For lunch big plates of oysters which gave me a bad time and saw me wrapped up in one of Diana's huge aprons. In the afternoon a coachman came in a jingling sleigh to drive us through the snowy streets. That evening there were guests for dinner. On condition that I wouldn't speak unless spoken to, I was allowed to sit at the table.

I had scarcely got over all this happiness when it was New Year's and everything began all over again. I remember everything, and it was a good thing I was so attentive, for twenty years were to pass before Christmas and New Year's were anything more to me than dreadfully painful days I thought would never end.

* * *

Then more and more Grandmother took to spending her days with Mother. She would go early in the morning, leaving me with Diana who looked after me with great gentleness.

At last came the thirteenth of March, the day that Marguerite began her life's journey. In eight years to the day, Mother was to end hers.

That morning Grandmother had taken me to church, a thing she did a bit too often to my liking. I was not born pious, and those interminable ceremonies bored me stiff. Grandmother took communion before mass, said a short prayer, then whispered in my ear:

"I have to leave right away. When mass is over you go back home by yourself. Ask a big person to take you across the street."

No sooner had she disappeared than I rushed out of church, crossed the street without asking anyone anything, and burst into Diana's kitchen.

"Don't tell me mass is over?"

"I don't know — anyway, the priest was at the foot of the altar."

"But that's where he is at the beginning too — "

"Oh, really?"

I remember this brief dialogue very well, for I can see Diana's skeptical smile as though she stood before me now, and I believe that was the first time I was truly aware of my own religious indifference. Grandmother came back that evening to announce that I had a new little sister, which seemed an incredible story. Where did she ever come from? It didn't occur to me for a second that she might be a baby.

"How old is she?"

This caused a general roar of laughter and gave Grandfather something to tease me about for years to come.

"Can you tell me the age of a one-day-old baby?" he would ask when he wanted to pull my leg.

It wasn't the custom in those days to explain the secrets of life to children. For that matter we didn't ask many questions. We felt certain that the grownups had no intention of informing us, and that there was a kind of frontier there that wasn't to be crossed either from their side or ours. So I was left wondering how a one-day-old baby had ever managed to get itself into my father's house.

All this excitement didn't prevent Grandmother from asking me about my return home from mass. I was scolded. But in doing so, as always, she kept a good sense of proportion.

A few days later there was the baptism. It was so difficult to break out of our family desert, especially in winter, that the three youngest were baptised in Mother's bedroom. On such occasions my father rarely missed the chance of sounding off.

That time I was the one to get it as soon as I walked in the door. Having lived normally for so many months I had got into the habit, I suppose, of a freedom of speech that, to say the least, was unwelcome under the paternal roof.

"I want the baby called Madeleine," I said with what was described as incredible effrontery.

The worst of it was that after he had finished with me, father turned on Grandmother and accused her of having suggested this intervention. At last the vicar rang, my father went down to let him in and calm was restored. When the ceremony was over, Grandmother and I left without further ado.

The plain fact was that my father did not know, and never knew, I think, that if Marguerite had been so named it was precisely, and secretly, because Grandmother's second name was Marguerite. As for her first name, Oliérie, one could scarcely have inflicted that on a second victim, even if this strange appellation did pay homage to Olier de Verneuil, the founder of the Sulpician Order in Canada.

* * *

During the weeks that followed, Grandmother worked on my first communion dress. Between fittings I stayed beside her and watched what she was doing. Until finally one morning I felt the urge to sew too.

"I'd like to make a dress for my doll."

Grandmother looked at me as though I had just made a statement of world-shattering importance. After many Oh's and Ah's she gave me a piece of white material with a rose check that she was prepared to let me cut out by myself, but I really didn't feel bold enough. I explained what I wanted, a straight bodice and a gathered skirt, and she took charge of the cutting. Then she threaded a needle and handed it to me.

I sat down near the window and eagerly began to sew. Several times I handed the needle back to be rethreaded. After nearly an hour had flown by, I exclaimed in triumph, "It's finished, Grandmother!"

"What? Already?"

I thought I deciphered a tinge of criticism in her voice. But there the dress was, draping my little fist, and it looked like nothing else than a dress.

"Well now, that's not bad at all."

I was thrilled. It didn't last long. Briskly turning the object inside out, Grandmother had discovered a jungle of thread ends and frayed edges.

"Good Lord! That child will never know how to sew!"

The way she said this I felt distinctly that I would be better dead than living, not knowing how to sew. Nor have I survived without learning the art.

I took up the dress again and set about cutting away everything that dishonoured its underside, and did such a good job that when I tried to put it on my doll everything fell apart. But Grandmother was not the woman to leave me in such a fix. Needle in hand she showed me how to stitch a seam, and how to finish it off. Then, most important of all, she explained that it took a great deal of patience to learn to sew and offered up pious hopes that I would learn this patience.

As much as I adored my Grandmother, I wasn't too keen on hearing her make what we children among ourselves called *un speech*. Dialogue between grownups and children wasn't at all the fashion in those days. More often than not, the adults did the talking and the children pretended to listen — in fear and trembling if the adult was angry, slightly bored if the grownup was in a good mood. As for me, true daughter of my father, then as now, I ran a little homemade blockade of my own against *le speech* and scarcely ever helped Grandmother turn it into a dialogue. I think she was perfectly well aware of what was going on inside me. So she never went on for very long.

Towards noon she tidied up her sewing and went to the kitchen where Diana had begun to get lunch ready. Grandmother cooked as she sewed, exquisitely. Her meals were always refined and infinitely various. She knew by heart what different seasonings were needed for every dish and took her dry herbs from a special shelf in the kitchen cupboard where they were arranged in little pots. The braided garlic hung close by. If tomatoes were required, she would peel them and take out the seeds. Onions were cut so fine they melted and disappeared in the pan. In no time at all wonderful smells filled the kitchen.

"How do you know what to put in, Grandmother?" I would ask.

"One learns," was her invariable reply.

Could everything be learned then? I certainly had a lot of work ahead of me. But from the tone of voice she used in answering me, I realized that this demanding woman would have judged it very ill had I not set about learning all those things myself.

* * *

One Thursday, after our weekly visit to my elder sisters who were already boarders at the convent, Mother, Grandmother and I stopped off at the registrar's office to arrange for my own admission at the beginning of May. I remember being very anxious that the sister in charge should admire my new coat.

"Grandmother made it. The collar is all hand-embroidered."

"Well! We're already quite sophisticated, aren't we," exclaimed the sister.

She said this as though I was suffering from some mild disease, not too serious, but one that needed watching. She pursed up her lips. I didn't like her.

In no time it was the first of May. The day before, Grandmother had carried out the last major fitting of my first communion dress: the long muslin gown with the little reticule tied to the waist, the embroidered petticoats, the tulle veil, the gloves and shoes. I took the memory of all that whiteness with me like a promise.

I also took a whole little boarding school trousseau. I was especially delighted with the things I had never had all to myself before, the soap, the talcum powder. No one to share my tube of toothpaste with. I would be able to eat it quietly all alone. I just loved it. My hair had always been combed with Mother's comb or Grandmother's. Now I was entitled to a sturdy one of my own which I still possess, minus three teeth broken out the following year in a fit of anger.

"So you will never forget the ugliness of anger, you will have to keep your broken comb," Mother told me.

"The ugliness of anger. . . ." The poor woman knew what she was talking about.

I also took certain things that seemed very strange to me: a white tulle veil for mass, and a black tulle veil for benedictions, vespers and other evening ceremonies.

The first fell on Thursday, on visiting day. I knew the parlour well for having gone there so often to see my sisters. The boarders sat on one side of the grill and the parents on the other, on the world's side. Kisses of greeting and good-bye were given between the bars. I was in such a hurry to be kissed that way I wanted to cross over to the other side at once, so Mother Saint-Henri came and opened the door cut into the bars at the far end of the room. But when I saw Mother and Grandmother go, I was overcome with despair and began to scream. Fortunately some lollipops were kept on hand for just such occasions. Not that they were any real consolation, but it was too difficult to suck and howl at the same time.

* * *

From that very first day I suffered acutely in my new state as a boarder. Apparently it had never occurred to the nuns that I might be totally ignorant of the rules of the house. I have often observed this feature of convent life since. What goes on within the walls seems so important to those poor girls who have cut themselves off from all contact with reality, that they simply cannot understand how anyone could not know what occupies every minute of their lives. I was expected to do what I was supposed to without ever being told what it was. The other little girls who had known all the rules since September seemed to think the same. Sometimes the sisters would give instructions, but they meant nothing to me because I was not familiar with the convent vocabulary. I was immediately taken to be disobedient by nature and in the first two days earned several reprimands. My fate for the next ten years was sealed from that instant on.

Still I was very lucky to get no more than scoldings. Corporal punishment was not as common as in my father's house, but it was not altogether neglected either. A few days before my arrival there had been a collective punishment that was still being whispered about. Here is the story. At the end of each of the morning classes — catechism, French and English — each pupil received a mark: very good, good, or fair. The morning in question the mistress of this division announced that girls who did not get their three "very goods" would be punished as an example to all. At eleven o'clock came the separation of the wheat from the tares. The tares were led off to the dormitory where they were ordered to take off their dresses. Then, arming herself with a stiff brush, the sister scrubbed their faces with laundry soap. It was a powerful detergent; even without the brush it left the skin raw in no time flat. Dark girls resisted a little better than the rest, but the poor little blondes — not to mention the redheads — came through the ordeal their faces peeling and oozing blood. I was quite shaken by this story, all the more so because my own sister, Françoise, was among the number of the skinned. I knew all about blows delivered in anger. But I had not yet heard of such meticulous and patient tortures. Decidedly, apart from Mother, Grandmother and Grandfather, grownups were not much good.

After the third or fourth day I found myself involved in my own first adventure. Even though a climate of strict puritanism reigned in our family, we were nonetheless used to calling certain functions by their proper names. At home we never used those ridiculous expressions which avoid the use of "peepee" but which, since they mean the same thing, are scarcely more distinguished for all that. I once knew a family where they said, "Do a wet," which is really the height of stupidity. But since there is no real ceiling to the ridiculous, these people went on to use the same word for the organ as for the function, all of which I find rather repulsive. The importance of a word lies in its meaning I should think, and if "chair" meant "whorehouse," the word "chair" in that case would have to be replaced by another word, which would in turn rapidly fall into discredit, and so on until we had no place to sit down.

In short, one day I had to "go upstairs," for that was the way the thing was said at the convent, even though we often might be on the same floor or the floor above. I happened to confide to my neighbour that I had a terrible urge to do a peepee. Hiding her mouth behind her hand, "Ah dzou!" she exclaimed. "Dzou," in that particular institution, was the strongest expression of horror imaginable. But, because I was so new, I didn't know the meaning of "dzou." The period ended just at that minute, and since we all went upstairs in a group, my problem was solved and I forgot the confidence I had shared with my neighbour.

At recess I was called over by the scrub-brush sister who made it her duty to get me to confess my sin. As it happened, I had completely forgotten it. One must really know nothing about children to think that they know what they said an hour earlier. Besides, since I had no idea of the organized tattle-taling that went on in convents, I couldn't understand what it was all about. I hadn't even spoken to that particular nun.

"You said a bad word."

To whom? When? The soul of good will, I tried to remember. But I drew a complete blank.

"So you want to add a lie to your bad word?"

Oh-oh! I had heard that somewhere before, and I realized that I had just earned myself a double punishment on the heels of the single. The more I saw of life, the more it seemed the same. But this time, weary of the fray, the sister dismissed me. I thought that was the end of it. But I didn't know who I was dealing with. That evening at bedtime I was taken to a room adjoining the dormitory.

"You're not going to go to bed without owning up? Just think, you might die in your sleep."

Good God! That didn't help matters much. Here I was now, to all intents and purposes threatened with death. I searched and searched. Nothing. The sister made me sit closeted alone with my crime, while the other little girls went to bed. From time to time she came to inquire into my disposition to confess. It wasn't good intentions that I lacked, it was a subject for confession.

I kept on searching and shivering in my nightgown. At last, after an hour perhaps, though it seemed as if half the night had gone by, she said: "I realize it must be embarrassing for you to repeat the word. I'm going to help you. It begins with a 'p' — "

It was good of her, but at my wits' end with all the unexpected, inextricable, petty, and insane confusion of the whole story, and overcome with sleep, "p" — wasn't much to set me on the right track. I kept on searching.

"Well,? p — p, e — "

"P, e" — ? I can't have been very brilliant that night. "P, e" — ? I couldn't see what it was. Finally the sister, who wanted to go to bed, I suppose, but for all that didn't want to let me risk my eternal salvation, lost patience.

"You said 'peepee.'"

She hid her mouth behind her hand, just as my little schoolmate had done. She made me say an act of contrition and then let me go to bed.

Next Thursday during the visit, my sisters told that I had been scolded but said they didn't know why. Mother insisted on knowing. Well, I was so convinced that I had done a thing, not really dreadful but running counter to the spirit of the institution, that I didn't want to admit to something in front of my sisters which might have caused them endless embarrassment.

"I said the food was no good, I said it was no better than cat shit."

In the end, that was not much better, but I felt there was an enormous difference between the two words: in the second there was no reference to human needs. The human had been duly rejected. Anyway, Mother laughed till the tears came, and my sisters too.

"Don't you worry about it anymore, it's all forgotten."

That remained to be seen.

I didn't like lying to Mother. It didn't happen often. With Grandmother, never. That was because though she might scold me for doing wrong, she never punished me. She thought that a scolding was enough. In Mother's case it was different. When we were quite patently at fault, when we had broken something for instance (I should point out that my father made no allowance for children's clumsiness and punished us just as severely for accidentally breaking a window as he would for deliberate badness), before inescapable evidence, Mother would have to tell what had happened. The first question my father would ask was, "Has the child been punished?" Mother couldn't decently say yes unless we had been. It is impossible to bring children up in that sort of duplicity. She had to reply vigorously in the affirmative or else he would have taken charge of the punishment himself. Mother wanted to avoid that at all costs. This didn't prevent my father, I must add, from often administering a second punishment which was never the same variety as the first. Mother made us stand in a corner. I can't remember ever being sent there by my father.

It isn't really so bad to be sent to the corner. The reason I hated it was for fear my father might come in while I was there. I will never forget my terror one day when I had been really intolerable and was left in the corner until I could hear my father's footsteps shaking the staircase.

"Mother, please forgive me! Please! I promise to be good."

Promptly pardoned and overcome with gratitude, for the next few days I behaved better than I ever had, and I was full of such tenderness for her — I remember this distinctly — that I even kissed her dress.

Lying to my father was quite another matter. It was a kind of vital necessity. Good sport, too. And vengeance, when you come to think of it. If all the lies invented by all of us over a period of, say, twenty years, had had to be totalled up, it would have kept a sharp accountant pretty busy. Children lie not only out of fear but also when they have to deal with people they don't respect. "That kind doesn't deserve to be told the truth." Truthfulness is not just a duty, it's a gift. To make matters worse, my father was not in the least observant. He always believed we were lying when we were telling the truth, and vice versa. The thoughts that such an attitude inspires in a child could hardly be called indulgent.

*   *   *

So I progressed towards my first communion. The days preceding the ceremony were spent in rehearsal. We were taught how to take communion and how to go to confession. It was on this occasion that my sin, my bad word, was trotted out again. Confession drill was said aloud between a sister and the five or six little girls who took catechism together. The sister would sit down, and one of us would kneel close beside her and confess "examples of sins." When my turn came, we passed rapidly from example to reality.

"You won't forget to confess the — well, you know what I mean — "

Crash bang! Again I had completely forgotten my crime. I looked at her with the blank eye of one who hasn't understood.

"Don't you remember? The thing you were punished for just after you came."

The little girls began to fidget and gave me a queer look.

Now I really became desperate. I don't suppose I knew the word "ridicule," but I had the distinct impression that if I let the sister get the better of me I would be in it up to my neck.

Then, to complicate matters even further, the sister second-in-command, the one who was called the second mistress of the division, took it upon herself, too, to help me make a good first communion. She knew that I had said a bad word, though she didn't know the ins and outs of it. But there was obviously a conversion to be worked here, so the private talks between us became interminable. Once again I was summoned to confess. I couldn't understand why, because I had already told everything to the first mistress, and in any case I was supposed to repeat everything once and for all in the confessional. I say "supposed to" because I wasn't fully convinced that such an avowal was necessary. On the other hand, perhaps I had committed a real sin. I didn't know where I stood.

At last, thank heaven, we had a lesson from the same chaplain who was going to hear our confessions. He explained that to sin you had to know that you were doing something bad. My problem was solved. At our next private meeting I felt like sharing my discovery with Mother Sainte-Mathilda, but on thinking it over I decided not to. With adults one always says too much.

Because of all this fuss I watched "the most beautiful day in my life" draw near without much fervour. If it hadn't been for the thought of the white muslin and tulle I would have been bored more than anything else.

When the time came for confession, the nun made a last little sign to me — what with all the undercover advice I was getting my companions were beginning to think of me as a leper — and I disappeared behind the curtain. The chaplain, M. Larue, was a darling. He took me on his knee, declared that at my age no one wanted to hurt God, and said that he would give me absolution anyway in case I had done anything bad. That was fine with me. I said my act of contrition, he gave me a lollipop and out I came, proud as a peacock, with the keen satisfaction of feeling that my two division mistresses had been properly done in.

That night in the dormitory I found spread out on my chair the long white dress, the veil, the embroidered petticoats, and the little reticule. Besides this, Grandmother had sent me another dress in embroidered muslin — I still have it, it is all hand-sewn and in stitches so fine they're a joy to behold — but this was a short dress meant to be put on after the ceremony so that I wouldn't be hobbled all day in long skirts. All this was fully explained in a letter that came with the package. I was in ecstasy.

The next morning the nun came to help me dress. Despite my protestations, she first put on the short slip, then the short dress, then the long slip, then the long dress. It was pure luck there was only one pair of shoes. I could hardly breathe, and I was monumental. I went down to the chapel completely preoccupied with this blunder and don't believe I thought of anything else all during the ceremony.

After mass, Mother, Grandmother, and Grandfather came to the main gate to get my two sisters and myself, and we spent the day together at Grandmother's. Diana had to press the short dress which had come through the adventure badly rumpled, and after that everything was happy again. That dress must have had an evil spell cast upon it. The last time it was used was for a school prize-day and my sister Margot wore it. They put it on her back to front and the poor child, unable to bend her arms, looked half-crucified. She was a sorry sight. On top of that, since the sleeves only just covered the elbows and the nuns refused to let her expose so much skin, they speedily concocted (I think the adverb conveys what I intend it to) a sturdy pair of sleeves in factory cotton which made an interesting contrast with the Swiss muslin.

* * *

Several days later I returned to my father's house. My first experience as a boarder had left me rather disgruntled — particularly because I had imagined it all in rosy colours. Nevertheless, without the slightest doubt I preferred it by far to life under the parental roof. My sisters felt the same. Whenever the last days of the school year came around, we were the only ones not to be swept up in a wave of impatience and happiness.

Sometimes when we returned we were lucky enough to find my father absent. He was a civil engineer and built roads for the provincial government. This meant that in summertime he did a lot of travelling. In the midst of our miseries we at least had this good fortune — four days' breathing space here, three there.

Mother was blessed with a strong predisposition to gaiety. Despite the painful conditions of her life, this gift of gaiety had survived. For that matter, most of her children inherited something of it. So, when my father left, he had scarcely turned his back before we were all transformed. I remember especially the difference in climate between our walks back from mass when he was away and when he wasn't. Until the road was built we used to walk along the railroad tracks. On Sundays when we were alone together the walk back was gay and silly. We would sing:

Whenever I find the wild hare's lair
I find that the wild hare isn't there.
When he gets up at the break of day
He carries his bed and bedding away.

Or:

Nearby the fountain a bird was singing
Fluttering, fluttering. . . .

"Mother, sing us the song about the ghost."

A brilliant ghost. . . .

"No, tell the story first."

"But I've told it a hundred times."

"That doesn't matter. It's still funny."

I've forgotten the story now. All I remember is that there was a story, and that it was about one of Mother's friends, perhaps Louise de Grandpré, who used to sing this song to make her friends laugh. But there was something about the origin of the song that has slipped my memory. After the story was told, at last Mother could sing:

> A brilliant ghost beguiled my youth,
> But when I came back to my senses again. . . .

We doubled up with laughter, and it was the same thing every time we came back from mass alone with her. The other times we returned in a funereal silence.

I think it is because of these moments of respite that we managed to hold out. That little hope of being able to breathe freely carried us on from one week to the next, from one month to another, until the convent took us back in September.

In the middle of August we began to get our trunks ready. That never happened without a scene. There were always things that needed replacing. That meant asking for money. Filthy money. Finally the day came when it was impossible to put off asking any longer, and all the children were warned. The night before, Mother would remark, in a seemingly offhand way:

"Tomorrow morning, I will have to ask your father for money."

No need to say more. That was as good as a thousand cautions. By dawn we were all properly furtive. We didn't walk, we slid. We were careful not to block the bathrooms, yet to get extra clean as befitted this morning above all others. We hurried into the dining room ready to spoon down imperturbably quantities of rugged wheat porridge, breakfast of centenarians. We asked for more. It's good, we said, with fine lack of foresight, not thinking of the obligations we were creating for tomorrow when we would have to take second helpings for nothing. Then breakfast was over. A wind of terror blew each of us into the corner where we would be least in the way.

In the kitchen, her handkerchief rolled up into a ball, Mother repeatedly wiped her face and hands. I can see her yet — if I forgot everything else I would never forget that — in her perennial grey cotton dress that she wore around the house, her hair too long — she wasn't permitted to cut it — tied in a heavy chignon that tired her and which she used to lift up with a mechanical gesture, her temples shiny with a mentholated ointment, for those were the migraine days — yes I can picture her easily, I saw her like that so often.

As the time drew on towards eight-thirty — his train left at the half hour — my father came out into the hall and began to get ready to leave for work. As on every other morning, he had forgotten to take a handkerchief, or his keys, or his cigars. He alone had the right to such shortcomings and he certainly wasn't slow to use it. One of us would fly upstairs and bring back the missing article. This was the moment that Mother had been waiting for in the kitchen. She waited, praying silently. To me this sight was almost unbearable. You could see her lips moving, her head bowed, her hands clasped over the moist little ball of handkerchief. She stopped praying and I thought the time had come. But no, she began again, and I knew she was strongly tempted to wait until it was too late. Suddenly she rushed across the distance that separated her from the hall, almost in one bound, as if to cut off all possibility of retreat. In a rush to leave, my father wouldn't have time to create a scene of much amplitude. But on bad mornings he preferred to miss the train rather than miss such an opportunity. In the first place, he knew very well that Mother had delayed her request in order to keep his violence down to a minimum and, since the subject of money always sent him off into his most majestic tantrums, he felt cheated. Secondly, if he didn't explode in anger, wouldn't we get into the habit of asking for money every time we needed it?

The next train didn't go until a quarter past nine. That left him three-quarters of an hour and almost anything could happen in that time. Three-quarters of an hour is a very long time.

I remember one morning in particular that was more horrible than all the rest. My father had replied to Mother's request by a truly exceptional explosion, difficult as it was to reach such heights. After three-quarters of an hour, during which he had treated all of us he could get his hands on with incredible brutality, at last he left the house. That day he was due to leave on a trip. Mother, poor dear, didn't want to let him go — who can tell what might happen on a trip or whether the return is sure — without attempting a reconciliation. She followed him out onto the verandah and held out her hand to him. Then, since he didn't show any signs of taking it:

"You're not going to refuse to take my hand?" she said.

By way of reply he sent it flying back with a blow that did credit to the great strength he was so proud of. Her little hand smashed back against the brick wall and began to turn blue instantly. By evening it was enormous and black, an awful thing that it hurt to look at. But Mother never uttered a word of blame. I must admit that I found this placid attitude in no way edifying; on the contrary, deep down it exasperated me terribly.

It had always been, and ever was to be, the rule that my father, once his anger was satisfied, docked the requested sum by a considerable amount. After this, he would start thinking about things he might need.

"While you're at it you can buy me a shirt, two ties, et cetera."

Without giving up an extra cent, naturally. Then, well pleased with himself — though this self-satisfaction didn't make him any pleasanter — he left. At last!

As my eldest sister used to say:

"You figure out that you'll need, at the very least, fifty dollars. You say to yourself, I'll ask for thirty-five. When the time comes you ask for twenty-five. And you get fifteen, out of which you have to take seven for the shirt or the ties."

As a matter of fact, my father was a great consumer of neckties. He soiled them constantly and would never trust anyone but himself to clean them. Ammonia, undiluted javex, cleansing powder — anything went. And so did the ties. The first result, as you can imagine, was a discoloured spot. To fix this he would apply ink, shoe polish. When that dried it would crack and shred and take the cloth with it. An engineer is not, of course, a chemist, but it seems to me that he might have had some inkling of the properties of chlorine. I have often thought that if, to our misfortune, he had been a lawyer or a notary, which is to say even more estranged from the properties of chlorine and the like, he would surely have succeeded in pulverizing the house during one of those cleaning sessions. As it was, he was obliged secretly to dispose of a great number of damaged ties, but nothing in the world would have made him ask for advice. He knew everything.

*　　*　　*

School started between the first and seventh of September. I was relieved to find on returning to the convent for my first full year that Sister Scrub-brush had been promoted to take charge of the third division. That year it was my elder sisters who reaped the benefits of the educational talents of that saintly girl, but before leaving her I would like to tell how she received the news of the birth of my youngest sister, Thérèse.

"Mother has just had a lovely baby girl," Dine burst out coming back from one of the Sunday parlours.

To her surprise, she was sent straight to the corner and learned, when she came to beg pardon, that she should have said:

"I have just got a lovely baby sister."

Not the same thing at all. Anyone can see that the arrival of a sister is a decent sort of event because the flesh doesn't enter into it, whereas the birth of a daughter, even for a mother who is Christian and all that, implies a carnal kind of hell that it is a duty to ignore — in words at least — for the thoughts of those poor obsessed girls must have been quite another thing! This one in particular would have got along fine with my father, both in thoughts and in silences. She was so afraid of impure remarks passing between the little girls under her care, and especially of the occasions that recess offered for such transgressions, that she made her whole division keep in one solid block while she pivoted around in the middle of them, all eyes and ears. Making her own the well-known principle, "Troubles never come singly," she went through life very proud of her discovery, repeating, "Never singly, never in pairs, always the whole division together." You should have seen the poor things, a good forty pupils forbidden to run or play, glued together around that black hen like so many sick chicks.

As for me, for a long time yet I was to stay in the little ones' division. The new division mistress, Mother Saint-Chérubin,[3] didn't like me much. She began by wanting to uncurl my hair — slicking it down with water, which made it curl twice as much; which is why, I think, she lost all faith in my docility. Besides, I always had the feeling that she had been told the story of my bad word and held it against me. Then, too, I was a reasoner. I have always been a reasoner. When Christmas time came around she had a chance to show her aversion for me, and I had a chance for a good laugh behind her back.

Our comings and goings in that season were like a ballet exercise: advance; retire; turn about — We went to midnight mass at the convent; we went home to spend Christmas day with our families; we came back again that night; the next morning we heard the first term marks read out; then we went back to our families again for the rest of the holidays. Poor parents, their festivities were quite spoiled by all this traipsing back and forth. Of course, I am expressing concern here for other people's families, for at home the festivities, well — anyway, it was customary on Christmas night for each of the four divisions to have a little celebration which we spent a long time preparing.

I sang very badly. Through my nose, it seems, more than was absolutely necessary, but nonetheless very boldly. So I was chosen to sing with two other little girls who had pretty voices but who suffered from shyness. They provided the quality, I the brass. We had got up "Three angels came tonight," the number that started off the programme. For the occasion we were strapped into rustling white wings. I loved to get dressed up. I was in seventh heaven.

"Anyone who comes in later than four o'clock will not take part in the performance tonight," said the sister, along with her Merry Christmas.

Now, to get out of the wilderness where we lived there were very few trains, even fewer on Sundays and holidays. On Christmas day we had a choice between one that would have got us to Quebec two or three hours too early, and another something like a quarter of an hour too late.

"You don't mean to tell me that the sister is not intelligent enough to understand that," Mother said.

Poor dear Mother!

I was greeted with, "You are a quarter of an hour late. You won't take part tonight."

The concert had been arranged by the second mistress of the division, the artistic one. She pleaded, but in vain, there was no help for it. After supper all the little girls began to dress up except for the few pariahs who were never chosen for this kind of thing, and me, the reprobate. The guests, a couple of dozen novices and postulants, took their seats.

The two unpunished angels, "who were to come that night" seemed scared stiff. Hesitantly, they shuffled on. The piano struck up the prelude. The moment they should have joined in came and went without either of the pair opening her mouth. The accompanist improvised a little fantasy and began the prelude again. Nothing happened. At last she loudly gave the note. Two feeble squeaks, as from two hoarse mice, stole out and shrank back immediately. One of the little girls started to cry. The other, not wishing to miss such a good way out, did likewise. They had to be collected and led off.

It was decided to move on to the second number. But the panic had done its work. Every little throat choked up, not an eye was dry. Self-confidence, memory, the fire of inspiration, all went up in smoke. The guests fidgeted, and cursed, I imagine, the tradition that willed that novices should attend the little girls' Christmas party. It became necessary to interrupt what could now scarcely be called the gala performance. And who took the blame? You guessed, it was me. Inescapably, because, as stupid as she was, the nun couldn't help seeing that deep in my heart of hearts I was having a good laugh at her.

Yes, it's true, I sang through my nose in a frightful manner. Despite that, I was often given a chance to display my talents. Because of my hair. All year long they tried to unkink it, but when it so happened that a Saint John the Baptist was required, for example, they were only too pleased that I was crowned with what in ordinary circumstances was considered a worldly adornment. I had worldly hair. But at midnight mass I led the procession into the chapel, my white dress partly covered with an imitation sheepskin, shepherd's crook in hand, my head half veiled in what I would call a compromise device (I was playing a boy's role but I was still a girl, and, besides, people had to see my hair because that's why I had been chosen). I entered the chapel then, singing. My sister Françoise claims that I sang:

> Sweet little Jesus so humble in the stable!
> Ah! Make me good like you.

I think myself that we sang that another time, and that for this occasion I sang:

> Now good shepherds, gather round
> Let us go and see the Messiah.

Anyway!

"Try not to sing through your nose too much," the sister would whisper just at the last minute.

I would have been glad to oblige her, but apparently I could never hear myself. For the chaplain's birthday that year I was entrusted, thanks to my hair again, with the role of a little Italian boy in a sort of operetta for two voices. The text was larded with words like "lazzaroni, macaroni" that we tossed off with a great rolling of "r"s. Though I've forgotten all the words except "Do not awaken the sleeping cat," I can still hum the main theme. The question of my costume caused grave uncertainties. It is hardly necessary to stress that they didn't want to put pants on me, but at the same time they didn't really want to dress me up in a skirt. They might have changed the role and made it a girl, but the character was really too bold for that. In the end they put me into a pair of big bloomers, covered with a pleated skirt just a trifle shorter, white stockings that all too fictitiously were supposed to resemble skin and, on top of that, knee socks. To cover my torso, two knitted sweaters, one on top of the other, one red, one yellow, to seem loud and Italian. To crown the ensemble, a jaunty little hat which, for once, completely hid my hair. That didn't matter. It was there underneath just the same, and everyone knew it was curly.

In the wings — which in this case was the corridor — the other actress, a big girl called Blanche, was shaking like a leaf.

"Haven't you got butterflies?" she kept asking.

I didn't know what that meant exactly, and anyway, I was too busy thinking about not singing through my nose. Mother Saint-Joseph, who had directed this show, would put drops in my nostrils, make me have one last good blow, and push me out onto the stage where I was supposed to take a few aimless steps, yawn, and then lie down on the floor, which, as everyone knows, is what Italians do. At each intermission Mother Saint-Joseph gave me a quick rub down — in all my woollies I was melting away — put in more drops and made me blow again.

"All right now, try not to sing through your nose."

All these ministrations didn't change a thing. If I sang the way I did, it wasn't because my nose was plugged, it was just because my voice chose to come out that exit.

*   *   *

We learned catechism, arithmetic, religious history, a little English — well now, saying that I suddenly remember that every other day we used to recite all our prayers in English, "Our Father," "Hail Mary," and the rest of them — and maybe a little geography. But though I ransack my memory, the only classes I really remember well are the ones in French: grammar, oral reading, dictation.

As regards dictation, there was a copybook that we called the honour book in which each child who had written a test dictation without making a single mistake was allowed to transcribe the paragraph in her finest hand. Although my writing was still very poor, I used to dream of winning this honour. The day I could announce this good news to Grandmother in my laundry (I used to send her my washing and this was the diplomatic pouch we used for our correspondence), it seemed to me would be by far the greatest day in my life. At last it came. I copied out my dictation, my tongue thrust firmly between my teeth. I was as proud as a peacock.

When the work was done I took the honour book up to Mother Saint-Chérubin, turned to go, but was called back at once.

"Aren't you ashamed of your handwriting? Just look at Cécile's beside yours."

Now though Cécile was in my class, she was three years older than all the rest of us. Such injustice broke my heart. "Cécile is three years older than I am."

I didn't have time to close my mouth before a heavy slap brought me around to a nicer notion of what partiality was all about. I was much surprised, after a day or two, to discover that Mother Saint-Chérubin was spreading the rumour that I was giving myself out as younger than I really was. It would be a mistake to think that stories of rejuvenation only circulate among actresses and fashionable women of a certain age. In the convent schools I know, in those my sisters and I went to, as soon as a child was ever so slightly ahead of the others a whispering campaign began to the effect that she was lying about her age. It often turned out, and this was my case, that you were accused before you even understood the nature of the charge.

After that slap in the face, Mother Saint-Chérubin began to hate me thoroughly. I didn't think much of her either, but my feelings were no match for hers. It wasn't surprising. I have often noticed that after the blows are over, the one who strikes hates more than the one who is struck.

Each new day now brought me some new trial.

By way of the package of clean laundry, Grandmother often sent us candy. Even in those days, drugstores were well stocked with goodies of all kinds. As there were often damaged boxes, or chocolates on display that got bleached by the sun, and as my sisters and I were ready customers for such unsaleable merchandise, we would sometimes receive parcels of candy a good deal bigger than the ones the other girls got. Mother Saint-Chérubin let that get under her skin. Normally the most she could do was talk endlessly about my piggishness, but she was lying in wait for me in Lent. Week after week she made me give up all the candies to the poor. What poor? That's what I never knew. Off she would go, the box under her arm, and that was the last I would hear of it. I was sure she stuffed herself with them at night in her cell, and it would have been hard to make me believe otherwise. I didn't dare say anything to Grandmother for fear of upsetting her. It was a long Lent.

A similar thing happened when this nun discovered that Grandfather used to give me twenty-five-cent bills, which we used to call paper quarters and which were thought of as money made specially for children, sort of baby dollars. I kept them lovingly as I kept everything Grandfather gave me.

One day, after morning prayers, Mother Saint-Chérubin launched into a harangue in support of the work of The Holy Childhood. Brandishing the little bank we were supposed to put our offerings in, she remarked that it didn't make very much noise. Everyone allowed that, and each of us, I think, was ready to contribute a coin or two. But she carried on treacherously:

"Now, as you know, money doesn't always make a noise. If one of you, for example, decided to give the paper twenty-five-cents that she hoards so avariciously, they wouldn't jingle in the bank, but think of the number of little Chinese souls she could save."

Everyone looked at me. I couldn't believe my ears. Give away something Grandfather had given me? Oh no! Never! I played deaf and blind. Besides, I knew very well that I wasn't the only one to have a little money set aside, and that certain little girls had saved a good deal more than I had. But while I was turning a deaf ear, the time for insinuations had slipped by.

"You're just a miser," said Mother Saint-Chérubin, pointing an accusing forefinger at me, "hard-hearted . . . blah-blah-blah."

The upshot of this was that I got out one of the little bills and went over and stuck it into the slot of the bank.

"Is that all? That's not much."

I put in a second one.

"Two? The fate of the souls of those little heathen Chinese doesn't really matter much to you, does it?"

She didn't leave me alone until I had put everything I had into that rotten little slot. In all there were not more, perhaps, than about ten bills, but it seemed to me the whole business lasted for hours, I have such a keen memory of how badly I felt. Yes, and I now declare in the name of truth (one has the right to use that kind of language when one is a saver of souls) that after forty years I still haven't really given that money with my whole heart, which strikes me as being quite a hazard for certain souls, even yellow ones, priced at twenty-five cents a pair.

It may seem that I suffered from a persecution complex. There were good grounds for it. But it mustn't be thought that I was the only one persecuted. Almost all of us were, each in turn, and each for her own particular reasons. I remember one little girl who was always suspected of throwing her crusts behind the radiator, which stirred up very moving scenes, "God's good bread," tears in the voice, the works.

"Is it you again, Pauline?"

Try as she might to defend herself, Pauline usually ended up by being forced to eat the dried crusts garnished with a good coating of dust. Sometimes she protested so sincerely that Mother Saint-Chérubin was left with her find on her hands.

"Since no one wishes to confess her guilt, I am going to take them away, and that will be my dinner tonight."

That didn't fool anyone, least of all me, for with my own eyes I had seen Mother Saint-Chérubin furtively stepping into the toilet with her little package of crusts and stepping out again empty-handed. But more often than not poor Pauline, sobbing and wracked with nausea, unmoved by the notion of "God's good bread," had to eat them up to the last crumb. It was a sorry sight to watch her dusting off her crusts.

In my case I know very well that the letters which Grandmother — and sometimes Grandfather, though, as a man, he didn't much like to write — slipped into my bundle of laundry used to irritate this nun. These letters, which she read, for it was she who opened the parcels, usually began: "My pretty darling." That had the effect of making all Mother Saint-Chérubin's Jansenist aridity squirm. Especially, as you can imagine, the word, "pretty."

Is it invariably the case that love shown to a child by one person always draws in its wake bad treatment from others? I am inclined to think so. Every time I was loved in childhood I had to pay for it dearly. For instance, the deep affection shown me by one sister, Mother Marie-du-Bon-Conseil, drew down upon me the animosity of two or three others, not to mention that of the girls for whom love always meant injustice — though that isn't always true. What does breed injustice is caprice. Much later I got to know a sister who went from one caprice to another, and when my turn came, for several months I profited from a number of injustices. But the fate of the favourite whose turn was over was far from rosy.

Many of us who went through the system complain that our minds were left uncultivated. And what about the heart, then, what about the heart? The very word brought on a blush. Of shame. And of anger, too, often enough.

* * *

That first year at the convent slowly drew to a close. When spring came the dormitory windows were left open at night, and one morning when I woke up before the bell I heard the distant clang of a streetcar. It was surely the one that, coming down from l'Avenue des Erables, ran along la Grande-Allée, la rue Saint-Louis, la Côte de la Fabrique, then down la rue Saint-Jean where Grandmother and Grandfather lived. Perhaps during the coming holidays I would be allowed to spend a few weeks with them. That would have to be paid for by more weeks spent with my father. I was ready to pay, because even at my young age nothing was free. At any rate, as I lay there listening to the bell of the streetcar, I learned something about the nostalgia of happiness.

In the meantime my sister Thérèse was born. The baptism took place, like the two preceding ones, in Mother's bedroom. Once bitten twice shy, this time I made no suggestion as to a suitable name for the child. It was not at all necessary. The growing vogue for Sainte Thérèse de Lisieux gave rise to innumerable Thérèses throughout the world, and to a great many plaster statues.

The only disagreeable memory I have of this ceremony is that little Marguerite was almost squashed under big Abbé Chouinard. She was twenty-two months old by now, and, like every child that age, her one thought was to get all the use she could out of her two little legs. At the application of the salt and holy water she took advantage of the general immobility to scamper about, almost fell, and resolutely clutched the Abbé, whose weight, rather than fixing him firmly to the ground as one might have expected, made him capsize on the spot. Everyone rushed forward, some to set the Abbé up again, some to free Margot from the avalanche. There were a good three hundred pounds of it, and it seemed more than likely we would find the child squashed thin as a sheet of paper.

The new baby held little interest for the three of us who were at the convent. All we knew was that Mother didn't come to see us any more, and that it was very long from one Thursday to the next. At last came the solemn and interminable prize giving, after several days given over to general hubbub and trunk packing.

I recall very little of the holidays that followed, except that I spent them convinced that I wouldn't find Mother Saint-Chérubin at the convent when I went back. On the strength of my previous experience, I thought that the first mistress changed every year. My disappointment at finding her long ferreting nose again, and her dry hands so quick to slap, was bitter indeed. I started the year off, then and there, fully discouraged, and nothing is sadder than discouragement in a seven-year-old.

Not more than a few weeks had gone by before we had our first "affray," or so my sisters and I used to call it. It was the affair of the letter to Billy.

Billy was the husband of one of Grandmother's nieces, the daughter of her brother, Ovide de Bondy. Great-uncle Ovide lived in the States and was an organist. His daughter, Antoinette, had married a charming boy whose family name, I must admit, was Connery. But in English that didn't mean anything.[4]

I had met him, perhaps during those holidays, perhaps the summer before, when he had come with his wife and mother-in-law to spend a few weeks with Grandmother. He seemed to me to be a kind of hero. He had been in the war and spoke enthusiastically about France. I used to sit on his knee after dinner and he would sing me American songs, translating them as he went along, just like that, without thinking twice about it. His songs about the war made it seem, the way he sang about it, like an endless succession of good times.

Don't want to get better, don't want to get worse,
'Cause I'm in love with my beautiful nurse.
Every morning and every night
She gives me the medicine that sets me right.

"Not '*le medicine*,' '*la medicine*,'" Antoinette corrected in her grave voice.

The doctor seems to worry 'bout my condition,
But, thank the Lord, I still got some ambition.

The idea of someone not wanting to get well seemed awfully funny to me.

"You see, if I was sick and you come to look after me — "

"Came," said Antoinette.

" — came. I wouldn't want to get better so's I could stay with you."

Confronted with such gallant sentiments, I decided I would marry him when I grew up, and told him so. Until the day he left, when we were together the two of us talked of nothing else but our engagement. I knew very well, deep inside, that it was all a joke, but I tried to believe that it was true, I was so taken with this handsome cousin.

It so happened that Billy was an American congressman, and that is how the story about the letter started. There was an election and he was re-elected, as he was, for that matter, until his death in 1937 — and Grandmother suggested I should write to congratulate him. After making a rough copy which I carefully kept, I rewrote the letter and gave it to Grandmother. Two weeks later she brought me Billy's reply. I put it, together with the rough copy, at the very back of my desk, determined never to be parted from such a prize possession.

As you can imagine, our desks were searched secretly. I knew this so I hid the letter between the cover of my geography book and its heavy brown paper wrapper. A useless precaution.

On Sunday mornings, the week's marks were read out. One after another we would stand up to hear the worst. When my turn came that Sunday, Mother Saint-Chérubin made a long pause. Then I saw her take out two pieces of paper which I recognized immediately from where I sat. I was more dead than alive. Without any commentary she began to read the letter in which I reminded Billy of his promise to marry me. In exchange, I promised never to have another beau. Then I congratulated him warmly on being re-elected congressman.

I was sick with shame. Not because the feelings I had expressed seemed silly, but because they were laid out for everyone to see, and I already sensed that the baby talk of love must remain secret, that for it to be taken in the right spirit, you have to be in a state of grace, the grace of being the special person in question.

Then came Billy's reply. He had learned to speak French in a rough and ready way at the front when flirting with various French Madelons, and had very few notions about grammar. Mother Saint-Chérubin knew nothing about this way of learning a foreign language. Every error was underlined with great guffaws, even mistakes in gender which are so commonly made in French by English speakers.

"He's an American," I tried to say in various places.

Each time my explanation was drowned out by a "be quiet!" which was extremely damaging to Billy's reputation. What vexed me most was that my engagement seemed to be taken for gospel truth, while Billy's re-election was treated as an enormous joke.

"Congressman? Why not President of the United States while you're at it? Congressman? With all those spelling mistakes?"

To say the very least, I was completely dumbfounded. I tried to figure out where the sheer stupidity of it all began, where the straight meanness came in, where downright dishonesty ended, or vice versa. But I couldn't fathom it. I had no respect for Mother Saint-Chérubin as it was.

After that, my scorn knew no bounds. And this old faker had the nerve to tell us every day that she was the bride of Christ. Poor Christ, he certainly hadn't chosen that of his own free will. He must have been pushed into it. A marriage of convenience at the least. To tell the truth, among all the brides of Christ I've known, I can only think of seven or eight a simple human husband would have taken. I don't expect Christ wanted the others either. Because they were blind to this, there they stayed — and there we were too, and we paid the price for these mismarriages.

This incident ended as everything ended at the convent, where nothing ever really ended at all. It was dragged out again two or three times a week, and as long as Mother Saint-Chérubin and I went on living face to face, she would start talking about it at the drop of a hat. As for me, what I remember most was that I never laid hands on Billy's letter again, and I couldn't get over that.

The most tiresome thing about Mother Saint-Chérubin was her unintelligence. Of all misfortunes that is certainly the worst. To give a fair idea of it, I should tell the story about the snakes. We were forbidden to brush our hair while sitting up in bed. Since it never occurred to anyone to do that, we all agreed wholeheartedly and obeyed the rule without undue inconvenience, and without asking why. Despite this, however, the interdiction was repeated constantly. (Nuns are given to forbidding nonsensical things. In my second convent we were forbidden one day, with a perverse insistence, to take our mirrors along when going for a bath. Nobody had ever done it — but it was done afterwards.) So the inevitable happened. Just to see, my neighbour, Adrienne, sitting up in bed and waiting for prayers, reached out for her brush and began brushing her hair for all she was worth. Mother Saint-Chérubin, pale as a sheet, arrived at a gallop. She made Adrienne get up and shake out her sheets and pillows.

"But what for?" the little girl asked.

"You poor creature! Don't you know that in the heat of the bed hairs turn into snakes? How would you like to wake up tomorrow morning in a nest of snakes?"

It wasn't explained why the hairs on our heads weren't also changed into snakes by the same bed-heat. Nobody asked. We knew better than to ask clever questions. Hypocritically, Mother Saint-Chérubin excused herself for having had to share such a terrifying secret with us, but necessity sets the law. There were some of us who got a good laugh out of that story, but many believed it, "The sister said so."

All old convent girls will agree that nights in the dormitory were always too short at one end and too long at the other. We were put to bed when we weren't sleepy and had to get up before we had slept enough. Apparently no one had ever thought of readjusting the balance. An alteration of one hour would have done the trick. But no such luck! The girls of 1660 had followed this schedule, and nowhere in the convent archives was there any record of their having suffered from it. Naturally enough, when you've always got the Iroquois on your heels, dawn doesn't come any too early. Nothing better than to be in a vertical position. But we, who were not threatened by anything worse than ordinary bed-snakes, would gladly have foregone being wrenched out of our sleep by a great jangling of bells. Maybe it was only a handbell, but in my memory the noise remains something enormous.

During my first year as a boarder, the children in the first division only went to mass every other morning. I really appreciated those mornings in between. But not everyone did. Mother Saint-Chérubin had two teacher's pets: Cécile — the Cécile whose dictation was in the honour book — and Marie-Jeanne who was, and still is, the cousin of one of our most brilliant journalists — that happens in families. These two little pests got the bright idea of asking if we might not have daily mass. Mother Saint-Chérubin was moved to tears. And especially because her two little pets, going quite over-board, threw themselves on the floor in front of everyone — yes they did — to obtain this favour. There was a kind of referendum. Next day we had lost our extra hour's sleep. The vote had been taken by a show of hands, and all hands went up. It wouldn't have been healthy to be in the opposition, and everyone knew it. A few little hands were a bit slow in moving, but not so you'd notice it.

* * *

Mass was all right. Once the rule was established, there was nothing more to say about it, except that the little piety I tried to muster was soon dissipated by the urge to sleep. But this wind of zeal soon enticed Mother Saint-Chérubin to irksome extremes, to say the least. As was fitting, we had always been encouraged to take frequent com-munion, but it had never been pushed to the point of real persecu-tion. Now things took a turn in that direction. One morning after mass the sister sat us in a semi-circle, then she took out her notebook:

"Marie-Rose, Pauline, So-and-so — "

And me, too, naturally.

"Step up here. Why didn't you take communion this morning?" Oh, that question! That abominable question that I heard all during my childhood, in the family, at the convent. I didn't know why the others had abstained and I wasn't curious. As for myself, I didn't go because I didn't like it. I wasn't born devout and nothing had occurred in my short life to persuade me that I should have been so. My mother's piety seemed to have very poor returns, my father's was a caricature. Mother Saint-Chérubin's brand was completely mad. Today, this was really the limit.

"I swallowed my toothbrush water," the first replied.

Every head turned towards the next to be interrogated. The best excuse had just been used up. What would the next one be?

"I felt sick to my stomach."

"I had something to drink in the night, I don't know what time it was."

It would be wonderful if I had the courage to say: "Because I didn't feel like it." I tried to convince myself that it was feasible. My hands were moist and the blood hammered in my ears.

"And you?"

I didn't say a thing.

"Well?"

Too late. I couldn't utter a word. I knew that state all too well. If ever I let the first question go by without answering, all of a sudden I would turn to stone. You could have beaten me to death, and I wouldn't have opened my mouth.

"Well?"

Now I didn't have the courage either to tell the truth or to lie. Just enough to keep on standing there, a little outside myself, feeling the way you do just before you faint. Only one thought: *It can't last forever, there's nothing to do but wait.*

Breakfast time came and I still hadn't talked. All the little girls, even the ones who had inadvertently swallowed their toothbrush water, looked at me queerly. They pursed their lips and were almost ready to close their ranks against me when we went down to the refectory. I knew well enough what they were thinking, girls and nuns alike. I had committed a sin. What sin? Why — Our sin! In Quebec we have never had more than just this one sin.

For that matter the whole inquisition was directed against this sin of impurity. That was plain as day to all of us. Sins that might be committed against justice, courage, or tolerance, we never heard a word about. But when Mother Saint-Chérubin observed that five or six of us hadn't taken communion, she concluded that those girls were up to something, and they should be shamed out of it, good and proper. The end justified the means.

I don't know what the others thought about these means. We weren't in the habit of exchanging views on such subjects. A general mistrust reigned, for we were all trained to inform on each other. When you are dealing with girls, it is always easy to install such a regime. As far as I was concerned, these particular means horrified me, to say the least. Of course I knew them well, my father took great delight in running this kind of interrogation. But I had come to think of everything connected with him as being abnormal, as not really existing, as something that had nothing to do with real life. But all of a sudden it all seemed hellishly real.

I wasn't pious but I still believed. I believed what I had been taught: that God was present in the host. If I didn't like to take communion it was precisely because of this belief, and because the act of taking communion not only failed to fill me with transports of devotion but upset me a great deal. The walk up to the rail and back under the critical eye of the supervisor, the taste of the host, the horror of feeling on my lower lip the touch — and sometimes, when the priest was old, the heavy touch — of a finger wet with the saliva of five or six little girls before me, all that turned my blood cold and I couldn't forget it, not for a minute. So it seemed to me much better to abstain since I wasn't cut out for the pious trance.

Sitting in front of the sickening bowl of coffee — we used to claim that it was made of old crusts of toast — nursing a lump in my throat, I thought things over. If the real presence was true, how could this bride of Christ force us into receiving her God in our hearts when we weren't properly prepared? Either communion was just an opportunity to blackmail and spy on us, or Mother Saint-Chérubin was a demon. I looked up at her presiding over the far end of the table. She looked much too much of a bumpkin to be a demon.

Next morning all the little girls, myself included, took communion.

At the end of the week we went to confession. I had decided to tell the abbé what was going on. I carefully prepared what I was going to confess.

"I confess to taking communion without being sufficiently prepared," I said to the abbé whose head came up with a jerk.

"What's that?"

"I didn't feel well prepared, but after mass the sister asks us in front of everybody why we didn't go to communion. So we have to go."

It was a bit mixed up, but I had got the main point across. The abbé sat for a long time in silence. He seemed annoyed and sighed noisily. In the end he chose to speak to me about preparation and let the question of obligation go.

"What do you mean by 'not well enough prepared'?"

"I mean that I didn't feel pious enough."

I caught another surprised look, and was sent away "in peace." I was sure something would happen. I let two or three days go by, then one morning I stayed in my pew at communion time. My heart beat wildly. We left the chapel and went up to the division room. My heart beat faster and faster. There was no interrogation.

When the week's marks were read out next Sunday, Mother Saint-Chérubin gave us a long lecture about being overscrupulous. She was against it, mind you, but she couldn't help talking about it with a certain gourmandise.

Thereafter she refrained from further inquisitions. The adventure had shaken her fleas up. But as soon as I changed convents, the whole thing began again. By this time, though, I had lost all interest. The role of righter of wrongs had lost its attractions. Now I, too, had swallowed my toothbrush water. Today, when the rules of eucharistic fast scarcely exist any more, I wonder what little school girls reply to the nuns, what children say to parents, what answer husbands find for jealous wives who suspect them of adultery, for I know this kind of surveillance is still practised in certain families.

*　　*　　*

My life as a boarder threw me in with a lot of little girls who, I had every reason to believe, were the offspring of normal fathers, who led pleasant family lives, and who fully enjoyed these privileges. And though I knew the taste of happiness and the pleasure of little attentions and of general well-being, from the moment I began my convent life I began to cultivate a sort of complex of destitution. Like most children, I struggled against this unhappiness with all sorts of inventions and compulsive fantasies, and, since lies didn't cost anything, I very quickly reached the point where I could no longer distinguish between the credible and the incredible. I was always being tripped up at this because the others, the happy ones, knew something I didn't: the limits of the possible.

I remember a French essay that year which caused me no end of trouble and humiliation. "Write an essay about your holidays, especially New Year's Day, and describe the gifts you received." As usual — except for those marvellous New Years' celebrations I have already described when I got truly magnificent toys — my presents were all of the shoes-socks-and-underpants variety, my holidays were a kind of claustration, and my New Years' festivities were of a kind unknown to anyone who was not my father's child. I wasn't going to write about that.

Did the nuns think everyone enjoyed an identical happiness? That we had all spent holidays apt to yield material for a pleasant essay? Were they so remote from reality? I think so. And yet they should have known what unhappiness was, since when the occasion called for it they doled it out so easily. Even now, after so many years, I distinctly remember the feeling of gloom that possessed me as long as my essay remained unwritten. I feel the same thing today whenever I undertake to do a job I dislike.

The little sisters who so piously waste away in our convents are very often remarkably sadistic. Our French mistress decided to read our essays out loud. This was never done, but she couldn't resist, I think, pointing out certain differences between us which, once they were known, would set a whole range of tensions working. All the exercises were read. There must have been fifteen or twenty of us in the class. We were thus privileged to hear an interminable listing of dolls, dolls' cradles and buggies, of games of chequers and parchesi, of bouncing balls and sewing sets (they were always in gold, those sewing sets, or at least in silver). Then we passed on to various parties, with full descriptions of all the dresses and all the menus — sometimes complete with champagne — of all the outings, fashionable and sporting, and so on, and so on, and so on.

"I got a lot of nice presents," the sister read when she came to my essay, "and the nicest is a watch in pure gold which must never be worn in the sun because it would melt." The whole class shrieked with laughter. Except me. My composition went on with a vividly executed picture of the receptions we had given. "Mother wore a satin dress that comes from France and my sister Dine (she was only five years older than me, that is twelve, but I considered her quite old enough to wear grown-up dresses if my father had been generous enough to buy them for her), Dine wore an evening gown in black velvet." And that wasn't the half of it. Velvet, satin, lace, gold, diamonds, pearls, I could let myself go without a care, and no one would have to pay the bill. Except me. For the girls nearly killed themselves laughing, and as for sister, tears of joy ran down her cheeks and took the starch out of her wimple.

The same thing held for the non-material side of life: family happiness, daughterly devotion, and so on. You had to invent. But in this domain my real difficulties didn't come until later. At seven, happiness is made up of material things. At least the kind you can talk about.

As luck would have it, such public disgrace didn't seem to harm or inhibit my studies. I worked well because I liked to, and above all because I liked to be able to tell Grandmother and Grandfather of my successes. "I stood first. Kisses to both." That was a love letter. Fervently, I would stick it into my bundle of dirty laundry.

French was the subject I preferred, but because I had so often heard Grandmother speak English fluently, I felt possessed by a fever of emulation and wanted to be able to do that too. It now seems scandalous to me the number of hours we spent studying that language, almost as many as we did French. Besides that, we had two English days a week — prayers and prattle in the language of D. H. Lawrence.

"Come along now! Speak English," Mother Saint-Chérubin would prompt us, passing from one group to another.

Only Ruth and Laurette who came from New York could really do it. As for the rest, our nugatory knowledge consisted in some useless vocabulary exercises (*The cat is black. I drink water. We are three sisters.*) that we didn't know what to do with and some grammar rules we hadn't found any use for yet.

This fad didn't last long. English prayers and conversation were dropped the following year. The colonialist Mother Superior had been replaced by a nationalist one. But the class hours remained unchanged. That was sufficient. It was so sufficient that when I arrived at another convent several years later, they thought that my mother or my grandmother must be English, my way of reading the language aloud had such a strong smell of porridge about it. This suspicion horrified me. No one in my family had ever believed in the sacrifice to ambition of an English marriage, which is, in fact, not necessary for material success, though it remains infallible if one aims at a certain moroseness in life.

All my clear memories about that school year's end are British ones. When the examination results were given out I proudly learned that I was the only one to pass in English. All the others had to stay in the fifth grade. Which just goes to show how much I put into it. Next year, when I reported to my first English class, I was so small beside the others that everyone burst out laughing. That froze me up so completely and so permanently that eventually I had to be put back into the fifth grade with the others. (In that particular convent the smallest were in the seventh grade and logic heaven knows where.) My career as a prodigy in plum pudding was at an end, I rejoined the herd and have never left it since.

*   *   *

That was the beginning of my third school year, not counting the month I had spent at the convent for my first communion. This year, for the first time in my life, I was to penetrate the unimagined world of extrafamilial affection. I was to learn that in the convent, as at home, love isn't all that simple. In changing grades I exchanged all my old mistresses for new ones, but kept my two division mistresses. French was now taught by a young nun who was slight and pretty, Mother Marie-du-Bon-Conseil. She's the one I'm referring to.

I was the youngest in her class and that became apparent when dictation time came around. I wrote too slowly. To begin with I would be a word or two behind, then a whole sentence, and soon I wouldn't know where I was, and would stop and start to snivel. Mother Bon-Conseil who soon saw how interested I was in her subject, decided that in future I should sit near her and stay there until I had learned to write more quickly. So with my notebooks and my pencils I settled myself at the same desk as her, at one of the narrow sides. She mothered me. She corrected my posture. She taught me to free myself of the bad habit I had of tensing up, which left me all glued together, fingers to pencil, notebook to nose, eyes, hair — all cramped into so small a space that nothing good could ever come of it, a sort of knot I used to tie myself into.

Between us there immediately sprang up a feeling of affection that was to bring me happiness and pain. It was the first time in that institution that I had encountered a truly human feeling, the presence of a real heart. I was enraptured. A fervent gratitude drove me on in my work, since it was all I had to offer.

I made rapid progress in writing as well as in grammar. Just the same I kept my place beside her at the desk all year long. When I began to stand first, it really began to rankle. The two division mistresses, whose pets were in this class, became alarmed. Every good mark I got inspired poisonous innuendos. Was it really so impossible to be left in peace? In the other classes — English, history, geography, even in arithmetic — I sometimes stood first too, for I liked to study, and besides, I was a vain girl, and it was music to my ears to hear the "excellents," one after another, when the Mother Superior read out my report card. But only the good marks given me by Mother Bon-Conseil caused me any trouble. I would have dearly liked to point that out to Mother Saint-Chérubin, but even if I had been bold enough I wouldn't have had time to finish my sentence. A prompt slap would have set me back before I had time to establish a bridgehead. I have a most painful memory of all such illogicality.

"Don't you reason with me!"

Reason, for the nuns, had only a pejorative sense, never any other. I never heard them use the word in its beautiful, original sense. Often that kept me awake long hours at night, when I would hold imaginary conversations with the sisters, conversations in which I had plenty of time to explain myself sensibly and which ended, of course, in my reducing them to silence and confusion.

Several months went more or less smoothly by. Wrapped up in my feelings for Mother Bon-Conseil, I endured the other nuns without much complaint. Love made up for all the rest.

The reading of reports took place on the first Sunday of every month. A few days before, the first mistress of the division circulated among her sister teachers a sort of wooden tablet on which a piece of squared paper had been fixed. After each pupil's name were twenty empty spaces or so for marks in French, English, arithmetic, and so on. Each sister filled in her own column. At the same time she could read the marks written in by her colleagues, as well as marks for good conduct, politeness, and piety, that had been given by the division mistress.

One morning, Mother Bon-Conseil greeted me in class with a stern face.

"I am sorry to see that though you have good marks in your academic subjects, you don't have such good marks in conduct," she said out loud. "Don't be surprised if I'm not present at the reading of the reports this week."

"What marks did I get?"

"Bad."

Thunderstruck — for it was a mark that was rarely given, and one which, if I can put it this way, was not easily deserved — I took my seat without saying a word.

I have often thought about what happened next, not because it was so important, but because the only motive I can see to explain it leaves me dumbfounded: I think that Mother Saint-Chérubin had drawn an advance on the satisfaction she would get in striking me down with a mark like that, and then couldn't resign herself to giving up this pleasure. When my schoolmates told her what had happened, she flew into an astonishing rage.

"It's not true," she screamed hysterically. "Your marks for conduct aren't even written in yet."

Fine. She went on shouting for a few more minutes, and then we sat down for study period. At the end of the hour she called me over.

"Just look. You can judge for yourself."

Wasn't it odd to set this proof before me at the end of the hour? I bent over the mark sheet. Though I am shortsighted — or rather because I am short-sighted — I see terribly well close up. As well as with a magnifying glass. The word "bad" had been rubbed out, but the pencil had scored the paper and I could see the disconcerting mark as plain as the nose on Sister Saint-Chérubin's face. What's more, since she was lazy into the bargain, I was the only one whose conduct-politeness-piety squares were empty. Well, almost empty.

I must have given the nun a look that betrayed thoughts that didn't please her, for she began to beat me immediately with a fury which I had never encountered yet outside my father's care. And she didn't stop until my nose began to bleed.

This was the kind of thing that barely bothered the author of my miserable days, and never prevented him from fully satisfying his pleasure. In such circumstances, the blood, obeying a trajectory imposed by the blows, flew now to one side as the head went that way, now to the other, and the room this happened in rapidly began to look like "the scene of the crime." Everything had to be cleaned up, the torturer, the victim, the walls. Whoever undertook this task found himself in a precarious situation. The least twitch of the face might be interpreted as blame, and often the whole thing would begin again with a second victim. Sometimes the floor had to be cleaned up too, because often enough, in such cases, the bladder lets go. If I spare no detail, it's that little or nothing was spared us in those days.

As for Mother Saint-Chérubin, at the sight of blood she couldn't help weakening. So I learned that there are degrees in everything.

At the next recess no one spoke to me. Nor during the afternoon one, either. The next day, after French class, I stayed behind to speak to Mother Bon-Conseil. I began to tell her everything that had happened.

"I swear," she said, "that the mark 'bad' was written in."

"I know. I saw it."

And I finished telling my story. When I had said everything, we looked each other in the eye a long time. Everything that we thought about Mother Saint-Chérubin and couldn't say, because a nun can't say or hear such things, went into that look.

"I won't ask you not to judge her. Sometimes it is very difficult to forgive. Try to forget."

Forget, don't hate, don't nurse a grudge. Wasn't it strange that those were the things that were always being recommended to me. Mother, Grandmother and now the sister, did they all think I hadn't good enough reasons for hatred? I ran up to the division room and got there late. As a punishment I was kept in for recess. That wasn't much of a change from my recreation periods ever since the incident.

At last came the day the reports were to be read. I hadn't slept a wink Saturday night, and all during high mass I felt like fainting because I hadn't been able to eat breakfast either. I could hardly breathe, my hands were wet with sweat, and my leg muscles were quivering so I couldn't stop them. I couldn't tell now whether the time was going too fast or too slow. When the chaplain began his sermon I couldn't hear anything. What he was saying was transformed into a kind of howling, my ears buzzed so. All things have an end. After mass we went up to the division room.

Mother Saint-Chérubin hadn't had the courage to withdraw the bad mark, even to back up her lie. Mother Bon-Conseil wasn't so stubborn. There she was, and she looked over at me with the ghost of a smile on her lips as the Mother Superior read out, in the midst of a horrified silence, and with long pauses in between:

"Conduct — bad, Politeness — bad, Piety — bad." Then she went on to the rest: "French — excellent, English — excellent, History — very good." And so on, right down to the bottom of that wretched little sheet which, when it was given to me, began to shake in my fingers in a ridiculous fashion.

"That's a funny kind of report," said the Mother Superior, "what's going on?"

What could I say?

"I don't know," I mumbled, like an idiot.

"She has a nasty disposition," Mother Saint-Chérubin explained.

At this clarification I dropped a curtsy which, in my confusion, almost sent me sprawling head first on the highly polished floor. Then I went back to my place, at the bottom of the class.

For the arrival and departure of the nuns who attended this ceremony, we used to sing a hymn, and I was the one who was supposed to start it off. Badly shaken by all this, I sounded off so high that we had to abandon it halfway through. On the spot I lost this job which they had somehow forgotten to relieve me of.

A nasty disposition. That's the bad name I dragged with me all through school. It should be said that all during these years I lived in a state of constant exasperation. I can't remember any explicit misdeed brought on by this exasperation. It was rather a displeasing attitude which attracted hatred. The nuns changed but the hatred remained. I would discover it, like a faithful dog, waiting for me every September. If I had been very ugly, or a cripple, or if my parents had been poor — children in any one of these categories were treated like doormats — it would have been easy to explain. But it was something else. A precocious whiff of sulphur perhaps.

The day after this memorable reading of reports, Mother Saint-Chérubin made me copy out, for the benefit of my father, a letter that she had composed in which I confessed to all the sins in Israel. It sounded almost like bragging: "I am the wickedest girl in the division and no one can manage me." The sister slipped my report in with the letter, and gleefully awaited the catastrophe.

It wasn't usual to send our report cards to our parents. In my day as a boarder, parents were expected to keep their mouths shut just like the rest of us. They weren't consulted. This first missive caught my father off guard. He saw the "bads" but he mainly saw the "excellents" and sent back a few desultory remarks. Which long after earned me reflections on "parents who don't know their own duty."

*   *   *

One Sunday morning at sermon time, the chaplain announced that he had a long proclamation to read to us and with an imperial gesture unrolled a crackling scroll. It was the decree — people of my age will remember it well — that forbade dancing in the diocese of Quebec. It was as though the chapel had been hit by lightning! The big girls looked at each other aghast and even the tiny tots were horrified. It should be realized that we were, in general, the offspring of the very cream of what the sisters called "society" in the city of Quebec, and stories about receptions, balls, evening gowns, et cetera, were the staple of our small talk.

Hereafter, under pain of mortal sin, the waltz, the tango, the foxtrot, the one-step, the two-step, the shimmy. . . .

The list seemed interminable. The chaplain drew a few chuckles with all these tongue-twisters, most of them English, which he mouthed as best he could. You realized that a team of real experts — and it was dizzying to think where they had been unearthed — had taken stock of every solitary thing that bore a name in the whole realm of jiggling to music. Nor was a single obscure polka or bourrée forgotten that nasty-minded people would, of course, immediately discover and put into practice.

The emotion aroused by this decree filled the parlour that Sunday afternoon with a bustle of whispering. What a shame! No, but really, what a rotten shame!

"Pooh! Mother said we'd go dancing in Montreal," said Bérangère with infinite scorn.

And that, in fact, is what people did for a while. Then, since the Chateau Frontenac kept its ballroom open, "for the tourists" — belonging to the Canadian Pacific it had, by that token, acquired a sort of extraterritorial status — little by little Quebec parishioners began to steal in there until, less than five years after the ukase, practically no one paid any attention to it, which may at first sight seem surprising in a populace as docile as ours. However, on second thought, it seems to me that the dance is such a good way for people like us to let off steam that it would have been impossible to forbid it for long. It should be added that, unless I am mistaken, this order was never withdrawn. I draw this, in passing, to the attention of all good citizens of Quebec.

*   *   *

One morning that same year, in December, I learned that Mother was seriously ill. The nun called me over and said: "Your mother is sick and your eldest sister has left." As dry as that. She was holding a piece of paper and gave it to me without further explanation. It was a letter from Mother in which she said that she had to leave the house and go to Grandmother's to be cared for there, and she was asking Dine to come home and look after the three little ones.

I read and reread that letter in its shaky handwriting and couldn't bring myself to believe it. I remember what a painful effort it was to understand it at all. Mother sick and Dine gone, it was really too much all at once. I went and knocked at the door of the junior division and asked for Françoise, who came out crying. She too had read Mother's letter. We fell into one another's arms saying, "Don't cry, don't cry." Until Mother Saint-Chérubin swept in to break it up. It was against the rules to hug anyone.

That night I hardly slept at all. Mother must have been really sick to wish such a painful fate on her eldest daughter of whom she was so proud. It was, in fact, the beginning of an illness that was to last a little less than five years and was to be fatal in the end. Mother had developed a pleurisy which her frail constitution, weakened by so many confinements and by the state of constant disillusion that she lived in, could not surmount. The pleurisy seemed to get better at first, but almost immediately tuberculosis set in. Fortunately I didn't know all this at the time.

As for Dine, I couldn't help but be terrified at the thought of what lay in store for her. I imagined her alone with my father and the three little ones (they ranged from one to five) in the huge frigid house, and I told myself that I would rather have died than be in her place.

To tell what the next six months were to be for Dine is no easy task. It seems to come straight out of a third-rate novel. As little as I say, I always seem to be overdoing it. Yet it may well be I don't know the whole of it.

She was fourteen. She was wonderfully good at school and so was very advanced for her age. That was her hard luck. It wasn't a question of school work now, it was the role of beast of burden she was wanted for. That may be a strong expression, and yet, to do a job that one hasn't chosen, that is beyond one's strength, for which one receives neither payment nor gratitude — there is no other way to say it. She arrived at my father's house just in time to take care of a whole household struck down by whooping cough.

For more than five years we had had an elderly maid named

Adèle, and Mother was counting on her to spare Dine some of the heaviest work. But Adèle left almost at once. My father, profiting from the fact that Mother was not there to remind him that it was usual to pay the help, quickly forgot such frivolities. But beyond that, as sure as I know him, he must simply have told himself that the maid was not indispensable. One day she decided she had had enough.

"I don't have to stay in this hell-house," she said, slamming the door.

There are times when it must be wonderful to be a servant and be able to slam doors.

Still she liked us well enough, old Adèle. She had stayed with us since the birth of my young brother whom she cherished with a wild passion. Her greatest pleasure was to take him with her on her day off and have his photograph taken. Soon she had dozens of photos which she would often spread out on the kitchen table and study amorously, lost in a kind of ecstasy.

Adèle was an uncouth, awkward, manlike type of woman, so deaf she never had learned to speak except in a guttural way, but she was uncommonly strong, which she owed, I think, to her semi-Algonquin parentage. Her mother, a pure Indian, sometimes came to visit her daughter. At first I didn't understand too well who the big woman was who looked so remarkably like her daughter's daughter with her crow-black hair, whereas Adèle's was all grey. I used to watch her from a good distance. Always silent, she used to sit in one corner of the kitchen, eyes lowered, her face immobile. After several days she would leave as she had come, without having opened her mouth.

Adèle detested my father — I often heard her say as much to Mother who would reply, "Tut, tut" — and I remember that one day my father and she almost came to blows on my account. She was washing socks and, since I was annoying her some way or other, she threw one at my head. That got my father's parental hackles up. Ah no! He wasn't going to let the flesh of his flesh be treated in that manner! He seized Adèle by one arm and dragged her outside where he began to curse her and threaten her with reprisals. Then, losing all sense of reality, he wound up saying:

"Aren't you ashamed to treat a helpless child that way?"

"You beat them, you do. They helpless too, when you beat them."

My father was flabbergasted. He let out a few additional yells, and went in quite sheepishly. The windows were wide open, and we hadn't missed a word of this dialogue, and he knew it. Many years afterwards — my father always seemed to believe, or hope, that none of us had a scrap of memory — he used to tell us his own version of this story whenever Adèle's name was mentioned.

"And didn't she have the nerve to strike one of my children? I don't rightly remember which one — "

"It was me," I would say. "I haven't forgotten a thing about it — "

"Oh, yes? Hmm. Well — I could never stand to have a servant strike one of my children."

That was understandable. When something gives you so much pleasure, you like to keep the monopoly. Besides, other people went about it so awkwardly, so feebly, and with so little perseverance, that it was pitiful to watch.

Once Mother had gone, Adèle felt strongly in her Algonquin heart that my father was going to take advantage of the situation and behave like a real Iroquois. She packed her bag, got hold of someone passing by in a sleigh, (ironically, the hard-packed track that led to the city gave us in winter the road we lacked in summer), slammed the door, as I have said, and went back to her village, Saint-Pamphile. I don't think she did it light-heartedly. She knew very well that Mother was counting on her strength and devotion to make Dine's task lighter. Moreover, hadn't there always been a sort of pact between us? She was crude and hardly likely to pick up decent manners but, on the other hand, our life was so lugubrious, the climate of our house so unbreathable, that we wouldn't have been able to replace her easily. She put up with our faults, and we accepted hers. But it was too hard to stay in hell, as she said, when you know you can get out.

*   *   *

So there was whooping cough in the house. This is perhaps a good time to say that the three youngest benefited from a preferential treatment which we older children had never known. We called them, among ourselves, the second marriage kids. The explanation for my father's preference was not hard to find: like him, they were all blond and blue eyed. It might have seemed likely they would resemble him, but on the whole this promise wasn't very well kept. As a result, all these little pets moved over to our side as soon as they grew up. For the eldest of the three this happened quite soon because he was a boy and, whatever his colouring, my father didn't like Mother having boys. Not that he preferred girls — he had, of course, a Moslem scorn for the female of the species — but he saw in the relationship, a rather intimate one after all, between his wife and another male, something unhealthy, and was constantly tendering Mother suspicious accusations on this subject. In the end, my sister Thérèse was the only one to keep certain paternal traits — the eyes, the mouth — which we never held against her and which gained her the appreciable advantage of being by far the least molested of the family. As for Marguerite, when she reached adolescence she began to look wonderfully like Mother, only blonde. Her fate was catastrophic.

Dine was put to work for the whooping coughers. As soon as she arrived she spent her days and nights running from one to the other. In an infernal round that seemed as if it would never end, coughing spell followed coughing spell, which brought on vomiting to be wiped up, and bleeding noses to be blotted. A doctor would probably have prescribed some sedative or other, but my father, who had no confidence in the medical profession — though his prejudices slacked off when he was the one who was sick — always cared for us himself. He had two tried and true remedies that were endowed, according to him, with infallible powers: dieting and hot baths. Two or three times a day, Dine had to plunge the whole little family into steaming tubs, which meant from six to nine baths of a long half-hour each, long enough to heat up the whooping cough. Then, so the child wouldn't catch cold in the frigid corridors, she would roll him in a blanket and carry him to bed. But the beds were freezing too, and as soon as the whooping cough cooled down the baby would begin to cough and vomit, and his nose would start to bleed again. Washing, mopping, and blotting followed. Then on to the second one. And the third. Then it would start all over again. And again, and again.

At night, when my father came back, another infernal round would begin. The house wasn't tidy, dinner wasn't ready, the children hadn't been properly cared for, since they weren't better than yesterday. As soon as she had bolted her last mouthful, Dine was sent back to operation steam-bath. In the midst of this my father would occasionally burst into the bathroom screaming out that things couldn't go on like this, the dinner dishes weren't done, the kitchen wasn't straightened up, there would have to be some changes made. All this accompanied by a welter of smacks. After days like this, what could have been the state of mind of a fourteen-year-old girl creeping up to her room which was too cold for her to get to sleep in. It's better not to think about it.

It was not surprising the house was so cold. Heat costs money. To meet this problem with minimum outlay, my father had a brilliant idea. He had acquired (very likely at a fantastic price, but it was the kind of economy he liked to make), a piece of forest where Pit, the farmer, went to cut wood, which he used to bring in endlessly and which had to be burned as it was, all dripping with sap or covered with a thick layer of ice, depending on the season. This — fuel — was intended for the kitchen as well as the central heating. When, with luck, one managed to get the fire lit, there was little cause for jubilation. One knew that when the time came to add another log, the ice it was covered with would melt and put out the fire already established. There are many poor people who have never known such distress. But we were far from poor. Though we could hardly have guessed it.

Spring came and revealed the little whoopers and their nurse reduced to skeletons. Dieting for some, operation steam-bath for all, had taken their full toll. You had to look sharp to see them walk past. Dine was allowed to come and visit us at the convent on Thursdays. I have never seen hands in such a state — cracked, bleeding, swollen, and of a rich lobster-red — it seemed as if some fore-runners of the Nazis had been at work there with their pincers and cigarette butts.

And she was gay.

Much later, when I was old enough to be taken into her confidence, she told me she had made it a point of honour to hide from everyone, so that Mother wouldn't hear about it, the kind of life she had led for those six months. That's pluck!

The picture wouldn't be complete if I omitted this: in December my father had promised his daughter a little fur piece if she "behaved well." When spring came, and the moment to untie the purse strings, he flatly declared that she hadn't deserved a thing.

For that matter, contrary to what happens in other families, furs with us were male attire. What am I saying? Male? — I was forgetting I had brothers. Paternal, paternal attire. My father was the only one who possessed a fur coat. It was a sumptuous beaver outfit, big enough to dress two women. He had bought it in 1917 and wore it nearly all the rest of his life. Every year when he took it out he rediscovered grievances as durable as the coat was.

"Everyone reproached me when I bought this coat. Just the same, I have worn it twenty-five years and I only paid. . . ." (We never knew how much he paid for it because the figure dwindled from year to year and at the end it had shrunk to almost nothing.)

None of us owned anything of a quality good enough to last twenty-five years or more. All we knew was the knack of making a thing last three years when it was only good for six months. I suppose Mother, who always had to count on her own mother to save her from going completely naked, must at one time or other have let drop some remark in this connection.

*   *   *

Up until that year, my father had abstained almost entirely from visiting us at the convent. None of us suffered inordinately on this account. But the weekly visits he paid Mother during her pleurisy were destined to change his habits. I can't help thinking that he used this as a good excuse not to stay at his wife's bedside any longer than the regulation twenty minutes of an official visit.

From the big window in their recreation room the pupils in the third division could see the parents arriving. In the other divisions we didn't have this advantage. Until then, like all the others, I had always been happy to hear my name called out by the little girl stationed at the door. That particular Sunday, I left the room at a gallop. Françoise, who was in the third division and could use the window, was waiting for me by the staircase.

"It's him."

We went downstairs with a heavy tread.

"You are both too pale," said my father in place of hello.

I looked at Françoise. She was green, in fact. In our confusion, the very confusion that had caused the green hue, we had forgotten to pinch our cheeks.

Our paleness always had the faculty of enraging my father. He was always afraid of doctor's bills, which was quite incomprehensible because he never called a doctor, but that's the way it was. Since we grew pale just hearing the sound of his footsteps, he often had occasion to reproach us for looking poorly.

"You're constipated again," he shouted out in that piercing voice of his to which I owe so many humiliations, for it is one thing to be insulted, but words can scarcely convey the mortifications of being insulted at the top of someone else's lungs, and your father's at that.

Neighbouring groups of girls turned around. Now we were in for it. The subject of constipation always set him going for a good while. Along with dieting and hot baths, the functioning of the intestines constituted the very foundations of his medical principles. Every health problem was caused by constipation: my short-sightedness, Mother's pleurisy, the slowness of a scratch to heal. He had found a formula that he was mighty proud of.

"If you were made of glass, you'd be a pretty sight to see."

As far as that went, if I may say so, I had no particular reason to feel guilty in this regard. But our denials went unheard. Once his premises were established, there was no stopping him on the road to his conclusions. He used to say: "You claim you're not, but supposing you were," and would go on just as he had planned.

When I was small that used to infuriate me. Then little by little I got into the habit of thinking that he was wrong in this matter as in everything else, and that one should never pay the slightest attention to what he said. Just the same, to hear him sound off right in the middle of the convent parlour was a bit thick. It wasn't to be the last time either. Fortunately, sufficient unto each visiting day was the evil thereof.

The evil didn't end, however, with visiting hour. A child who is humiliated in front of other children doesn't escape his troubles that easily. Coming back to the recreation room we found that news of our disgrace had preceded us, and we were given a scornful welcome. Instead of feeling sorry for us for having such a father, the girls held it against us. They jeered at us.

"Say, your father's got a good voice, hasn't he? You can hear him a mile away."

And they dissolved in laughter. I went off to my corner while the ones who had been in on the incident brought the others up to date. While the whispering went on, they kept glancing over at me from a distance and I didn't know what to do with myself, as if having such a father was some kind of bad deed.

When I look back on all those wretched years, I realize that the thing that was lacking in our convents was kindness. No one was kind, neither the sisters nor the children, and no one ever told us that we should have tried to be kind. No one ever told us that kindness existed. If, by chance, we encountered it we couldn't recognize it because we were so unused to it, because we had never heard it called by its right name. It was called preference, caprice, cajolery, favouritism, but never kindness.

Next Sunday we made sure to pinch our cheeks. It was my sister Dine who had taught us this trick. It had to be done firmly but gently. The first time she tried it she went at it with such passion that two enormous bruises, very difficult to explain away, appeared on her cheeks the next morning.

That was a bad year for all of us. It is always a disaster, even in a normal family, when the mother is sick. We weren't a normal family and our disasters rarely came singly. We two boarders didn't experience anything like the misery of our eldest sister, still our life underwent some sad changes. With Mother bedridden, Grandmother busy looking after her, Dine taken up by her whooping coughers, we didn't see anyone we loved, and the visiting days when we were called were much worse than the ones when we weren't. It had become our custom for ten months of the year to let a crust of forgetfulness form over our abscess. Boarding school life brought wounds of its own, but a child knows very well, despite the fact that life moves so slowly for him, that this is just a hard moment to live through, and that it has no place in his true destiny. But now it became impossible to forget. Sundays succeeded one another with terrifying rapidity. My father was becoming almost as much of an obsession as he was during the holidays.

It is a distressing predicament to have a father whose physical existence is such a scourge but who, deep in the child's heart where the feeling of filial love takes root, has absolutely no existence. I was, at one and the same time, terribly concerned and monstrously detached. It was a destructive dualism. My father was nothing but a physical force that one had to avoid unloosing. He was that with a vengeance. But I have never in my whole life known anyone so unanimously rejected by his family. Apparently he never felt this. Since he never sought to impose himself except by violence, since he never believed you could impose yourself any other way, he was satisfied with the situation. From time to time he sensed that our filial affection wasn't exactly delirious. For example, he used to say after what we called "a beating session" (session/*séance*: the time one spends uninterrupted in some occupation — see *Dictionnaire Larousse*).

"You haven't got the right to hate me."

Yes, he caught the occasional hint. As for us, we would have preferred never to have had reason or opportunity to feed our hate. But my father was a stickler for our rights. On the whole, apart from these intuitions, he was well pleased with himself. Of course he had his own way of being self-satisfied. Year in, year out, he never put aside his anger. *Never.* It was the only thing he really liked, anger. He enjoyed our cringing silence. He wanted us chronically terrified. We were. He could take full credit for that.

They always say that laziness is the mother of all the vices. I am inclined to think that it is the mother of all the lively vices. The mother of all the lugubrious ones is anger. The success of his rages inspired a kind of desperate pride in my father. Pride engendered egotism, nothing counted except himself. Egotism is the brother of avarice. And avarice bred that lack of sociability which, after Mother's death, made him close his door to all comers.

I should say that this lack of sociability was not encouraged by avarice alone. To save money on tea and cakes and a dress decent enough to receive guests and go out in, was, naturally, an important matter. But there was something else.

What could it be?

What indeed! In Quebec city! Yes, yes, that's it, you've put your finger on it, in a manner of speaking. Sex. He thought about it all the time, that poor father of ours, in the wrong way of course. Except for his own marriages — four in all — but anything that pertained to him belonged to another world altogether. He thought about it incessantly and tracked us down on this ground to our last lines of defence. Though we had little enough time to think whether we were walking straight, let alone anything else, we were remorselessly suspected, accused, and finally convicted of guilt. So he had enough troubles with us, without letting any strangers into the fold. Besides, "strangers' children always have bad parents who never keep a close eye on their offspring, and let them grow up swamped in vice."

Those were two good motives for keeping us prisoners. There was another even more important. It is a powerful motive, the very one that makes dictatorial governments forbid travelling outside their borders: the fear that we might discover that our family was not a family, that our home was not a home, that our life was not a life.

*   *   *

The school year ended on a less mournful note, at least as far as my relationship with the sisters and the girls was concerned. It even ended in quite a comical way. Every year we celebrated the thirty-first of May, the last day in the month of Mary, with a procession. It was a very exciting occasion. On that day, granted a special permission, we ventured into a part of the convent where the laity were not allowed to set even the shadow of a foot. Then we went through a huge garden from one end to the other, another place we never went. A garden full of fruit trees and flowers and raked gravel paths which has left a wonderful memory. Finally, after crossing a little cemetery, we entered the chapel by a mysterious door hidden from view on every side, whose exact location we could never remember from one year to the next. It was really something.

I was sturdy for my age. A hereditary gift from my father, no doubt. There was only one girl in the division who could rival me in this regard. (We actually came to blows the next year and I came out on the bottom, but not before I had pulled out a good handful of hair and left her with a kind of off-centre, eczema-ridden tonsure, the sight of which pursued me everywhere.) The year before, she had been the one to carry the banner in the procession. This year something had gone wrong, she had sprained her wrist perhaps. I think you can guess what I'm driving at with my little piledriver. When it became apparent that the wrist would not be better in time, a sweet wind of forgiveness began to blow over my sins. All of a sudden, it was noticed that I didn't talk any more during the study period — I didn't even have anyone to talk to at recess — that

I didn't go on playing after the bell had gone. Who would I have played with? I even got a few compliments.

Two or three days before the procession, the facts of the case became self-evident: if the banner was to be carried at all, I was the one who would carry it. At the end of catechism class, Mother Saint-Chérubin had me stand up and read me the speech of the prodigal son's father. I was forgiven, and from a full heart. And since, in like circumstances, there is nothing better than some striking tangible proof, I was to have the honour of being entrusted with the banner. I couldn't get over it. My eyes were moist and my heart melted within me. At recess they fought to play with me.

"I thought Marie-Jeanne would be the one who was chosen," said one little girl innocently.

"She's not strong enough," replied another just as innocent. "She's got arms like match sticks."

"If Marthe had been able to — "

Suddenly I had a bad taste in my mouth. I gathered up my little things and took my freshly won glory over to another group.

The custom of handing out as rewards tasks that required a maximum of vitality and a minimum of timidity was a great nuisance to the nuns. Docility was usually found elsewhere and if the so-called honours had been given out as punishment everything would have been easier.

I have already said that I was as free of timidity as could be. A childhood like mine results either in a precocious hardening of the epidermis, or in being stripped raw. I wasn't a trembler. That got me into another hilarious adventure the next year which is so like the banner episode that I feel like telling it right now.

The highest reward we could win for good conduct was a ribbon that changed colour and recipient division by division, and which could only be earned once, no matter how many years one had been in the same division. In the lower division it was pink and was called the Infant Jesus ribbon. It was presented with great pomp at the same time as the red and blue ones, in the chapel, before the whole convent, after one of the recipients of each colour had read an act of consecration. I was never one of them.

Then came this year when there was no one left in line for the pink ribbon but a few of the shyest girls. According to the rule you had to have been good since September to get it. Along about the end of April they realized, it seems, that they had run into something of a dead end. The sister summoned me, and in the course of a long lecture it came out that I hadn't been quite so bad as in other years. If I could be good for a month, I would get the ribbon. Moreover, I would have the honour of reading out the act of consecration. I was a little surprised, but that's all. I applied myself to the task. But before two days were out I had forgotten my good resolutions. I was given a second sermon. I had been thoughtless, but I wasn't disqualified yet. I would do better in future, they were sure of it. In short, from sermon to lecture, and from pardon to clean slate, I reached rehearsal time. These were held in the chapel. With my stentorian voice there was no risk: I would be heard right to the back of the organ loft.

Then one day, on my way back from chapel, I happened to linger in the cloakroom where it was always as black as pitch. Suddenly I heard the two division mistresses come in.

"She doesn't deserve the ribbon," said one.

"Well, what can you do ? I haven't anyone else to read the act of consecration. Everyone that could is already a ribbon-holder," replied the other.

Small children are good-hearted. It might have seemed natural for me to press my advantage to the limit, just to see if perhaps that memorable panic of Christmas Eve might not be repeated again. I didn't even think of it. I left the cloakroom as soon as the path was clear and was as good as gold right up to the big day. Since there were only a couple of days left, that was feasible. I don't want to take any undue credit, but I think the impulse I followed was a kind of pity. At that age one feels it often.

* * *

I believe that was the year we prayed so much, day and night, for the miracle, and made all those sacrifices and offerings to God. From September to June that was our one abiding preoccupation. The miracle did not take place.

The thing they were trying to obtain was the beatification of our venerable foundress, and we didn't have a sufficient number of miracles for that. The religious community decided that this was the year for it. By an unparalleled coincidence, that September there arrived among us a little girl who had been crippled by an accident in another convent. Due to lack of proper attention — the nuns had not even called a doctor after the fracture — little Jeanne had a shrivelled leg. She limped very badly. Heaven had surely sent her to us, for though it is true that ills to cure are in no short supply in this sad world, it is always preferable to have the potential subject for the miracle close at hand. That way there is no risk she might be cured by some other miracle worker. This very thing had happened a few years previous: the mother of one of our pupils had been cured by Saint Anne, which was a little hard to take.

We hadn't finished unpacking our things before Mother Saint-Chérubin had got Jeanne to stand as candidate for the miracle. She was radiant. One morning she would wake up with both legs the same size, there wasn't the slightest doubt about it. Prayers began immediately. From the "I give my Heart to God" in the morning to the same prayer at night, with all the day's prayers thrown in, there was only one concern among us, between us and God, between us and the venerable foundress: Jeanne's leg. It was our first thought as we climbed out of bed. Considering the possibility that the subject might be too moved to cry out "Miracle! Miracle!" we all craned our necks to see with our own eyes if Jeanne was walking straight. For it was commonly agreed that "it" could only happen at night. Though we had great faith in the powers of our foundress, it seemed to us the thing would have to take place in the secrecy of the bed and the mystery of the dark. The undertaking was difficult enough without our requiring it to happen in broad daylight. One must know the bounds of discretion.

Morning after morning went by without the leg lengthening. Jeanne grew, and it was the other leg, the one we weren't praying for, that grew longer. We multiplied our prayers and promises, in vain. Nothing happened. The venerable foundress remained insensitive, and little by little Jeanne lost her smile. The month of June found her just as she had come to us in September. All she had got out of it was not having had a single day without hearing her infirmity talked about. She wasn't allowed to forget it for a second. Every step she took was a deep deception incessantly renewed, both for herself and for the whole convent.

"Perhaps you don't deserve a miracle," Mother Saint-Chérubin used to say sometimes; she had a fine stock of kind sentiments.

Jeanne would begin to cry, and we to wonder, with some annoyance, if all this time we hadn't been praying and making sacrifices for a leg destined to remain short forever.

Admittedly, we were somewhat unpractised in obtaining prodigies. We were often told, for instance, that extreme docility was one way of inciting the miraculous, and that once, no one knew exactly when or where, a child who had obediently closed her notebook at the sound of the bell, without even finishing the word she was writing, had found her work completed for her by her guardian angel. Angels use nothing but golden ink, and that's the way you can recognize their interventions. After that, how many of us closed our books without even taking the time to use blotting paper! Not only did our guardian angels prove to be a lazy lot, but we were even scolded for blots caused by our exemplary docility.

And Jeanne went on limping. It was one of two things: we were too bad for our prayers to be granted, or miracles were out of fashion. In either case it was a depressing speculation. One must admit that the indifference — not to say slackness — of a good forty guardian angels, plus a venerable foundress, gave food for thought.

*   *   *

Mother came back just before the summer holidays. Until her death four years later, her health followed a particular rhythm, always the same: springtime and summer her condition improved and she would spend these seasons more or less normally. In October, when the infernal cold set in — yes, Hell is cold — and added its rigours to the fatigue accumulated during the holidays, she would be bedridden until the end of the winter. I can't think of those holidays without remorse. I was really impossible. At Grandmother's I was good enough. But at our house, as soon as my father left for work, apparently I thought up all kinds of mischief. Though I adored Mother, I think I resented the fact that she had married that man, that she had given him to me as a father, that she was too weak to bring him down to size. All that, of course, stayed deep inside me, unformulated.

She was bedridden every winter, but she never went back to Grandmother's except to die. She knew, I think, after her first relapse, that her fate was sealed. From then on it was useless to leave Dine alone to face the madman. As long as Mother had a hope of getting better and, by leaving, could hope to protect us better later on, there was some purpose in her momentarily abandoning us. But now she preferred to forgo a very slim chance of recovery and not abandon us until death. I overheard her telling Grandmother about the decision she had taken one day when Grandmother came to visit us, which didn't happen very often, for her visits used to send my father into a rage. I was just about to walk by the open living room window when I was stopped by Grandmother's tragic voice. I can hear it now. She could — for tears didn't choke her as they choke me, for instance — hold a long tearful conversation, and that used to cause me — for we had several sessions like this later on, she and I — an indescribable sorrow.

I didn't understand very much of what they were saying. I heard them talking about death, and about Mother's death, but at that age a child easily persuades himself that the death of those he loves is improbable, that it is only mentioned as a kind of threat, a kind of mild blackmail — "You'll be the death of me" — and that being good is enough to avert the danger. I was very upset, however, for several days. Then, since nothing happened, and since I didn't know what the future was or what it was to anticipate it, I didn't think about it any more.

*   *   *

It was probably that same year when we came back for the summer holidays that we found my father deeply engaged in his agricultural enterprises.

For a long time we had had chickens. We also had a cow that old Adèle used to milk morning and night in her time. Having no road made the question of supplies somewhat uncertain (Adèle made bread and, when we had two cows, butter also), and these creatures were very useful. But now we had passed the stage of such modest operations. My father had become a gentleman farmer. He had acquired some adjacent land, hired a farmer, bought two mares — Belle and Maggie — more chickens, bees, and pigeons that were always flying back to their old coop where we had to go and reclaim them from their first owner. Besides this, all the appropriate machinery.

"Did you get a new summer dress, Mother?" I asked on my arrival.

"No, dear, I haven't got a new dress, but we do have a mower, a binder, a hayrake, and Lord knows what else — "

I had never before heard my father's activities spoken of in this ironic tone. I was astonished, and thought to myself that this new paternal fad must really be a mad one. It was. A dozen years later, when he had the sudden inspiration to start keeping accounts, he discovered that his profits didn't amount to a tenth of his expenses. Meanwhile, we had lost all the calves our cows had been imprudent enough to have, the chickens died without telling us why, the bees perished during hibernation. As for the pigeons, they proved as faithful as they had been on the very first day, and lavished all their love on their first master.

Though he had become a gentleman farmer, luckily for us my father remained an engineer. The task of running the farm fell on our shoulders. There was, of course, the farmer. We even had several of them, one after another, but they must all have been recruited from among the race of leaners on hoe handles. Or was it that they were so poorly paid they felt free, in all conscience, to act as if every day was Sunday?

Every morning before leaving for the office, my father handed out the chores: hoeing, watering, transplanting, pruning, digging, and raking. But none of that could equal the potato bug fatigue. Nothing was so repugnant. Nearly every day we had to pace through the potato field armed with empty tin cans to put the "beasties" in.

For the benefit of children assigned to the capture of these insects, but not yet up on their metamorphoses, there are two sorts of potato beetles: "hard" and "soft." The soft ones are more or less inert, pinkish, and round. They yield a little between the fingers. The hard ones wriggle around, cling to the skin of your hand with all their little legs, and persistently try to scurry away. You have to shake them back into the can, and when it's already almost full to the top, this isn't so easy.

When the can was full, we would go and throw our harvest into a stick fire specially lit for the purpose. They sent up an indescribable smell. After that, off we would go and fill up another can. And so on, all day long. I never saw creatures demonstrate such courageous obstinacy in their will to reproduce: for every one we caught, a thousand more seemed to spring forth.

We were supposed to have the right to a cent a canful at the end of the day, but there was always some hitch that did us out of our salaries. We had been too silly about it, or hadn't filled up as many cans as we said, and were therefore nasty little liars who didn't deserve a thing, et cetera. After a while we caught on: in this particular operation there were only two real things, the potato bugs, and the inescapable order to collect them. It would be a waste of breath trying to argue that we were all, boys and girls alike, developing an ardent love of the land. For that matter we were already, all seven of us, dyed-in-the-wool urbanites. The assertion "French Canadians are all very close to the soil" always makes me smile. We're the same as anybody else: some of us are close to the land, others — sons, grandsons and great-grandsons of city dwellers — have been estranged from it for years, and this forced initiation into the charms of country living did nothing for us but sharpen our natural tendencies.

* * *

One of our farmers, Pit, perpetrated a fantastic number of blunders. But he knew so well how to flatter my father that, whatever he had done, he was always pardoned, and lightly at that. Pit liked the bottle. My father had always held that to swallow down a single gulp of wine was a mortal sin, but he always absolved Pit when he got drunk, which frequently happened with catastrophic results. Once, on the day before New Year's, for instance, my father had commissioned him to go to town to do the rounds of our relatives and pick up the presents they had for us. It was, in fact, a terribly complicated business to bring presents out to the end of the world where we lived. But Pit was there, he had the team and the sleigh. Everything became wonderfully simple.

As for doing the rounds, as soon as he had finished with the relatives, he started on the bars. Alcohol whipping up the native ingenuity in the man, he trustfully left the sleigh full of beribboned packages each time he went into a *buvette* as my father used to call them. He didn't think about coming home until the sleigh had been completely emptied by the passers-by. He didn't get a very warm welcome from my father that time, but not too sharp a one either.

I can still see myself writing a thank you letter to my godmother the next day for a pair of gloves I had never seen. It's easy enough to imagine a pair of gloves. But you had to avoid mentioning their colour. Every sentence I concocted had a gap where there should have been white, blue, or brown.

When Grandmother heard what had happened, she came out herself, bringing us other presents. New Year's Day had passed, that was true, but New Year's Day hardly counted anyway. First and foremost, it was a day when my father stayed home. Give me a good working Monday any time. A perfectly ordinary Monday amongst ourselves, us children and Mother.

Pit and his wife — a real prune called Blanche — were the ones who stayed with us longest. Before them there were Richard and

Victoire — Acadians, who spoke a kind of music — and after them someone called Lachance, about whom there is nothing to say. There were others, too, that I have forgotten. Since they all came from distant parts, they spoke in languages that were very strange to us. No Anglicisms, no, but archaisms, slithering meanings. One of them, I remember now, always used to say *quitter faire* for *laissez faire*. They were generally loaded with children who must be about the same age as we are now and who remember, perhaps, that they played while my father's children spent their holidays picking "beasties."

*   *   *

Harvesting potato beetles is a useful occupation, but the time came for us to tear ourselves away and go back to the convent. I wasn't to see Mother Bon-Conseil again except by accident in the corridor. In French I was to fall — that's precisely the right word — into the hands of Mother Ange Gabriel.

I spoke before about the capacity of a child's memory — without it, I would have ended that year as illiterate as a newborn babe. In theory we were supposed to have five hours of French a week. Under the reign of Mother Ange Gabriel we didn't have ten minutes.

She was a fat, ugly woman with red cheeks and a noisy way of walking. She came in every morning with the hurried manner of someone who can hardly wait to start dispensing knowledge.

"Come along now! Prayers! Prayers!"

Everything she said was so important that she repeated it twice. Once prayers were over she sat down cautiously, for there was a great disproportion between the chair and what she brought to bear on it, and looked us over with a woebegone expression, always the same.

"Yes, indeed, we certainly need to pray, we certainly need to pray. These days you can't tell who is living or who is dying. Or who is dying. To begin with there's the doctors. You can't trust them any more, can't trust them. When you put yourself in their hands, you might just as well write your will. Yes, write your will. Just think, they've come up with an invention to treat the sick with iodine. With iodine!"

She surveyed us with a satisfied eye. The eye of a woman bold enough to dare denounce a well-concealed crime that threatens the very survival of the human race. Bang! on the desk with her fist.

"Iodine! The autopsy shows their insides all rotted away. But those doctors just carry on anyway!"

Sometimes she stretched condescension to the point of saying:

"I am not referring to your father, So-and-so. His name was not among those communicated to us."

But mostly scruples of this kind didn't stop her. Once she had weighed anchor, she sailed on, full steam, right through to the end of the class. Neither time nor space was the slightest obstacle. No sooner had the medical profession dreamt up the iodine treatment than we were up to our necks in autopsies. Good Christians were dying like flies, "as many as from the Spanish flu," only now, not only did they take plenty of time to bury them — which had sometimes been lacking during the epidemic — they also took plenty of time to dissect them. Could you believe it!

This rigmarole began all over again every third day, for she had only three hobby horses which she rode in turn. They were invariably offered to us as mysterious revelations served up red-hot by some shady messenger to her convent cabal.

The second day:

"Yes, indeed, we certainly need to pray. Great need to pray, and that's the truth of it. We were informed yesterday that the Jews and the Freemasons met together two days ago [we were always full of

admiration for the freshness of the news] and arrived at some terrible decisions. Terrible!" There followed a knowing silence which
was supposed to cast us into an agony of terror. We stifled our
laughter in our handkerchiefs. Slowly the nun would sweep her eye
over us. She saw herself as the lighthouse whose beam saves
mariners in distress. The most distressing peril that threatened was
the danger that we wouldn't learn any French grammar, but that
wasn't the one she was aiming at.

"And do you know what they decided?"

A second silence, more prolonged than the first.

"That this year women's fashions will be even more indecent
than last. We are going to eradicate Catholicism by working
through women. That's what they said. Those are their very
words."

She lifted an intrepid chin.

"They don't suspect that their plans are already known to us. Yet
what I am telling you happened only the night before last in New
York. You all know that New York is a city of Jews and Freemasons
. . . blah, blah, blah."

Every three days these same bandits remade their plans, and
made them over again the evening of the third day after. It seems
certain they were suffering from seventy-two hour amnesia.
Nothing less than the ten o'clock bell could interrupt the description of this sombre judaeo-masonic world, and the scarcely less
sombre world of woman — still in the clutches of the devil, as
everyone knows.

The third day:

"Yes, indeed, we certainly need to pray . . . et cetera, and so on."

These days were the funniest, because the subject was the state of
innocence of her young niece when she first entered the convent as
a boarder. Such innocence was nowhere to be found today. The
niece had lost it by coming into contact with us. Hadn't one of us

taken it into her head to share the news of an upcoming blessed event with her? "Mother's expecting a baby." From that day on, the niece had started to get nervous. She cried easily, and didn't sleep well at night. To be sure, it was her innocence alone that was worth saving. Ours wasn't worth a fig. Which was hardly surprising when you considered that in this very class there were certain little girls whose mothers used makeup, and we all leaned forward to look at the Landry girls, for they were the ones she was talking about.

Fat and sallow, with straight, greasy hair, the niece seemed the least nervous of any of us, but her aunt tried awfully hard to persuade us that she was as shy as a startled doe. She hid this under a cow-like calm. She listened to the funeral oration preached over her lost innocence with a listless air, and didn't seem to suffer much hearing her most intimate pruderies paraded in public. Like the rest of us, she was waiting for the bell. Sometimes at recess someone would go over and challenge her directly.

"It's a funny thing. I sleep quite close to you and I never hear you crying at night."

"I'm going to tell my aunt what you said," the startled doe would bawl out, her fat shaking with sobs.

So we would often see them, aunt and niece, chattering away in some corner and we knew perfectly well what it was all about.

Despite all the tips we kept getting, I, for one, didn't know where children came from. My innocence was made of sterner stuff than the startled doe's. I gathered, from all the mysterious talk, that they must come from some not very Catholic place and, well, gad! the not-very-Catholic place I was thinking of seemed quite impossible. It didn't stand up under analysis. Whoever, and whyever would anyone stick the little urchins into such a minute cranny. I hadn't a clue, and I must say I couldn't have cared less. I find my ignorance quite admirable when I think of all the suspicions I was the butt of, both at home and at school, for it remained profound and unassailable.

For instance, I often wondered by what strange accommodation my father and mother shared the same bed. We girls were not allowed near the boys any more than was absolutely necessary, and yet my parents, who were not of the same sex, slept in the same bed. I thought that Mother had inexplicable tastes. If it had been me, I wouldn't have wanted to sleep in my father's bed for all the gold in Peru. That must have been awfully disagreeable. (When Mother came back after her pleurisy, my parents slept in separate rooms, which was a great relief to me.)

Even when I was very small, though, I had a feeling that beds weren't just meant for sleeping in. It was an unformed notion, but if I refer back to two dreams I remember very well, I must conclude that it was firmly present in my subconscious. The first of these dreams occurred when I was about six. I was having a loving conversation with someone whom I couldn't identify very well, and all of a sudden I realized it was the devil. But that didn't frighten me. On the contrary, I seized the opportunity and gave him a good talking to, explaining that he should have asked to be forgiven ages ago, and assuring him that I would pray God to pardon him. After which he lay down beside me and snuggled into my arms. I woke up quite excited erotically, if I remember rightly. The second dream resembled the first, and I place it several years later. The Iroquois were invading the convent. All the nuns (hmm!) and all the girls were dead. I was hidden under a table covered with a green baize cloth and I was going to suffer the same fate as the rest, for I had just been turned out of my hiding place by a young Iroquois brave — a handsome one, it goes without saying, and very prettily feathered. I made him a little speech too, and I must have convinced him, for I opened my bed to him as well. This predilection for "bad boys" — and what a pair! — as well as for sermonizing, leaves me quite stunned.

*   *   *

So all this while grammar and spelling sank deeper and deeper into a distant fog. Here and there, when Mother Ange Gabriel's muse was silent, we might be treated to a dictation, but nine times out of ten we never got our copies back.

"We'll correct them tomorrow, we'll correct them tomorrow."

But the next day, the devil take dictation! All we had time for was figure-hugging fashions, desecrated hosts, iodine and transparent stockings. Occasionally some zealot would ask, just as the bell was going:

"Do we have any homework for tomorrow?"

"Study pages fifty and fifty-one."

"But we're already at page seventy-five."

Mother Ange Gabriel would shrug her shoulders wearily. What was all this talk about grammar when she was engaged in saving the whole of Christendom, body and soul?

I don't bear her any real grudge. That year, thanks to her, I acquired a strong faith in medicine and in doctors, as well as a lasting indifference to the evil deeds of all Freemasons. Besides, I developed a passion for the history of France that has never left me. During the holidays I had got hold of my sister Dine's textbook. As soon as I had Mother Ange Gabriel's rigmaroles by heart (at first I used to listen because they were so hilarious), I spent her class, otherwise a dead loss, studying the history of a country I worshipped already for a number of reasons, not the least of which was that my father, who couldn't stomach little old Combes' politics, detested it furiously.

Fortunately, other branches of knowledge were better handled. I have a pleasant memory of Mother de la Trinité, for example, who taught us geography in a way that was truly divine. Instead of rushing into the novitiate on leaving school she had taken a trip around the world. She came to class, her arms full of photos, maps and rock samples, and her memory well stocked with anecdotes. She always knew where we had got to in history, and never failed to stress what had happened here or there, what monuments there were, or what ruins. Suddenly Quebec wasn't the only place in the world. Someone had actually seen all those other countries and cities, quite unreal till then, and had brought back objects from them you could see and touch.

Nevertheless, deprived of what I wanted most — a real class in French — I pulled through the year with only mediocre marks. In addition it was the year of my first solemn communion. In those days you didn't make solemn communion with your class, but at the age of ten, no matter what grade you were in. Unluckily for me, I was the only one that age in my class, all my companions having "done" their catechism the year before. This meant that my absence from class was scarcely noticed, and it never occurred to anyone, since communion was behind them, that I might need help to make up my school work. I was even scolded for it.

"What's this? You haven't done such and such? You haven't copied this out yet? You haven't taken notes on that?"

"I was at catechism."

"How come you didn't make your solemn communion last year with the others?"

"I wasn't ten then — "

Whereupon I was ordered to be silent and sit down. My refusal to be ten at the same time as the others was taken to be another sign of my nasty disposition.

* * *

Ever since I had been at boarding school, I had always spent Holy Week at Grandmother's. If I remember, only the littlest girls of the fourth division — because the services were too tiring, I think — went home that week, and they were not joined there by their big sisters until Holy Saturday. Usually, then, I wouldn't return to my father's until midday Saturday, at the same time as Françoise. But that particular year, because Grandmother wasn't well, I spent Holy Week at the convent along with Lauretta from New York and Marthe who came from far away too, I forget where. It was, in fact, during this period that I yanked out that hot handful of her hair that still burns my fingers and my conscience. Anyway, Saturday at noon Grandmother came to get Françoise and me and take us to my father's. He was on holiday too.

Grandmother rarely came to see us when my father was there. Whenever that did happen, the family climate became even more unbearable than usual. My father outdid himself finding ways to prove he wasn't afraid of her, or anyone else. He swaggered and huffed. We were all caught, one by one. He knew very well that in order to avoid big scenes, with Mother in the role of first martyr, Grandmother was ready to tolerate some minor ones. And the minor scenes multiplied in due course!

When we arrived at the house, we found a new occupant, a dog, Dano, who was, you guessed it, a great Dane. Young and crazy, he tore around all over the place, and it so happened that one day, getting up from my chair, I found a soft paw squirming wildly under one of my feet. The room was filled with yelps, the dog's, mine, then my father's. Unable to disentangle myself from this four-footed dervish, I stumbled clumsily around. I was promptly brought back into line. In a rage that was totally out of proportion with what had happened, my father seized me by the shoulder and came down on me with his whole weight, crushing my foot under his own enormous one, saying that would teach me a lesson. The dog, who hadn't asked for this kind of support, was already racing around on all four feet. I thought I would die with the pain, and through my tears watched my white tennis shoe turning red with blood. I am sure everyone else saw it too, but nobody dared to move. Grandmother, pale as a corpse, kept her eyes bent over her work, and the needle trembled so in her fingers that later that afternoon she had to rip out the whole hem she had been sewing at the time.

It's one thing to wound a child. It's another to sit still and watch the blood flow, especially when there's company. After a few minutes my father suddenly thought of something that needed attention in the orchard. He got up violently, and sure enough, came down on one of the dog's paws, too. But the only compensation Dano got this time was an energetic kick in the ribs. As soon as my father had gone, I was stretched out, the shoe was removed, the foot was bandaged. I had a nail torn out to the root, and it has always grown crooked since. Above all, I was comforted for my pain. But is "comforted" the right word? Mother covered the hurt foot with kisses. It was a lot more than comforting. It was taking sides.

Poor Mother! She was so small, so frail, and my father was so big, so strong, and so mean, that she could only take sides once a wrong had been done and the wrongdoer had disappeared. He could have killed us all, I used to think, and no one could have stopped him. But the time was soon to come when I would realize that Mother's presence protected us more than I thought.

*   *   *

I never liked Dano. We had got off to a bad start. I didn't like the two dogs we had afterwards either, the Newfoundland called Trim or the spaniel, Miro. For that matter it took me thirty-eight years to become reconciled to the canine race, and the little blond Nicou from St-Cézaire-sur-Siagne (Alpes-Maritimes) who belongs to my friend André Serval was the first one to profit from this reconciliation.

When he bought a dog my father always wanted expensive pure-breds. When it became a question of feeding them, the purse strings tightened. He gave them pig food that the poor animals had to eat to keep alive. Never a piece of meat, never a bone. They immediately became ugly, snappish, with rough coats and bleary eyes. They were kept outside in all seasons. In summer, if we were cooking with the windows open, they became absolutely wild. Except for my father, whom they too cringed before in panicky fear, they would throw themselves at anyone imprudent enough to step outside at such times, and tear his clothes. And God knows we didn't have enough clothes to give to the dogs. I think it was Dano, who in a frenzy one day, jumped right through a closed window when he saw a ham cooling on the other side.

It was the same thing for the horses. Thoroughbreds. But so poorly treated that both Belle and Maggie became dangerous animals who bit and kicked. One day, one of them tried to bite my father. This gave rise to a truly Homeric scene. Mad with anger, the outraged hero seized a whip and beat the mare until she fell to the ground, rolled up in a ball like a mouse in the claws of a cat. Then, his clothes soaked with sweat, a brow like Jupiter's, and a mouth spewing forth oaths, he made a crashing entrance into the house.

"Tried to bite her master! To bite the hand that feeds her! That damned horse! Her master!"

In her big horse heart Belle didn't perhaps share this idea of the word master, and that was the cause of all the trouble. Since we lived as far from the S.P.C.A. as from the Children's Welfare Society, my father got away with just being hated by his horse, too.

Whenever he had reason to complain of us — animals or children — he automatically defined himself as the hand that fed us. That didn't impress us unduly. His was mainly the hand that beat us and, as it could switch in a flash to this more important function, allusions to the fist that fed rather put us off our food. But for all that we were forbidden to say we didn't feel hungry.

"Clean up your plate."

Nothing but the bones could be left. Before the table was cleared, he cast a sweeping look over the plates and we were often invited to move our forks so he could see what we had left underneath. He served us abundantly with the things he liked least, and kept all the choice morsels. If a nice piece remained in the platter, he would secure it rapidly for himself as soon as one of us looked like asking for a second helping. He bought calves' liver for himself, pork liver for us, and drew our attention to it quite unashamedly. "The calves' liver is for me," he would say simply. When we had a large iced cake, he used to scrape all the icing over onto his piece. Those are little things, and we would have accepted them easily if someone else had been permitted some of them too. However, we knew very well that if he had caught one of us scraping the icing —

Every morning at breakfast there was the scene about the sugar spoon. We had given up sugaring our coffee with brown honey — I don't know why, a countermanding opinion from some new naturist or, more likely, a large hike in the price of honey — and now we had the right to use granulated sugar. As frequently happened, the steam from the hot coffee would condense on the cold spoon and a little sugar would stick to it. In winter, when the temperature in the house hit Siberian lows, this phenomenon took on major proportions, blown up to our scale like everything else. Well, every blessed morning this created unbelievable scenes. One of us had dipped the sugar spoon in the coffee, and had put it back wet into the sugar bowl. Who was it? Aha! Well, this morning he was going to get to the bottom of it. He wasn't going to leave the table without knowing who had puddled around in their coffee with the sugar spoon. There was a limit to kindness and patience. Since gentleness hadn't worked, he would be forced to be strict. He made that choice between gentleness and strictness every single morning and, gentleness or not, one or several of us would be bound to pick up a few knocks in the battle that followed.

I don't want to suggest that my father didn't know anything about the condensation of water vapour. It wasn't a question of ignorance or knowledge, but of pleasure. That the sugar stuck to the sugar spoon was nothing more than a pretext for anger, a regular daily pretext that didn't require the least effort of the imagination. Anger for him was like morphine for the drug addict. And just as you never hear of a morphine addict who only takes it when he comes across it, here and there, now and then, so he needed his drug first thing in the morning, every day. The sugar spoon was his hypodermic.

When you think of anger in these terms, that is, when you consider it as a drug, it becomes less difficult to give at least a partial explanation of my father's behaviour. Otherwise, the method of education he practised — if I can call it that — remains impossible to understand. Strictly speaking, we didn't have the right to do anything, or the right to do nothing. It's not difficult to imagine the number of fits of anger such a programme permitted in a household like ours. If you multiply the number of us, seven children, plus my mother and the cook, by the number of things it was forbidden to do — without counting those which, without being officially forbidden, became so on the spur of the moment for the sake of the cause — you reach quite a healthy total. And he reached it. We might be cautious to a fault, but in vain. When we were too careful, and the pretexts dwindled down accordingly, he found others like these:

"What are you looking at me like that for? Do you think I eat too much? Do I disgust you?"

None of us had a voice strong enough to make our denials heard above the shouting and banging of dishes that followed. Once he had exhausted this subject, he would take just enough time to catch his breath and then:

"What are you looking so stupid about? Why do you have to look like an idiot when I speak to you? Why? Answer!"

Answer — Each time he asked one of those questions there isn't any possible answer to, he began to shout like a maniac, "Answer! Answer!" Any other time, he didn't give a hang for an answer. For that matter, he never got many. To have a lump in your throat is not just a metaphor. We tried painfully to get something out, a "yes" or a "no" according to the inspiration of the moment, but we never managed more than a few strangled gurgles. Sometimes, on mornings of high sadism, he would go as far as to ask:

"Are you afraid of me?"

A Machiavellian question. As everyone knows, there is no room for fear in a child's love for his parent. So you couldn't say "yes." On the other hand, maybe it wouldn't be such a good idea to say, "No, I'm not afraid of you." More mumbling.

"Are you trying to make out I'm an ogre?"

At last, an honest question! We heaved an "Oh, no!" with heartfelt conviction, and settled back to catch our breaths for the next one. The intermissions were not gay. I have known hot-tempered people who weren't disagreeable between crises. God willing. In my father's case it was rather a matter of one and the same fit all day long, a fifteen-hour anger, with its fever peaks at more or less regular intervals.

*   *   *

When I went back to school I changed divisions. All that entailed was crossing the corridor. Yet despite this proximity, the only contact I was to have with Mother Saint-Chérubin was limited to the briefest of nods. We seemed to be mutually pleased with the arrangement. Often, on leaving my new room, I would see a little girl, always the same one, standing in penance near the door. I had been as fully replaced as the first wife of a newly remarried widower. (When you are the daughter of a man who was to marry four times, such comparisons spring to mind of their own accord.) Well, that's life!

I haven't any very lively memories of this last year in that particular convent. The two division mistresses were nice. We had a good librarian, and if we did our homework and knew our lessons we could read as much as we wanted to. I couldn't have asked for more. Since the year before when I had spent all those French classes reading French history, I had developed a flaming passion for Napoleon Bonaparte, it was a real love affair. I devoured every book in the library on him. My nights were filled with heroic dreams.

I also loved to read stories set in chateaux equipped with cellars, dungeons, hidden staircases and secret passages. I would have given anything to discover a mysterious passage somewhere, and thought it extremely stupid that people had got out of the habit of digging them under their houses. I felt they had quite frivolously sacrificed the best things in life, and moreover that, if from time to time I had been able to go and feel over old walls which would open when my finger touched the hidden spring, all my troubles would have been as naught.

* * *

In December my paternal grandfather died. Beyond "Hello, Goodbye," he had never really spoken to me except once. It was during one of the two visits I paid to his house, and he had called me into his study.

"Do you want a mint?"

He took the cover off a big well-filled jar and gave me one. One. For a good part of the afternoon I waited to be called back again. In vain.

That December morning, the first mistress took me over to one side. This kind of news was always announced in the same way.

"Is it long since you last saw your grandfather?"

This precaution was prompted by a good intention, but it was wasted effort. At our age, the thought of death didn't come easily. The poor nun would have to insist more and more heavily, and put on a longer and longer face, before we at last began to become concerned. When, after many circumlocutions, she told me what had happened, I felt my whole emotional world reeling.

"Grandfather de la Chevrotière?"

"No, your paternal grandfather."

I threw myself sobbing against her white linen wimple. "I was so afraid — so afraid — so afraid."

I had been so afraid, in fact, that I couldn't stop saying it. Mother Marie-Jean let me cry myself out, and then stood me up again. She looked at me curiously. I was so embarrassed at the way I had behaved. Used to Mother Saint-Chérubin's inhumanity, I thought it indispensable to make amends. I tried to find something to say in that line, but without any luck.

"Well now! You must thank God, and ask him to keep your Grandfather de la Chevrotière safe for you for a long time to come."

That reply, so full of tenderness, tolerance, and presence of mind, amazes me still. I went back to the division very puzzled. Was what had just happened really possible? Were there really sisters who could understand a little girl's heart, her preferences, her need of reciprocity? I wouldn't have believed it. To be sure, there had been Mother Bon-Conseil, but I thought she was unique of her kind, a stray among the hundred Mother Saint-Chérubins.

I never saw Mother Bon-Conseil any more. They said she wasn't well, and was resting. I hardly dared ask about her. We had been the cause of so much trouble for one another. By mutual assent we had begun by avoiding each other, and suddenly I discovered it wasn't necessary any longer. She just wasn't around. She didn't teach

French, or anything else, to anyone. Even on days of high religious ceremonies, days of taking the veil or the habit, she wasn't there with the other nuns singing the *Veni Creator.*

Several of us had been her students, and it would have been normal for them to speak to us about her from time to time, to ask us to pray for her, since she was ill. But never. It would also have been normal for me not to feel embarrassed to ask about her. But how could I have felt otherwise? I knew that my questions would have given rise to nothing but mockery. In those days, it was pretty difficult to love in this country. It either made people laugh, or set their teeth on edge.

Then one day she came to ask for me at the door of the division. In spite of her enormous skirts, she seemed unbelievably thin. But her cheeks were so red they looked rouged. She was to be put to bed in the infirmary the next day, and she had come to say goodbye to me. At least I understood later that she had come to say goodbye.

"What's wrong, Mother?"

"Glands."

"Whereabouts?"

"All over."

"But glands are nothing. You'll soon be better."

"Yes — "

In the shadows of the corridor her eyes seemed to be glistening in a curious way.

"Are you crying, Mother?"

"Why no."

And to prove it she started to laugh in a way that seemed to me a little forced, a little miserable.

"You'll be better by springtime, you'll see."

That was a hope I often heard. Everyone said it to Mother when she took to her bed in the autumn.

Mother Bon-Conseil didn't get better, and I never saw her again. She died in September. The news reached me in my new convent.

Was it possible that she had had her funeral service in that same chapel I knew so well? The white pine box placed near the choir screen must have been very, very small — and I wasn't there. I hadn't seen it. I didn't believe it. Besides, it was a day-girl from my first convent, who lived close to my second one, who had tossed this piece of news off to me on the run. It was a mistake. What did day-girls know about boarders' affairs? And for years, each time I met an old school friend, I would ask her if it was true that Mother Bon-Conseil was dead.

*   *   *

In June I left the convent not knowing I wouldn't come back. The older I got, the more I dreaded the approach of the summer holidays. The last night in the dormitory, nobody slept. Happiness made the girls nervous. In my case, it was fear that kept me from sleeping. From that year on, I always suffered from indigestion, nausea, and diarrhoea, those last days before the holidays. I knew nothing about the influence of psychological factors on physical health, and thought it was really bad luck to be sick just when I was feeling so upset. This time I had to leave the reception hall where the prize-giving was taking place, before the ceremonies were over. I just managed to get through the door and collapsed in a faint in the empty corridor. When I came to, I was stretched out — in my pretty white muslin dress, too, on that dusty floor that had been trampled over by all those feet that same morning. It was strange to find myself on the ground without knowing how or why, and without anyone to help me up, or tell me what had happened. For a child, fainting is a mystery. It is an important experience, too. All the more so because adults always refuse to be serious about this horrible thing that makes a child afraid he is going to die. "It's nothing, you just feel a little bit faint."

Nothing could compare to the feeling of lightness that flowed through me when I regained consciousness. It was like being relieved of half my weight. None of the disagreeable sensations remained. Gone was that clamour in my ears, as though I was surrounded by swarms of giant grasshoppers, that darkening of vision which came on long before the loss of consciousness — how often did I have to leave the chapel my hands stretched out in front of me like a blind man? — that wish to be dead rather than go on feeling so helpless. All those symptoms disappeared at the same time as I lost the sense of my body's weight. All that was left was a delicious void, and a little sweat on my forehead.

I couldn't enjoy this bliss long. My dress was causing me too much concern. I had vomited a little, I was dusty from head to toe, one of my prize books from Mame et Fils was beginning to lose colour in my moist hands, and there was red everywhere. I went to wash my hands and face at the sink in the little ones' room, I cleaned my dress with my handkerchief and threw it behind the "crust" radiator. The prize-giving was over at last, and my sister Françoise finished up repairing what was repairable.

Then I put on the marvellous hat that Grandmother had sent me. It was the custom for our parents on the eve of prize day to send us "a worldly hat," as we used to call them. These hats were laid out on a long table like a young bride's wedding presents. Mine was a straw hat with an openwork brim through which you could catch a glimpse of finely pleated pink silk. "It's the nicest," my school friends declared. And so we departed, the two of us, by the main door. Adieu!

*   *   *

We found my father's pseudo-farm considerably enlarged: a pigpen, rabbit hutches, various other sheds, and a collection of farm machinery no less various. Several new chunks of land belonged to us. This regime had been functioning for some time and had brought in practically nothing. On the contrary, it was costing a pretty penny. You don't become a farmer casually, especially when you spend your days in an office and have to entrust the upkeep to people who don't like you, and don't like what you do. The dear man had started off on the principle that you are always a winner, even if only a small one, when you grow almost all the food for the family yourself. He could never bring himself to believe that the taxes, machinery, fertilizers, salaries, and all the rest, blew up the cost of a single home-grown tomato until it equalled that of a precious mango devoutly packaged in the tropics for consumption in Iceland. In short, this disparager of the imagination and of its evil effects was a born dreamer who spent his life cherishing every illusion that strayed within reach.

So the money was going fast. To plug some of the leaks my father got the idea of not paying any of our year's fees for boarding at the convent. Determined not to sacrifice a single calf, he decided to send us to another institution, planning to pay off his debts to the first one after the farm had brought in a fortune. All that for a few hundred dollars it would have been easy to dig up. But my father adored these little dramas. He liked nothing better than to stride through the whole downstairs — study, hall, living room, dining room, kitchen, hall — like a wild beast, cursing this family that cost him so much that he could never make two ends meet — take that debt, for example, that he didn't know when he'd be able to settle. The next day he would buy five hundred dollars' worth of I don't know what, that the farmer had asked for.

I was at an age when any change is attractive, when any old bird in the bush seems more than worth whatever poor fowl you happen to have in hand. In short, we asked to be admitted to a convent much nearer my father's house than the first one. It was all right with me.

A change like that would have displeased me greatly in the days when Grandmother came to visit us every week. But there was no question of that any more. All during the past year she hadn't come once. Grandfather had sold the drugstore on la rue Saint-Jean. Now he was looking after the one on la rue Canardière which had been acquired several years before to make a job for my uncle, Mother's brother. My uncle was a charming, but light-hearted fellow who had grown bored behind the counter. He had let the business run down, and Grandfather had to take it back. For this reason, Grandmother and he now lived far away from the convent. Then, too, Grandmother was ill: serious hyper-tension, brought on, it would seem fair to judge, by her distress at her daughter's misery. Besides, Diana having left her to get mar-ried, all maids, compared to this priceless pearl, seemed unac-ceptable. Grandmother, therefore, spent long periods without help. For all these reasons, it wasn't possible for her to come to see us any more.

About this time, many things had started to disintegrate in my grandparents' life. During their last years an uninterrupted succes-sion of misfortunes befell them. A good many came from my father, and it was also due to him that the outcome of them all was has-tened: death.

*   *   *

Speaking of misfortunes, one befell Mother that year that affected her deeply. Her best friend, Claire, died without their having seen each other for I don't know how long, probably since the time of what I scarcely dare call my parents' reconciliation. On my mother's side of the family, it was accepted that my own first name came from this Claire. On my father's side they believed it came from one of their grandmothers. In that matter, as in almost everything else, there was the official version that was false, and the other, secret and true.

Mother often spoke to us about this friend. Especially during her last year. I don't know how she got news of her, from Grandmother perhaps. At any rate, news of her was always most extraordinary. It should be said that Claire had lost her husband ten years or so before. He had died quite suddenly. One evening he felt ill. The doctor came and ordered some medicine. Claire sat up with him all that night, but towards morning she fell asleep, and when she woke up he was dead or dying, I don't know which. Anyway, it was too late for the last rites. Since he was not much of a believer, Claire developed a strong sense of remorse because of this.

"If one day I have the revelation that my husband is saved, I'll do something, some good action," she often repeated to my mother.

Then she went back with her young son to the little town where she was born. Years passed. It seems that the desired revelation suddenly came to her, I don't know just how, but I am inclined to believe by some third party. In short, it was learned one day that she was giving her vast and beautiful house to a religious order that she was having brought out from France. Some edifying stories came out of that transaction. The day of their arrival, the Superior of these saintly girls handed Claire some little hemp sacks she was supposed to have filled with bran.

"Can you guess why? Well, to be used as pillows."

Despite her piety, or perhaps because of her piety, Grandmother wasn't very keen on ostentation. She would add a little "hum!" at the end of the story, accompanied by a slight shake of the head which seemed to say, "I don't much like that kind of thing, but it's none of my business."

Claire's gift was made at the beginning of summer. In September, she died in three days. From typhoid fever they claimed. From anger and vexation, her son told me. It seems that the poor woman had been cheated so frightfully, that she wasn't able to live through it. Her generosity was used as a starting point for burdening her with all sorts of heavy obligations. "You're not going to go and give us the bridle without giving us the horse, too!" Above all, she was chased out of her own house, when it had been clearly understood that she should keep two rooms, outside the community cloister but still within the shadow of the walls, so to speak.

You can imagine how important it must have been for this woman of mystical inclinations to live thus in her own house, now become a convent! But as soon as the sisters were installed, they let her know that she would have to leave — their sacred rule did not permit them to live under the same roof as the laity. Under the malicious eyes of the whole little town, she had to move out. She never got over it. I think that Mother must have got wind of all these catastrophes. "Poor Claire," she often used to sigh, "poor Claire, how I wish I could have seen her again."

Mother never saw any of her childhood friends. A short time ago, I received a letter from one of them, Louise de Grandpré, who wrote: "After her marriage we never saw each other again." Even if Mother had been free to go out or receive visitors, I think she would have refused, for fear of exposing the sadness of her life to those who had known her in her happy childhood.

Now and then, however, one or another of these old friends would turn up as a witness. Madame Lépine and her children, who were so noisy that Mother had to take to her bed after their visit; Madame O'Leary and her sister Cornélie Dostaler who, long before other women, drove her own car "like a man" and spryly turned the crank while her two nephews, Dostaler and Walter, sat soberly in the back seat like two blond cherubim. All in all, seven or eight visits in ten years.

*   *   *

Anyway, here we were changing convents. I remember my frame of mind — madly optimistic. I thought I had escaped the danger of falling under the rule of some new Sister Saint-Chérubin. Françoise didn't share my enthusiasm. Of the two of us, she was the one who proved to be right.

The first nun I had anything to do with was called Mother Saint-Protais —

"I used to have a friend who entered the religious life in the convent you come from," she said to me. "I wonder if you know her — Mother Saint-Chérubin?"

Ouch! What a great beginning. I learned in the next breath that Mother Saint-Protais was to be my teacher. In this small convent there were no specialists. The same nun took us in hand every morning for catechism and dropped us in the afternoon after geography. She also watched over us during study period. So, if you were mutually displeasing, you were mutually displeasing all day.

I noticed right away that the nuns I came from were not viewed with favour by the nuns I came to. Mother Saint-Protais took it for granted that I knew practically nothing, that I was far behind for my age and that she would have a tough time driving anything into my head. She just had to look at me to see that I wasn't up to scratch. The reason was that she had always been uncommonly demanding, especially in French. Her classes had always been outstanding for her pupils' proficiency, especially in French. Anyway —

The first day was spent choosing which girls would go into Section A in the class, and which into Section B — the latter, on principle, were not likely to pass at the end of the year. I sensed at once that Mother Saint-Protais had decided to put me into Section B. I had with me what we pompously used to call a diploma, a kind of certificate stating that I had completed the previous year in good standing. But who could trust the diploma of the convent I came from?

Halfway through the day it only remained to choose between Fernande and me. To take both of us into Section A was out of the question because merit wasn't the only consideration. Number also had to be considered: so many girls in Section A, so many in Section B.

"I am going to give you a little test in irregular verbs. The one who knows them best will go into Section A."

I had learned my irregular verbs with Mother Bon-Conseil three years ago, but I knew them all by heart. The choice of exam surprised me. At that age one's feeling for knowledge is like the self-made man's feeling for money: "I've already had it for a long time." Deep down, I decided that I had erred into a kind of bedlam of ignorance.

As a matter of course, the examination began straight off with the imperfect subjunctive.

"Fernande, the imperfect subjunctive of the verb *fuir*."

"*Que je fuiye, que tu fuiyes —* "

"Claire?"

Dear Mother Bon-Conseil, how strongly I felt at that moment the love and gratitude I owed her.

"*Que je fuisse —* "

"Fernande, of the verb *clore*?"

"*Que je closisse —* "

"There isn't any," I said with a fine show of assurance, for I knew now that I wouldn't miss a single one. I saw those irregular verbs, I heard them with all their persons, numbers, tenses, moods, kinds and forms, all of them, the easy ones, the risky ones, the crazy ones.

"And of the verb *mouvoir*?"

"There isn't any," said Fernande, who had just remembered that when it's too difficult there isn't any imperfect subjunctive.

From time to time Mother Saint-Protais had to consult her text-book to decide which of us was right. That left me wondering, even though I was pretty hard pressed. And though the match had begun in mid-afternoon, the day ended without any final verdict. The next day right after catechism:

"Fernande, the imperfect of. . . ."

I suddenly had the very strong suspicion that a single wrong answer from me would put me into Section B. Mother Saint-Protais' voice began to drip gall:

"And you, my little prodigy?"

The verb to sow, the verb to graze, the verb to be tantamount to! I was always questioned second. I realized that if ever Fernande replied a single time, *"Que je cousisse, que j'équivalusse"* the examination would stop, and my fate would be sealed, because she would know her irregular verbs quite well enough. Finally, the time came to put an end to the tournament. I was exhausted, I had burned up all my phosphorus, but I hadn't missed a single one.

"Oh! Mother Bon-Conseil, Mother Bon-Conseil," I kept repeating silently over and over again, like some pious and amorous litany, not knowing that she was living out her last week. I had the keen feeling that I owed her something very important, and had just grasped how important it was.

Fernande, who had learned her irregular verbs the year before with Mother Saint-Protais, was not, I think, preoccupied with the same kind of litany.

"All right, you'll be in Section A. But I'm sorry about it, because Fernande is very good in arithmetic."

We hadn't been examined in arithmetic, and I judged the remark worthy of its speaker. I was disgusted. Whatever might happen after that, I had lost confidence in my instructor's knowledge, in her sense of justice, and in any word that might issue from her lips. The long and the short of it was, that I had rediscovered Mother Saint-Chérubin. Serpents in the bed couldn't be far off.

Mother Saint-Protais had other manias. More than anything else she was against food. According to her, any kind of nourishment dulled the wits. The thing was not to eat. Eleven-year-olds are usually hungry. But the needs of growing children didn't touch her. We were all accused of filling our faces, of wolfing down our food, of stuffing ourselves. If a child didn't know her homework:

"You've been eating like a pig again, your mind is completely dulled," she would say, with a grimace that seemed like an attempt to remove her long nose from the vicinity of her mouth.

The girl she singled out would be submerged in shame, feeling that she had indulged in some base and disgusting materialism. At the next meal, she would scarcely dare nibble. Personally, even though I couldn't have cared less about Mother Saint-Protais, the thing I feared above all was her verbal attacks, administered in front of all my schoolmates in a vocabulary so offensive you could hardly believe your ears. I began to melt away. About one morning in two I had all kinds of pains, and at least once a week I would have to leave the chapel groping my way, with my hands stretched out before me.

"It's indigestion, you eat too much," she would say, looking disgusted.

I began to get nervous. When we went to chapel I was so scared of fainting that I couldn't breathe properly. As a result I began to feel faint almost immediately.

"Mother Prefect will be with us for prayers tonight," Mother Saint-Protais said one day. "I forbid anyone to leave the chapel for any reason whatsoever. Those among you who are in the habit of giving way to certain weaknesses should consider themselves forewarned."

I was so well forewarned that even before I reached my place I felt crushed by fatigue and a foreboding of disaster. Most of the prayers went by all right. There were hardly ten minutes left to go, when I felt the first stirrings of what I dreaded. With what has so justly been called the strength of despair I fastened myself to the *prie-Dieu*, my arms clasped around the elbow rest and, in an attempt to re-establish the circulation, tried to bend my head forward as far as possible. Then I passed out. When I came to, I was still clutching the *prie-Dieu*, but had done peepee on the holy chapel floor. This earned me, as you can well imagine, far weightier insults than I had ever got before.

*   *   *

No, I have never experienced a chronic fatigue comparable to the one I knew that year. Yet I was basically a strong and sturdy girl. But I had too many battles to fight, and while fasting into the bargain.

First, Mother was getting sicker and sicker. She always claimed to be on the verge of recovery, but I began to hear her predictions with a skeptical ear. Then, my father had bought a car. (I haven't said that in the spring of the year of grace 1925, heaven and the government had blessed us with a road which linked us to civilization — a little road, about one horse wide, but at the time it seemed to us to be one of the boldest realizations of human genius.) So every Sunday now my father came to the convent to visit us, with Dine and the three little ones. We would install ourselves in one corner of the parlour, the same deadly boredom stamped on every face. The nuns lost no time in singling out my father — he was the one who bawled out his daughters so loudly. Result? The nuns' scorn for those same daughters. And though I hesitate to admit it, there wasn't a grill in this parlour. My father used to take advantage of this shamelessly in front of everyone. Finally, to cap it all, for six months he obstinately refused to pay the bill for the school books my sister and I had to buy.

"Have you got the money?" Mother Saint-Protais would ask every time we came back from the parlour.

I would cover my mouth with my hand, just like the guileless girl in the drawing room comedy who is caught out in some giddy slip.

"I forgot — "

For another thing, my sister wasn't much more appreciated than I was. I was implicitly made party to the things they reproached her with, and vice versa. The nun who was in charge of her was called Mother Saint-Pamphile. She was a champion at insinuations. She would scold us in public for crimes which she would only designate by, "You know what I'm talking about," or "I don't dare say it in front of your schoolmates, but you know very well — " which left room for the most abominable suspicions.

"I found near your bed," she said one day to Françoise, "something unspeakably vile, something that decency forbids me to name. Even to speak of it turns my stomach. You must certainly be a disgusting creature to . . . et cetera."

All the girls who were "in the know" calculated Françoise's age, and naturally concluded that "that" was what the nun had found. Poor Ti-Fan didn't know where to look. Large reddish patches came out on her face and neck, as they still do when she is upset.

Fortified by a clear conscience, she went over at the next recess to ask Mother Saint-Pamphile to tell her, once and for all, what it was that had been found near her bed.

"Nail parings, from the feet," murmured the dear woman, whose turn it now was to blush painfully. At least she had the good fortune to be spared saying outright the word, "toe," which, as everyone knows, dishonours the mouth that utters it.

I was badly shaken by this story. I tried to tell the true version to some of the little girls to make them understand that it wasn't what they thought, but I got a cool reception. Since Mother Saint-Pamphile had said it was something unspeakably vile (ever after my sisters and I never used another term to refer to nail parings; in my own home it has been shortened to "unspeakables"), although no one had ever suspected it before, toenails must be something horrible. And when something is held to be horrible in a convent, you don't shake the conviction all that easily. To do that the girls would have had to be impervious to the general atmosphere. Neither Mother Saint-Pamphile nor Mother Saint-Protais was obliged to admit to such an ignominious defeat in this case.

A moment ago, I alluded to the signs of puberty. Everyone was preoccupied with them. There were those who had reached it, and those who were still waiting. Among the latter, there were those who knew, and those who, to use the expression current in both my convents, were ignorant of "the curse." I was ignorant. Or rather, I knew there was something I didn't know, which let me act as though I did. This attitude bore fruit; after a week in the new convent I knew what to expect. The unfortunate part of it for me was that I mainly learned that it was a shameful thing which you could laugh about with your girlfriends, but which it was impossible to discuss with adults. My female condition began to seem absurd to me, because I had inquired about boys to see if they went through something equivalent and had learned they didn't go through anything at all. Another pretty kettle of fish. So that was what the future promised me, all those troubles and, on top of that, the prospect of marrying a man who, in time, would probably turn out to be for me what my father was for my mother. If there was ever a time in my life when I felt hatred for men, it was then. But times change.

One morning, one of the girls woke up "with something new," and not knowing what to do, went off to confide in Mother Saint-Protais.

"It's a punishment from God," she exclaimed, brandishing her fists.

The little girl came and told me about this at recess. I was shattered. Contrary to what I had been given to understand, this thing didn't happen to everyone, since it was a punishment. Moreover, I thought immediately, since you are always punished where you have sinned, it must really be something when it hits you. However, I didn't find anything illogical in that. We were so used to being ashamed of our bodies, to thinking that every last thing that happened to them was a punishment for some unknown crime, that even the growth of a single hair disturbed us greatly. When I first noticed them growing in my armpits and pubes, I was overcome with despair. What could I have been doing? Was it all in vain that I had been going to sleep with my hands removed from my body as far as the width of the bed would permit? Punishments rained down on me from everywhere just the same.

I tried not to think about all this, because I knew that bad thoughts were as bad as bad actions, and I walked around as though on eggs, careful not to sit down on any hot radiators either, so I wouldn't give "the punishment" any chance to surprise me. As it was, I had quite enough to worry about with my three hairs. At last I found out that this stigma was an integral part of original sin, and part of every woman's fate. It would have been even worse not to suffer it though, because that meant that one hadn't long to live. It was either death or defilement. Well!

Though it was something that happened to all women, it wasn't any less shameful for all that. How could I ever bring myself to ask Mother about such a scabrous subject, Mother who was so scrupulous, so shy about this kind of thing and so marked herself by all this nonsense. If by chance I had a pain in my stomach, I immediately choked up with anxiety. What would I do when the time came, I asked myself endlessly, at the same time trying to dismiss this bad thought. When the time did come, I didn't find the courage to speak of it. It happened during the next holidays, and there was no one to notice but the maid. For several days I nourished the hope that she would take it upon herself to report this secret, but it seems

she wasn't any more courageous than I was. I got around my difficulties by raiding my elder sisters' bureau drawers — they had had
the good luck not to have been exposed to the punishment theory.
As for Mother, she was living her last months. I think that she was
preoccupied by graver concerns about her children. Perhaps, too,
she didn't think of me as being as big as I really was. Our children
must seem very small when we are about to leave them.

*　*　*

But for the time being, there was almost a year ahead before that
was to happen. I was settling into my new convent, and every day
brought new reasons for bitterly missing the old one. My greatest
disappointment was to discover that French history was not on
the curriculum. At first I thought it was just not on this year's
programme of studies, but that it would be on next year, or the
year after.

"We don't study French history here," Mother Saint-Protais told
me, hammering each syllable, with a particularly loud bang on the
"here."

There followed a long diatribe about that infamous country that
had expelled its priests and nuns. To the point that it had been necessary to take in a good number of them ourselves, out of pure charity. To listen to her one would have thought that she was feeding
the outlaws at her own expense and that, since those poor creatures
were ignorant of the fact that food dulls the wits, it was costing her
a pretty penny. Every day I thought to myself that if I had been old
man Combes, and it had been my job to settle the hash of Sisters
Saint-Protais and Saint-Chérubin, I couldn't have got the door
open fast enough.

So I continued to bone up secretly on my French history, using
my old text whose cover I had torn off and replaced by a binding on

which I had written "History of Canada." (Mother Saint-Protais went through our desks too, but apparently she was always taken in by this subterfuge.) However, after a while, my pleasure began to pall. To freshen it I got the idea of looking up the names of all my favourite heroes in the dictionary. That led me on to other names, which led to others — I couldn't see an end to it. The end came unexpectedly.

"What are you looking up in the dictionary? Dirty words?"

I can't have been very bright, I must admit, for I would never have thought of that myself. Besides, the words I knew I didn't have to look up definitions for, and those I didn't know, how could I ever have found them anyway? Now that I think back on it, I understand the poor sister's turmoil. Dirty words gave her a hell of a bad time. They were all over the place — even in the Gospel. For here was another difference, among many others, between my first convent and this one — here we learned the Sunday Gospel by heart, and recited it on Monday morning. It was a decision that had been taken without sufficient forethought. At the end of November, without anyone being able to do anything to stop it, along came the twenty-fourth Sunday after Pentecost.

"And woe unto them that are with child, and unto them that give suck in those days!" There it was, written out as large as life, and as impudent. And, good gracious! it's Jesus himself who is speaking! It's a sure bet he wouldn't have used those dirty words if he had been French-Canadian. But Jesus was Jewish, and the Jews, well, what do you expect!

That won't get by without making some fur fly, I said to my little old self.

The Monday of the twenty-fourth week after Pentecost, everyone was on edge. If only she doesn't pick on me, was the expression clearly marked on every face. I don't remember who got picked, but what I do remember is that Mother Saint-Protais' eyes couldn't move fast enough — to the right, to the left, in the front row, in the last — to be sure, absolutely sure, to surprise the least smile.

"So-and-so, you smiled. Why?"

It wasn't so much that poor So-and-so found these Gospel threats particularly funny, but under the inquisitorial eye of this wimpled Torquemada, she just couldn't control her cheek muscles.

When the all-clear sounded, we could breathe again until the third Sunday in Lent, when it began all over again: "Blessed is the womb that bare thee and the paps which thou hast sucked." Ugh!

Even geography had disagreeable surprises in store for us. *L'île de Sein*! Those darned Frenchmen! "Breast Island," really, I ask you, always the same obsession. But there was worse than that: weren't the South Americans so dirty they even called one of their lakes "Titicaca"?

"Lake Titica*na*," the nun said, to my utter stupefaction.

And all the little girls, relieved of considerable pressure on their prudery, repeated "Titica*na*" after her. Nobody was taken in, neither the nun, or the children. But that wasn't what mattered. The important thing was not to blush. And perhaps to hint, from a distance that would allow the whole thing to remain quite platonic, that we disapproved.

For the sake of memory, I might mention *Pie le Septième* whom all Quebec school children in my time knew very well from studying the history of the Church. I also remember hearing in a sermon: *Le pape Pie, septième du nom . . .*" and all the congregation sniggered.

I was forgetting the letter Q. We pronounced it "que" everywhere, in all schools, boys and girls alike, and it wasn't until my husband specialized in the transcendental science of mathematics that he learned that everywhere else in the world it was pronounced "cu."[5] I was lucky enough to be initiated much younger than he was, by a little girl who came from another convent — run by

French sisters, it would have been impossible otherwise — where, by some kind of sadistic prudery they used to say "indecent letter."

"Why indecent?"

"Because the right pronunciation isn't 'que,' it's 'cu.'"

"Are you sure?"

"Yes, I'm positive. But don't tell anyone."

I wasn't used to much broad-mindedness, but such extreme narrowness really bothered me.

As a consolation, I began to write novels. Napoleonic novels. I would write three pages, then get a better idea and begin another. They were always stories about heroic young girls, usually nieces unknown to the Emperor, for incapable as I was, in my ignorance of the facts of life, of inventing daughters out of wedlock, I had to rely on secret nieces, offspring of the marriage of Jérôme and Elisa Paterson. They were always giving their lives to save their uncle, who always refused to receive them. It didn't take long for Sister Saint-Protais to get her hands on my notebooks. One can imagine a normal person saying in such circumstances: "So you like to write, eh? That's fine. Go right ahead. Learn by doing, et cetera." Not on your life. She treated me to a long sermon in which the salient points were: *primo*, I had suspicious inclinations; *secundo*, it was impossible that I could have made up what I was writing all by myself, for I was far too stupid ever to write a book in my life; *tertio*, there had never been any kings in Canada, and my Napoleon was a ridiculous invention. Quite aghast, I lost the thread of her discourse and didn't hear if there was a *quarto* or a *quinto*.

With the exception of Mother Saint-Chérubin, I had never in my first convent encountered what is so justly called crass ignorance, and as for Mother Saint-Chérubin, care had been taken not to give any classes to such an ignoramus. Except catechism (but catechism was nothing but answers learned by heart and regurgitated by the little word machines) and — to give her her just due — a few sermons on the importance of preserving our purity and on the equal importance of giving our pennies to the Holy Childhood. So you can guess how the ignorance of Mother Saint-Protais, in a subject that fascinated me, roused my scorn. From that minute on, she could say whatever she liked, I was deaf, I wasn't the least interested. It just didn't concern me any more. In my research in the dictionary I had found the word *autodidacte*. "One who instructs himself without a teacher." That was just what I needed. I was going to be self-taught. That's a strange decision to make when one is at school and only eleven, but with sisters of that kind there were too many risks involved. I felt the same suspicions about her as I did about my father: whatever she said couldn't be anything else but wrong.

I improvised my little course of studies as the fancy struck me. If a subject pleased me, I would do my best to get to the bottom of it — I spent hours in the dictionary — if not, I would settle for the minimum. Since Mother Saint-Protais didn't understand the sense of what she was teaching, she required word-for-word answers for lessons and the end of the month tests as well. My system wasn't geared to the word-for-word, and I was always among the last in the class.

French composition gave me a sadistic pleasure. Each time I discovered a word whose spelling might lead to possible error, I noted it down. *Imbécillité*, for example. With a good deal of finagling, I managed to get *imbécillité* into my essays quite often. My paper would come back every time with a red mark through the second "l." It cost me one mark, but that was the least of my worries. I didn't argue. This waste of imagination served no purpose, except to give me a kind of morose pleasure by proving to myself just how often I was right, and that stupid creature was wrong. The next week I would start over again with *caparaçonner* or *voire*. My essay would come back with *carapaçonner* or *voir*, written in red ink. Or else, adopting a dry formalism, I would write, *il faisait soleil* or *il faisait froid* just to have the pleasure of seeing myself corrected to *il faisait un soleil ardent*, or *il faisait un froid glacial*, and landing, in the margin, "You have no sense of style," which was what I expected. In reality, it was a pretty sad form of amusement, and I think that was the time in my life I was in greatest need of a psychiatrist.

But the saddest thing of all was that the dear woman prided herself on her reputation for forming outstanding scholars in French.

One December evening I felt sick in the chapel. I had to go out in the hall where Mother Saint-Protais, who had followed me, found me sitting on the floor. I couldn't have taken one step more.

"Get up," she shouted. "Get up! If you could only see yourself sitting there on the ground. What a sight you are."

She dragged me off into a study room, saying that I was behaving like an animal, really! That she had found me sprawled on the floor and, naturally, when you ate like a pig what else could you expect.

"Indigestion again! You're always getting sick with these indigestions of yours. It's disgraceful!"

I tried to explain that I had been coughing a lot the last day or two.

"Anyone can pretend to be coughing."

So there you are!

The next day, when the rising bell went, I sat up in my bed to say the "I gave my heart to God" like everyone else. But I didn't feel up to much. Suddenly I saw Mother Saint-Protais bearing down on me.

"Lie down! Will you please lie down! And don't scratch."

Did I have something you could see? As soon as she moved off I grabbed my mirror. I had the measles. I was all decked out[6] in red spots, which just went to show the stupidity[7] of Mother Saint-Protais. I was delighted. It was the measles, of course, that had made me cough, and the Sister would certainly be forced to admit that I wasn't a faker. True enough, you could pretend to have a

cough, but you could hardly pretend to have the measles. I convinced myself that Mother Saint-Protais couldn't get out of offering
me an apology.

An apology?

"Yesterday, when she had to leave the chapel, I immediately
thought she must be catching something," she said, in a voice full
of compunction, to the Superior who had been summoned to my
bedside.

They smiled at me tenderly. They called me "poor little thing."

"Poor little thing," is what my father said, too, when he came to
get me. "She's really a pitiful sight. Do you feel pretty sick?"

I had never heard that milk-and-honey tone before and didn't
reply. Anyway, I was rolled up in a couple of blankets, hoisted into
my father's car and off I went.

"That's what you get for always being constipated. You pick up
everything that comes along. But you're just like your mother,
you'll never listen to me. Answer when I speak to you!"

At last we got there. The house I walked through was deserted.
Dine had made up a bed for me in my father's bedroom, where no
one but himself would have right of entry. That way he could keep
a closer watch on me than if I was in my own room, and he also
hoped, in this way, to prevent me from contaminating the three little ones. I went to bed. Then he went off to work.

"Well, someone has got to look after you," said Mother, pushing
open my door. "I'm certainly not going to leave you alone there all
day long. And besides, when there's measles in the house — "

Sure enough, a few weeks later the little ones came down with it,
too, all three of them. Only they didn't have to sleep in the paternal
bedroom, not them.

It was a huge room with large windows, through which the sunshine fell profusely, right into my eyes. My father maintained that it
was old-fashioned to believe that sunlight was harmful to the eyes

of measles patients. Lots of air and light. I was never short of light, for he read a good part of the night. Every time he woke up, three or four times a night, he would turn on the light and read. That woke me up, and when I got bored I would read too. This routine lasted as long as the measles, after which, since I was already a little short-sighted, I couldn't see much more than a mole. Besides, I was so short on sleep that I felt as tired as if I were at the gates of death.

*   *   *

Yes, my father read. He even read a lot. But I never saw him with any really good book in his hands — though there must have been a time in his life when he studied some of the great English writers, for he occasionally quoted Shakespeare, and even Milton. He used to buy what the Americans so aptly call "trash" and also so aptly publish in great quantity — stories of murders, or charlatans' cures, and the thousands of horrors you have to eat to preserve perfect health. That kind of thing had the double advantage of corresponding, alas! to his tastes and also of being written in a language, English, which we didn't know very well yet.

He read a lot, but whenever he caught one of us looking into a book he turned red with anger. When I was small I could never reconcile those conflicting attitudes. I finally understood what it was: women shouldn't read. That was an occupation that must remain strictly masculine. If you let women read they risk, first, imagining that they understand, and second, concluding that they have brains in their heads. Whereas women have nothing in their heads.

"Fundamentally, the only advantage that women have over animals is that they talk," he used to claim.

Now it must be agreed that there is nothing more painful than to cohabit with talking animals, who refuse to accept their condition and meddlesomely wish to read like men. If only his scorn for women had led him to practise silence, so as not to resemble them! On the other hand, for the man was contradiction incarnate, he expected us to stand at the head of the class, as though we had been in possession of real brains, in perfect working order, and all the rest of it. But perhaps that ambition was just the wish to get full measure for his money. Full measure? What am I saying? More than full measure. His dream was to get us to take two or three years in one. Deep down, he cursed this age that required girls to be educated. If we were speaking among ourselves about one of the subjects we were studying:

"I really wonder what good that's going to be to you in serving a man," he would exclaim with a sneer.

Serving a man? There wasn't anything I aspired to less, and the least allusion to it revolted me. At the convent some of the girls were beginning to dream about boys. When we went to the parish church, they would lavish on the pupils of the Christian Brothers looks that seemed to me to be a clear sign of early softening of the brain. Never would I condescend to look at a man in that fashion.

I stayed at home until after the Christmas holidays. For my New Year's gift, breaking with the tradition of socks-gloves-underpants, I asked Grandmother to give me a book. This book, naturally, was published in France, for in those days French-Canadian publications —

"I trust you will be responsible enough, if you find something indecent in that book, to put it aside of your own accord. You know, of course, that anything that comes from France nowadays is not worth much."

So saying, my father cast a look heavy with reproach towards Mother, whose parents, there was no doubt in his mind, were quite capable of giving indecent books to his children. Mother was scarcely strong enough now to reply to this kind of accusation.

My father's francophobia was, in the first instance, simply one of his many phobias. He didn't like the English or Americans any better. There was only one race for whom he felt a trace of respect, the Germans, because they were good at kicking people around. But in general he hated all races and all individuals, with a double dose for the French. He had spent part of his youth with them, when he was starting up on his career as an engineer on Anticosti Island which belonged to the chocolate-maker Menier, and he remained permanently scandalized by these people. It was not so much that they led profligate lives, but they had a kind of freedom in their heads that used to drive him wild. Despite that, though he never suspected it, he had been quite marked by them, in his manner of speech, of swearing (when he was angry he would say *merde* quite easily, which was a rarity at that time), and of eating, especially when he was ready to forget his ambition to live to a hundred. But he would have been peeved at having this pointed out to him.

When the January term began I took my book with me back to the convent, where it was no better received than it had been at home. Mother Saint-Protais, like all idiots I have ever known, frequently used the expression "waste your time reading." In one corner of our classroom there was a library, at least that's what it was called. There were all of a dozen volumes, lined up on one shelf of a piece of furniture which contained mostly inkwells, chalk, and dusters. Only no time had been set aside in the schedule to waste on reading and, in any event, we didn't have permission to touch the books, which had got there the devil only knows how.

I continued to cultivate my sullen delight in catching out Mother Saint-Protais. In this pursuit, I discovered that she didn't know who the Knights Templars were — even though we saw them every year passing discreetly through the history of the Church, under the reign of Clement V. But the sister didn't feel the slightest need to know anything more about them, and that, after all, is the beginning and end of all ignorance. This discovery gave me curious pleasure. I spent half my time checking on her without her knowing it. And if, one fine day, I had been convinced that she knew neither how to read nor write — I pride myself on having discovered so young that this is the depth of abjection — no doubt I would have been delighted.

It should be said in my defence, that I wasn't any too healthy. I was growing very fast, and on a starvation diet. For that matter, we were all in the same boat. You never saw so many pale faces, transparent hands, and calfless legs! It's bad enough to be constantly accused of stuffing oneself like a pig, but the real bind is to be fed like a pig. I know nothing about porcine taste buds, but I remain convinced they are considerably different from human ones, and that the two menus should differ accordingly. Of all the days in the week, none was more dreadful than Friday. All the more so, because, from the point of view of smell, Friday began on Thursday, when the delivery truck came in with the fish. An unholy odour began to creep under every door, even into the chapel where our meditations, thanks to it, were effortlessly guided towards the spirit of mortification. The day-girls, who ate at home, turned up incredulous noses. The next morning, just when we were beginning to get used to it, the smell of the cooking which was being perpetrated in the kitchen reopened the issue, with a heightening of effect you can well imagine. We had no need of exhortations to frugality, and as for Mother Saint-Protais, who got the smell like the rest of us, for once she refrained from her dietary lecturing.

About three o'clock in the afternoon, the whiffs of fish which still slunk around in every corner were subjected to a sudden onslaught from the peas in white sauce. For this other fast-day dish, Sister Cook had her own home recipe: take milk on the verge of turning — there was always some of that around that could be revived this way at the end of the week — a little flour, and peas the size and consistency of common or garden marbles. If it was one of the cook's good days, and she was feeling strong in arm and spirit, the number of lumps wouldn't exceed the number of peas. If, by some unlucky chance, Friday coincided with a despondent period, the peas would be definitely in the minority. This mixture languished and finished souring at the back of the stove until dinner time, when we would make our way into the dining room with dragging feet, holding our handkerchiefs to our noses.

Sometimes we were brought under olfactory attack from the moment we woke up. Those days we knew what was in store for us for breakfast — oatmeal porridge. Here again Sister Cook used one of her own special recipes: she always let it stick to the bottom of the pot. Not once every five times, not every other time, but every time, religiously, without fail. You wouldn't believe the stink.

One of the girls at the convent was being educated by the sisters out of charity. There was no secret about it, for she was reminded of it several times a day, in front of all of us. In exchange for this charity they made her wash the dishes, both the nuns' and the girls'. It took all of her recreation time. Her name was Marie-Paule, she looked like a whipped dog, and suffered, year in, year out, from whitlows, which the greasy water kept open and sore. She was the one who told us the story about the pin.

One day, when she was mashing potatoes, Sister Cook suddenly noticed that a pin was missing from her headdress. There were ninety-nine chances out of a hundred that it was in the mashed potatoes. Throw out the potatoes? Not on your life. Warn the sixty girls who were just about to sit down to eat them? That wouldn't do either. Never admit anything. There was just one solution left. Pray. I don't know if God was addressed personally or whether there exists some saint who looks after such cases, but I do know that the invocations went up at a good rate all during the meal. And it was a good job too, for the pin was never found, either in the mashed potatoes or elsewhere.

Besides Sister Cook and her slave, Marie-Paule, the staff included a man whom we ingenuously called the sisters' Man. He smelled of manure, copiously and continuously. Any day, even on Sunday, you could smell out where he had been. And as the scent most frequently led to the refectory, where one of his jobs was to place the cut bread — mountains of slices, naturally — into a cupboard, it scarcely improved our appetites. It was in a corner between this cupboard and the wall that two of my friends and I saw him fooling around under Sister Cook's bib, and you have to be pretty smart to get in there, while she clucked like a regular floozy, "You old fool, go on, you old fool." That kept us in stitches for the rest of the year. One of us would just have to whisper "You old fool" in the other's ear for both to break out into gales of laughter.

*　　*　　*

In all convents, life gets more and more difficult as the weeks pass. Exasperation builds up day by day. The interdictions multiply, and so do the punishments. Every morning brings its new load of "henceforth it will be forbidden to. . . ." a load that is more or less onerous according to the nuns' imagination, and those who despise this faculty the most are not the least skilful in inventing thou-shalt-nots. There was a girl in our class who aroused our secret admiration. Mine at any rate. She was a day-girl and her name was Simone. She let all the it-will-be-forbidden-to's sail over her head with an abstracted eye, and opposed to all the bawlings-out she got for her ignorance of these, a stony little face, absolutely expressionless, that shed insults like rainwater.

Especially during Lent, day-girls were required to attend mass on week days at the parish church. Unlike the boarders, they could sit where they liked, which didn't prevent the sisters from seeing at a glance who was there, and who wasn't. Simone was never there.

How could she have been? She always arrived last in class, and most times with her dress not all buttoned up yet, the last bite of toast and jam in her hand, looking for all the world as if she had got up less than a quarter of an hour before. That set me dreaming! The family life I imagined for this child was easy, relaxed, utterly fascinating, and totally foreign.

"You're barely out of bed yet," Mother Saint-Protais would say to her. "And what about mass? That's for another day, I suppose."

Simone didn't reply, she never did. She had no excuses to offer, and didn't hunt for any. I thought to myself that she must surely have a father who stood up for her, otherwise she would have been more timorous.

On the first day back after the Christmas holidays, she appeared on the doorstep, ah! with her hair cut like a boy's. On seeing her, I experienced an extraordinary sensation, a sort of rapture, a confused joy, as if I had seen, as it is said in the Bible, my enemies reduced to serve me as a footstool. It must be said here that in this convent there was only one permissible, orthodox way of wearing one's hair: on each side it fell straight down over the ears, while the middle part was all drawn straight back and tied with a black moiré ribbon. Any other way of doing it was considered a criminal offence. We looked horrible, and that was, I think, exactly the desired effect.

At the sight of this shaved neck, Mother Saint-Protais turned green. Never before had a pupil flouted her in this fashion and, for one dreadful moment, it seemed that she might remain tongue-tied. Words came back to her only by degrees, in shrieks. Simone was compared to a plucked hen, and all sorts of skinned animals, each barer than the last. Standing there with her head bent, she seemed to listen to all this in a kind of inner peace which she was certainly the only one to feel in the midst of the general excitement. At last she was ordered to sit down. Afterwards I had to crane my neck, and I must have done it a hundred times that day, to see her. The more I saw it, the prettier I thought her hair looked, and I was bitterly sorry that Simone would have to let it grow in again.

Not a bit of it! Right up till the end of the school year not a fortnight went by that she didn't have it freshly trimmed. Finally, tired of the struggle (it was Simone who told me this), the nun telephoned to her parents who replied that their daughter had her hair cut during the time she was under their jurisdiction. Just like that. I was full of wonder.

*   *   *

With the spring Mother Saint-Protais began to look poorly. More and more often she had to get someone else to take her place at the desk. Then she got really sick. Nothing delights children more, to be frank about it, than to see people they detest fall ill. They are rid of them for the moment and, since primitive instincts are never very far below the surface, in their imagination they consign them to death without a tremor. In this spirit we wondered, curiously, what could be wrong with Mother Saint-Protais, and if it was something she was likely to recover from.

"Mother says, at that age women who haven't had a man yet are always sick," my neighbour confided to me.

"Why's that?"

"Because they go mad, that's why. Gosh, you're stupid!"

For all I knew about men, it seemed to me I would have been madder with them than without. And then, my little friend had laughed in a special way that I recognized at once when she said "who haven't had a man yet." In my perplexity, I had to admit that there were still things I didn't know. Were there then many more chapters to this business? Babies, monthly periods, and now men. What could be so "un-mad-making" about a man? I didn't ask any questions, such things were never learned by asking questions. It wasn't done. The only way to learn the facts of life was to wait until one of the girls slipped you the information — wrong most of the time — information which, to all appearances, she had become incapable of keeping to herself. I didn't have long to wait.

Thanks to Mother Saint-Protais' illness, drawings began to circulate around the classroom. Sometimes we were an hour or two without supervision, and that was the time, if ever, to get on with the thing. The information was revealed to me in a crude fashion. The first drawing I was passed showed a horrible woman, endowed with enormous breasts, who was receiving attentions from a male partner no less well equipped. I turned so red I felt the blood pounding in my ears as though they would burst. My neighbour took fright and snatched back the sheet of paper.

"You're not going to tell?"

God knows I wasn't a tattletale. I would have been closer to the sisters' hearts if I had been. But I came from a family where silence was learned early.

Mother Saint-Protais recovered, and it was almost immediately time for the final exams. We never spoke of them except in most solemn tones. For this occasion, our teacher served only as proctor. Examination questions were not her province; they came to us from another convent on which we were dependent, and our exam copies were also sent there to be corrected. This procedure plunged the little girls into a respectful terror.

"Was that the way it was in your last convent?"

"No, it wasn't like that."

"Then it wasn't such an important convent as they say."

It was in vain that I explained that in my first convent we weren't dependent on anyone, that we were "the Mother House." I didn't succeed in getting my point across. Anyway, I couldn't see what possible interest this trans-shipment of exams had. But the scales were soon to fall from my eyes.

I wasn't expecting much from those exams. All year long I had been almost at the bottom of the class, and I was resigned to go back to my father with a shabby report in my pocket.

"There'll be some surprises for you on prize-day," Mother Saint-Protais told us one of the last days of class. "If I hadn't supervised the exams myself, I'd think that some of you had been cheating."

I listened to these predictions with only half an ear. I was preoccupied enough already with my annual colic. We spent the last days spring cleaning the convent: windows, woodwork, even the floors. The pretext was instruction in domestic science. (The following years, on the same pretext, they made us do everything: we had lessons in washing, ironing and mending, and every week, too. The raw material? The nuns' things. Smart thinking, that's the least you can say.) We went up to get our prizes with hands covered with splinters and cracks, hands of apprentice charwomen just starting their labouring life, when the skin is tender and still won't withstand the least abuse.

When my class's turn came around on that famous prize day, Marie-Louise was first and then, with only a few marks between us, I was second. Marie-Louise had been at the tail-end of the class for the whole year, even more regularly than I had. When we passed each other, she coming back and I on my way up, we exchanged incredulous glances. Back in our seats, we were possessed by mad laughter, which we had a hard time stifling in our handkerchiefs. From that moment on until the end of the ceremony, I didn't hear a word. Complete stupefaction, a strong feeling of having been avenged for everything I had put up with all during the year, the disappearance of the uneasiness I had been nursing as to the parental welcome awaiting me, my amazement at this entry of Justice on the scene when I wasn't expecting it, the mark I had got in French composition, my highest, when I had been skirting zero for the last ten months — all these reactions plunged me into a kind of hypnotic state of contentment. Which explains how impossible it was for me to listen to things that concerned the rest of the students.

After the ceremony, I went to say goodbye to Mother Saint-Protais, who replied with a curl of the lip. She can't have been enjoying herself much, and I don't blame her. I never saw her again. The poor girl with her South-American lake, her dirty Gospels, her singular spellings and her ignorance of the Templars, she gives me a chapter that I rather enjoy, and in return I forgive her all the slaps she gave me. I must say that as far as slaps were concerned, especially when they were handed out one by one, since I wasn't used to such stinginess they didn't amount to much.

* * *

The holidays that followed were to be of inestimable value to me. Summer 1926. But, as always happens, I lived through them without recognizing them for what they were. When we arrived my father was away on a trip, and I took advantage of this to ask Mother to send me for a few days to Grandmother's. Her state of health had prevented any visits for the last few years, but it had now improved. We had hardly seen each other, she and I, for two years, and when I opened her door we fell weeping into one another's arms. We couldn't stop crying. I wept for the emotion of being with her again and for regret at not having seen her for so long, she for quite different reasons. I wasn't only her long-lost granddaughter, but also a little orphan-to-be. I found her thinner and older and sad. Grandfather had grown older too, and if he wasn't sad he still wasn't as gay as he used to be in the old days, which was a great change.

I was twelve. We spent the week talking like grownups. We talked about the future, mine. Grandmother asked if I wanted to get married later on, and told me that, if so, I would have to think it over very carefully before deciding. I replied that I would never marry anyone unless he was like Grandfather, a peaceable, good-humoured man (I kept my word). We understood each other without saying things outright. My father's name was never mentioned a single time, but when we spoke about the kind of husband to shun, we both knew he was the one we meant. I said that if I couldn't find a man like Grandfather, I'd be an old maid, and Grandmother asked me if I had ever thought about becoming a nun. Then, for the first and only time in the whole of my childhood, I spoke to an adult about what went on inside convents — their meanness, injustice, and cruelty — all the reasons that induced me not to become a sister. Then I talked to her about Mother Bon-Conseil, said that she had died, and started to cry again, and Grandmother, who must have been upset at the very mention of this word, started to cry again too. But I liked to cry with Grandmother. You could really let yourself go and sob as long as there were any sobs left. It wasn't at all embarrassing or silly. When the handkerchiefs were soaked, you went and got new ones, sat down again and simply went right on crying. When I cry I can't talk, but Grandmother talked on just the same as if nothing was happening. But never once did she allow herself to share her real grief with me. We often talked about Mother, but always as if the only possible conclusion to her illness was recovery. She would say to me, for example:

"It's been so long since your mother took ill, she must be going to get better soon."

That seemed strictly logical to me, because I wanted to believe it. How moving are those lies inspired by love, and how sweet they remain in memory!

When the time of my visit was up, I was loath to go. If I had only known — if I had only known, well I'd rather have died. I wouldn't have had the courage to face all the unhappiness that lay ahead of me, had it been shown me all at once. The misfortunes came in series, one developing out of the other like a family of monsters. When I had undergone the first of them, I was almost incapable of feeling any more pain. I was nothing more than a bunch of nerveless scars. I say, "I'd rather have died," and "I wouldn't have had the courage," but you don't die when the heart is a strong young muscle, and lack of courage doesn't prevent us from bearing unhappiness.

That summer, Mother made a last effort to regain her health. There was a French doctor; everyone at the time said he was wonderful, and later everyone said he was nothing but a charlatan with false credentials. Whatever he was, Mother decided to go and consult him. My uncle, her brother, came to get her in his car one morning. We had heard such good things of this doctor that we thought she was already cured, just seeing her leave for a consultation. We were seized by a kind of fever. We set about polishing and scrubbing the house, putting flowers in all the vases as if, since everything was bound to change when she came back, short of beginning life over in another house we could at least make this one shine like new.

At last my uncle's car appeared at the turn in the drive. We rushed out, and since my uncle had to get back to work, he left at once and we had Mother all to ourselves. On the verandah there were a table and chairs. Before sitting down, she leaned on a table just long enough to catch her breath. She was wearing, for the last time perhaps, the lovely black suit that Grandmother had made her, a suit with a very long coat, almost a redingote, and it didn't fit very well any more, the top floated loosely around her.

"What did the doctor say, Mother?"

"Well, he said that he was going to make me better."

Ah! We knew it. It would have been impossible to imagine anything else.

"He examined me very carefully. He says that I have a shadow on my left lung, and another on the right, but with the treatment he's going to give me, they'll heal up very soon."

She took several sheets of paper out of her purse which explained at length the marvellous treatment that was going to cure her.

"I'm supposed to drink red wine with my meals. I don't know what your father will say about that — "

As luck would have it, there was some red wine in the basement. My father often received gifts of this kind from road contractors who apparently didn't know him very well — cases of champagne, cases of whisky. He would keep them for a while, then end up giving them to someone less virtuous than himself. The Christmas before, he had been given a case of old claret. And that was exactly what the doctor had written on the prescription, "claret." You would have said it was a sign, a good omen. One of us ran to get a bottle. We felt as bold as brass.

Mother smiled. To what extent was she really confident? I don't know. She had two pretty pink spots on her cheeks.

"You look better already, Mother."

But she was so tired she had to finish the day in bed. She started the treatment the next day. It was an exhausting business — mustard baths, wrappings-up, cupping glasses — I suppose its only real use was to give the patient the impression that she was giving herself intensive care, and to keep her so busy she had no time to think about her illness.

My father greeted the news of this therapy without enthusiasm. Not that he found it too strenuous — didn't his American oracles extol the treatment of tuberculosis by exercise, forced marches, et cetera — but it was his habit to oppose any new treatment. He said he knew better ones, dieting for example, but Mother had never wanted to listen to him, otherwise she would have been cured long ago. The doctor had prescribed a menu to build Mother up. Every day we would have to ask my father to buy this, or that, and he never missed the chance to start off again on his diatribes about dieting. Then, when the stock of claret ran out, he refused to replenish it. Mother drinking wine at table was a bad example for the children. He's afraid Mother will get better, I thought to myself. He wants her to die. And you'd have had a hard time convincing me I was wrong. At last Grandmother brought some claret, and I could go back to the convent reassured. As soon as we had left, Mother was obliged to go back to bed and give up the tiring treatment. I never knew it, and was still full of confidence. Besides, I didn't know what it was to be sick unto death. I wanted her to get better, but it never occurred to me to think that she would die if she didn't get better. It had all lasted so long that I never imagined the outcome might be fatal. I thought that at the worst she would go on being sick, that she would live on as an invalid. There was, of course, that conversation between her and Grandmother that I had overheard so many years ago, as it seemed to me — so many years ago that it had lost all importance, it had already been remedied. And the accusation I mentioned above — the one that in the depths of my heart I held against my father — it wasn't connected to reality in any way. I wished he'd die, didn't I, and that didn't seem to affect his health very much.

* * *

So back I went to the convent with my brand new puberty a proud secret. The first thing I learned was that Mother Saint-Protais had gone, and had been replaced by a fat sister with a turned-up nose and a red face, the butcher-boy type, whose name was Mother Saint-Jules. Mother Saint-Pamphile had gone too. In her place we found a long sister who oozed bile from every pore of her yellow skin, Mother Saint-Fortunat. I immediately began to think about the pleasant year I had spent after I escaped from the clutches of Mother Saint-Chérubin, and that seemed an auspicious omen. After the rain comes the sunshine, so people say, so it must be true. Mother Saint-Fortunat might be yellow, but she had beautiful eyes, black as jet. With eyes like that she must be nice. For that matter, Mother Saint-Jules seemed to be a nice fat old thing who wouldn't hurt a fly. That was a common saying too. It's true, of course, that fat Nero used to pull the wings off flies.

Mother Saint-Fortunat taught the biggest girls, and on that account was also first mistress of the first division. On the second day she preached us a long sermon on all the things that would be forbidden under her reign: writing letters without showing them to her; wearing skirts that revealed so much as the lower part of the calf — she managed not to use the word "calf" of course, she said "the hem must be so many inches from the ground"; receiving visits in the parlour from people who weren't close relatives and, above all, it was strictly forbidden to curl our hair. Several girls had come back from the holidays with waves. That was to be all washed out and never mentioned again. Mother Saint-Fortunat's beautiful eyes seemed to lose a little of their velvet quality.

The next day, as we stood waiting to go into the refectory, a nervous hand pulled me out of the ranks.

"So! That's the way you begin the year, is it, by disobeying the rules?"

As she said this, she pushed my head from side to side with angry little pokes of a perforating index finger, first on the right temple, then on the left.

I was born with a good conscience. When someone accuses me of a crime and doesn't say what it is right away, I don't understand, I try to think and I stand there round-eyed, and round-mouthed too. Besides, I had already forgotten all yesterday's recommendations because they didn't apply to me. One look at my mop was enough to see that no hairdresser had ever touched it.

"You haven't uncurled your hair yet?"

"It's natural, Mother."

"What do you mean, natural?"

"Well — natural — "

"Do you expect me to believe that you don't curl your hair?"

"No, I don't. I was born with it just like that."

"Go into the refectory. I'll look into it."

How, she didn't say. But after all, that was something she'd have to work out between herself and my Maker, and I didn't have to worry about that. It was the same old story: the nun believed in God, but in a God who was not too sharp, clumsy with his hands, and, to say the least, grossly ignorant about the rules of the convent.

When I go to sleep, I pull the sheets up over my head. That evening, just as I was about to doze quietly off, the probing forefinger of Mother Saint-Fortunat brought me to with a start.

"Aha! I've caught you. Uncover. Show me your head."

I pulled the sheets down, and she ran a fumbling hand through my hair without, of course, finding a single curl paper.

"Don't think you'll get off so easily. I've got my eye on you."

She was as good as her word. For several nights in a row, my sleep was interrupted by a long dry hand that came foraging around in my mane at diabolically various times. I was beginning to get pretty fed up with Mother Saint-Fortunat, who despite her religious vocation, was afflicted with a fragile little heart of a rare inflammability and hence of a rare inconstancy, a heart that would have created a fantastic number of cuckolds had it been turned loose on the world, when she became madly stuck on my sister. By a lucky ricochet, I received full and unquestioned authority to have naturally curly hair.

However, at Mother Saint-Fortunat's instigation, and all the time her suspicions lasted, the nuns had talked about the thing so much that it had become an institutional problem. Their little consciences were quivering. There were already repercussions. Each time I passed through "the community corridor" someone there would say after me, rudely, "What a head of hair!" Was it a spell? A curse? Who knows?

One morning, on the stroke of five, I was wakened up by a nun whose name I forget, though she was pretty yellow too. She had brought with her a basin of hot water and a rung out of an old chair. The functions that this sister filled were not very clearly defined. All I knew about her was that she lived in Mother Saint-George's old room — another one who never did much of anything, it came with the room I suppose. Anyway, at this particular moment, there she was holding this chair rung. She had got up at the crack of dawn and had climbed six flights of stairs just to trick me out in what we called *boudins*. French children call these curls just plain *saucisses*, but since we are such close cousins they are still sausages.

"At least it will make your head smaller," said Mother Saint-George's heir.

Thereupon she set about soaking my head, dividing my hair into strands, and rolling each one around the chair rung with the help of my hair brush, which was soaking wet too. She worked like the devil at it. The hardest part was to pull the chair rung out without disturbing a single hair, for when that happened, she had to begin the whole operation all over again. My bed and nightgown were soon wringing wet like my hair and, since it had never occurred to anyone to heat the convent dormitories, my teeth were chattering madly.

"Just stay there, sitting up in bed, till the bell goes," she told me on leaving when the deed was done.

And in her mind it was a good deed, too, beyond the shadow of a doubt. There was about half an hour left. I spent it sitting up, drying out, while other heads around me, capped with regulation hair, exhaled the noisy sounds of sleep. But not for long. I was

suddenly seized by an uncontrollable fit of sneezing which drew
unkind observations from every corner of the dormitory. All day I
was the laughing stock of the whole school with my "sausages,"
some of which, badly deformed, stood straight out, away out of
line with the rest.

The next day it began all over again.

"If you're a good girl, I'll come and do your hair every morning,"
the sister whispered with an angelic smile.

The poor imprudent thing! She sometimes used to supervise us
in the refectory, and I wished with all my heart that this would be
one of those days. It was, she came, and naturally I couldn't think of
enough ways to make myself disagreeable. At my first outburst she
gave me a pained look that filled me with remorse. But it wasn't a
question of listening to my heart. I would have to obey my head
only, otherwise it would be flooded out every morning of the year
and, Good Lord! with winter coming on I was beginning to dread
an endless succession of colds, bronchitis, ear infections and chills
of all sorts.

"I won't be coming to comb your hair tomorrow," Sister Saint-
Figaro[8] said to me as I came out of the refectory.

The next day was Homeric. As soon as I put the comb into hair
that had been tightly rolled into sausages for two days, it began to
take on outrageous proportions. It sprang out every which way in
an inextricable confusion. In height, breadth and thickness of mane,
Absalom didn't hold a candle to me. He was another one who didn't
fit the rules. I didn't lose my life, but the whole convent lost its
straight face. Besides, circumstances seemed to conspire to give a
heightened lustre to my Absalomism. That morning we had mass in
the chapel, as we did from time to time. For all ceremonies held in
chapel it was customary, instead of wearing hats as we did when we
went to the parish church, to cover our heads with a white tulle veil.
Mine was new, the tulle was stiff. Long before the fashion designers

dreamt of creating styles designated by the letters of the alphabet, that day I launched the O-line. Or, if you will, I looked like some rare specimen of a strange nomadic species which, as the tortoise carries its house on its back, carried its igloo on its head. I had to wait until my wedding day before I would again play such a starring role in a church. All during mass there were three or four girls in the front row looking back over their shoulders. And giggling. And looking slyly over towards Sister Saint-Figaro who had turned quite red under her yellow skin, which gave her a lovely brick-red hue.

Funny things happen! Here was a child who had been punished, and the result of the punishment was that she found herself even more in opposition to the rules than ever.

"It wouldn't be hard to believe it's the Devil himself who curls your hair," the Mother Superior said to me as I came out of chapel.

Mother Saint-Fortunat was laughing. When her heart was captive, her indulgence knew no bounds. She didn't know how to resist her crushes. She was the Ninon de Lenclos of the institution.[9] That particular morning she had the air of one who couldn't bridle her gaiety. She fluttered coquettish glances at my sister, she twitched her nose in a delicate gesture, which was her way of showing the height of amusement. It was a nose which, in the realm of noses, had no call to play second fiddle to my hair. To each his own specialty. Whenever she felt an excess of sprightliness, there was much twitching. That happened often now, for everything her treasure did (or her treasure's sister, it was the same thing) made her light-hearted — even the most flagrant mischief. Sometimes another little girl tried the same tricks, but Ninon's shouts quickly brought her back to reality. One man's peck is another man's bushel.

And sometimes the peck could be remarkably small. As Mother Saint-Fortunat loved, so she hated. To counterbalance a favourite, there was always a scapegoat to persecute at the other end. I experienced both extremes. While the former role was quite various, the latter simply consisted of taking upon one's back all the misdeeds committed in the school. An opinion scrawled in a very childish hand on the toilet wall which read: *Mother Saint-Fortunat is crasy*, was attributed to me without a moment's hesitation. To think they could believe me capable of writing crazy with an "s" made me almost beside myself with rage. Yet I couldn't claim the chief martyr's crown myself. That went to a little girl whose name I've forgotten, a sickly little blonde, shy and a bit backward. Her parents were not rich, and this was a vice that Mother Saint-Fortunat never forgave. If the little blonde so much as moved an eyelash, an avalanche of abuse was released on her.

"You're just one of the poor. Your parents are poor. You are only kept here out of charity. At home you'd go hungry."

The little girl had the faculty of secreting enormous tears which plopped out of her eyes. This phenomenon always surprised me greatly, even though I could observe it nearly every day. I don't know how the others felt. Personally, I despised myself so much for not having the courage to get up, put my arm around the girl's shoulders and console her, that sometimes I couldn't sleep at night. Even now, to remember that young face, flushed with shame, brings a lump to my throat. To impose such degrading complicity on a child is surely an unforgivable sin!

But where Mother Saint-Fortunat really shone, and it was marvellous to observe her, was when she fell into the toils of infidelity. Suddenly her attention would be drawn to a new object, though no one, not even herself, could unravel the how or the why of it. It just happened, like that. For several days she would let herself float between the old object and the new, cherishing, I think, the illusion that she could choose between them. None of us had enough experience in the province of the heart to understand these sentimental fluctuations, and the old object never suspected that she was under threat of being replaced. But that was inevitable; the new object always won. Never once to my knowledge — and God knows it would have been difficult to remain ignorant of those devouring passions — never once was the dear woman able to remain faithful to her old flame. Never once was she able to choose. The lure of novelty fascinated her to the point of stripping her entirely of free will. And away she'd go! It always wound up the same way. One day, worn out by the old ties, she would violently shake them off at the first pretext. A slap, a zero for misbehaviour, a recess spent in penance in the corner, and the poor abandoned child would suddenly realize that she had ceased to please, and that from now on Mother Saint-Fortunat would be twitching her nose for someone else.

*　*　*

Don't misunderstand me. All this was purely platonic. Besides, if the little girls entered into the game, it was much more out of self-interest than from any reciprocity of feeling. For all I know, convent love affairs are always platonic. Most girls are too dormant sensually for it to be otherwise. If their senses are not completely asleep, they keep it to themselves. In the first place, they wouldn't trust a partner, for girls of that age are terrible informers, and secondly, on the whole it's usually the heart that's involved in such cases. When they do come alive a little, about the age of fifteen, then it's boys of their own age they begin to turn to, with a few exceptions.

The exceptions — I once happened to surprise a couple locked in one another's arms. I had been sent to take a book to one of the sister's rooms and hadn't even knocked, because it was class time and I thought the sister was at her desk. But she must have taken some time off, for there she was with a little girl, naked to the waist, holding her in her arms, and caressing her back.

Although I drew back hurriedly, mumbling out a frightened

"Excuse me," I wasn't quick enough to disappear unidentified. I found that out next day when the marks were read out. The nun began to carry on at some length about slander. We listened drowsily until we were brought to by a shout directed at me.

"Get up."

A little lost, for I couldn't see how I was mixed up in this, I got to my feet. Here it was my turn again. Oh well!

"Children," she said, with horror in her voice, but determination too, "you see before you the greatest slanderer you could ever hope to find."

I hadn't breathed a word to a soul about what I had seen, so my schoolmates stared at me agog, as though I was some kind of sideshow freak, the tallest man in the world, or the bearded lady. For some time past, I hadn't said anything unusual, nothing that could be called questionable. Sister — though I hesitate to accept the implied relationship — stood there with bent head and clasped hands. If only I could manage to catch her eye. But she went on, interminably.

"I warn you, children, everything this pupil says is prompted by the Devil. Lying comes to her as naturally as breathing. Even the most filthy falsehoods are not beyond her. She has the most debased soul I have ever had the occasion to know."

At last, however, she raised her eyes. This was the moment I was waiting for. I shot her the purest look I could muster, and added a sad half-smile, in the style of Saint Agnes, virgin martyr.

"Sit down," she burst out, losing face completely.

Once I was seated again, I turned around to see how the sister's accomplice, a soft little pink-and-gold thing, was taking all this. She seemed to find it quite to her liking. She returned my ironic stare with another of the same kind. Evidently, she was ready to pay the price required for pleasure received, which is a happy frame of mind to be in.

After the marks were read out, several girls came over to ask me what it was all about. They had never noticed such satanic tendencies in me and they smelled a rat. I didn't have time to decide whether I'd talk or whether I wouldn't, if I'd reveal all, or nothing. The Sister rushed over, seized me, and led me off to the farthest corner of the room where, she said, I would spend all my recesses until further notice. That meant until my classmates' curiosity had died down. She didn't say as much, she didn't have to. It wasn't necessary, because we both knew what it meant. So once again, my debased soul and I spent a couple of weeks in the corner without thinking too much about it. The sister, who seemed to have more trouble coming to terms with hers, became very high-strung after that. She yelled at the least pretext, like one of the damned.

*   *   *

If the favouritism my sister basked in acted as a shield for some things, for others it wasn't worth a fig. The second mistress of the division didn't set much stock in these kinds of sentimental goings-on. To show her disapproval, she took a strong dislike to all of Mother Saint-Fortunat's sweethearts, one after another. She wasn't the nice fat old thing I had thought. She was a fat old thing. She had a heavy hand, and it didn't take us long to find it out. She was rather like my father in that she had a hard time resisting the temptation of her own strength. Her punch to the head — she had us kneel down before she beat us — made you see quite a complete collection of stars. But she was a good teacher. Only we weren't at an age when the latter could excuse the former. I think she was really bored to death with her vocation, a choice that perhaps her ugliness and obesity had pushed her into. From time to time, I would have a talk with her on one of her good days, which were rare, and I must admit she had a fine sense of humour. With that impassive face that always makes witticisms irresistible, she struck off some wonderfully well-chosen remarks.

Born before their time, into a society where women either married or simply didn't exist, in those days countless plain girls took the path to the convent, where they became bogged down in the dreariest stupidity, and where their talents, often very real ones, were never used except for developing good technique in slapping or punching. We were totally ignorant of the fact that such violence was a release of frustrated sexuality. The sexuality of the nuns — that would really have made us laugh.

Sexuality or no, this particular nun, having acquired a certain velocity, began to give in more and more to her fits of violence. It was even said that once in an argument she had slapped another nun, although I wasn't there, and in the convent this kind of rumour was current coin. But I was there the morning of the last dramatic act. It was one of those days dogged by pure bad luck that come into everyone's life. One of those days when your horoscope says, Don't do anything, Don't start anything, Stay very quiet, the stars are against you. Singularly innocent of astrological science, the fat sister stepped straight into the snares of destiny.

She had got up that morning, as they used to say in my youth, "the big end first," and right off began to nag, now one, now another. Not ten minutes after we had all offered our day to God, and the sister with us, the blows began to rain down. Then her anger crystallized around one of the little Leblonds, whom she began to chase, fists in the air, the little girl scampering away in front of her. At the end of the dormitory there would have to be a stop. But beyond the end wall, a staircase opened tempting jaws. The fat sister couldn't resist. She threw the little Leblond down it. On the way down, with magnificent presence of mind, the little girl started shouting out choice abuse. It was all incredibly dramatic, and we were positively delighted to hear the sister called "fat cow," so much so that we scarcely gave a thought to our little friend, whose fall was making horrible noises as a background to the shouting.

"What's going on here?" thundered a voice from the depths.

At the end of her headlong descent, the child had fallen into the arms of the Mother Superior, and it was the heavy asthmatic voice of authority that we were hearing, without being really able to believe it, it was such an unexpected godsend. Never in boarders' memory had the Superior been seen in that particular stairway at that particular time. Pure bad luck. Sister Saint-Jules had turned a beefy, apoplectic red. As for the little Leblond, she was painfully climbing up the stairs, supported by the Mother Superior.

"You will come to my office after mass," she said to Sister Saint-Jules.

Though it's unfair, that kind of thing always takes place behind closed doors. After this confrontation, none of us ever saw Mother Saint-Jules again. They only spoke of her once to tell us she was tired. There was good reason. They told us the same thing again when they had to replace her replacement, the next year at about the same time.

* * *

Now it was my little sister Marguerite's turn to make her first communion. It was decided that this would take place at Christmas, and at the beginning of December she came to join us at the convent. Though the margins of her heart were beginning to get quite congested, Mother Saint-Fortunat welcomed this second sister of the object of her affections with open arms. She was so delighted that the very evening of Margot's arrival she organized an entertainment conceived for the sole purpose of starring the whole family, and of showing that she knew how to pick her pets. I sang, I recited fables and, when I ran out, some little girls were called on to fill in with childish babble. During this time, Françoise and Marguerite, hidden behind the piano, were being organized and costumed for what was to be the hit of the evening, something the nuns called "a living picture." Marguerite was supposed to be Sainte Thérèse of Lisieux as a child, and Françoise was her mother. They had made the little saint put on long white stockings which didn't go at all well with her black uniform, but the idea behind it was, I suppose, that that was the best place to wear the symbol of purity — when the legs resist, everything holds. Only they hadn't attached the stockings, believing that they would stay up by themselves. Ah! Those symbols! Always such a letdown! And this one began to slip as soon as Margot stepped out onto the stage. Now, since she was well brought up, Margot was indoctrinated with the necessity of keeping one's stockings taut. So, while with her right hand she presented a bouquet of paper roses destined to shed a shower of petals on the ground, she thought that the only proper thing to do was to grasp the tops of her two stockings in her free hand and by a brisk twisting motion to try to get them to stay in place, seeking meanwhile, with all of her terrified little body that was left unoccupied, to hide her confusion behind Françoise's skirts.

The essential of a living picture is that it is supposed to last as long as the audience, and the picture, can stand it. Nobody dared laugh, because all the girls knew from experience that you didn't laugh at the sister of the chief pet. So there they sat, watching Marguerite struggle with her symbols, and the whole thing lasted just as long as Mother Saint-Fortunat felt like watching her little ducks.

Marguerite made her first communion at midnight mass on Christmas Eve. She did this in a white tulle veil torn into tatters, thanks to the ingenuity of Sister Saint-Arsène, who was in charge of the little ones. This nun, who had become dissatisfied with the way the veil was gathered, undertook to rip out the ribbon, and fixed it up according to some idea of her own. Her initiative resulted in four or five long gashes, as though the sister had been stricken with St. Vitus Dance, scissors in hand. Just before the ceremony, Françoise and I went up to the little girls' dormitory to see that our sister was properly dressed.

"Have you seen my veil?" Margot asked, pointing with disgust. "Honestly, have you seen my veil?"

And all during mass you could see her reaching up to take a triangle of tulle net that was floating loose, and pushing it towards the middle of her head; then another, then the first one, which had fallen down again. In short, there was another first communion spoiled. It became a tradition in the family. It was almost like a collective plot on the part of the nuns to plunge our whole family line into eternal damnation.

*   *   *

The next day we left the convent for the Christmas holidays. Mother was confined to bed and only got up for a few minutes in the afternoon on New Year's Day. My half-brother, Gérard, who was gravely ill himself, had come to visit us with his wife, Yvonne, and it was to welcome them that Mother came down.

That's all I remember, that one hour. The rest of the time we spent trying to be as calm and quiet as possible. By we, I mean we children. When Jupiter came back at night it was always the same old thunder.

But there's one thing I remember — and it's the word thunder that makes me think of it. That was the year my father bought his first radio set. As soon as dinner was over, he would sit down in front of the knobs, turn the volume up as high as it would go, and start to twiddle the others, as though he expected a message on which the future of the world depended without knowing the wave length on which it would be broadcast. He never wanted to listen to a programme, he just wanted to know what was going on, here, there and everywhere. A band, that's good. A political speech, fine. Opera, splendid. Symphony orchestra. Static, well now! It must, alas, have been a very good piece of equipment for those days, because we could get every station on the continent, and perhaps some others. (I say "we" figuratively because neither Mother nor we children were ever allowed to touch the set; it was turned on by a key which my father always kept in his pocket.) About eight-thirty at night, the children went up to their rooms to settle down for a sleepless night, for already those benighted Americans had invented broadcasting that ran until four in the morning. We tossed and turned in our freezing beds. Behind the wailing of the soprano and the hysterical shouting of the prohibitionist, we could hear Mother coughing, coughing. Then, after he had been unable to get anything but static for half an hour, my father would decide to take his big inconsiderate feet up to bed. He slammed the door. He threw his shoes on the floor. We might have been able to get to sleep then, if anger hadn't kept us awake till dawn. Utterly futile anger — one of the rights my father had acquired at birth was to make an enormous din whenever someone else was resting.

✳ ✳ ✳

We had been back at the convent for a fortnight, when Françoise was summoned to my father's house the same way Dine had been. She left in such a rush she didn't come to say goodbye to me, and didn't take any of her things with her. At recess Mother Saint-Fortunat came to tell me the news with red eyes and a crestfallen expression.

"Your Mother has gone to rest at your Grandmother's," she said, "and Françoise has gone home, so your eldest sister won't be alone."

What had happened was this. Feeling that she only had a few more days to live, Mother had decided to go and live them in peace. She had been strongly seconded in this decision by my sister Dine who, at eighteen, was mature enough to realize that every human being has the right to quit this life in serenity of spirit. (But it wasn't until the year after, when my brother Gérard came back to die in his father's house, that Dine realized what ultimate danger Mother had escaped.) So that morning Mother had telephoned to Grandmother, and had told her what she wanted to do. Then she had telephoned my father. I never knew the nature of his reply, whether he agreed or not. All I know is that my uncle came to get Mother late that morning. They dressed her and wrapped her up in blankets, and she left that accursed house forever. If it is true that after death one comes back to haunt the places where one has been unhappy, that house stands to be visited by more ghosts than any Scottish castle.

Despite all the commotion, it never occurred to me that Mother was going to die. Is it normal that a girl almost thirteen should be so little aware of what's going on, especially when it's a question of her own mother's sickness and approaching death? Nothing happened to stir my suspicions. For example, a little before Christmas, one of Françoise's friends had asked her, in my presence:

"How is *madame ta mère?*"

The phrase, which wasn't often used by children, made me want to laugh.

"What's wrong with her?" Rolande went on.

"Tuberculosis," replied Françoise.

All of a sudden the laugh died in me.

"You're crazy," I exclaimed.

But the study bell rang and smothered my cry. My sister was the only one who heard it. She looked at me in a funny way and went off to get into line. I remember my dismay very well, but I don't know what became of it. I think that I didn't want to know any more about such a thing and that, with the marvellous ease children have for doing this, I simply shuttered myself in ignorance. At any rate, after having seen the state she was in during the holidays, and though I had been very upset by it, when I heard that Mother had "gone to rest at Grandmother's" I took this to be nothing more than a reason for reassurance and rejoicing. All this time, apparently, everyone else around me knew perfectly well what was happening.

"Doesn't your father take you to see your mother?" Hélène asked me one day in February.

I turned very red. Though I had thought about it often enough, I hadn't dared ask my father. I knew he wouldn't ever understand such a request. Basically, I wasn't supposed to love Mother any more than he did. But if I had known she was dying, I would have found the courage. Hélène had a sick father whom she went to see every week. I didn't like to share confidences about my father with my school friends, for I knew from experience the cruelty that is triggered in children by the unhappiness of another child, but it seemed to me this girl was likely to understand.

"If you would, you might speak to the Mother Superior about it. I prefer that to asking my father."

Now it was Hélène's turn to blush, and her eyes began to fill with tears, and seeing them I started to cry too. Next Thursday morning, the Mother Superior called me in to tell me that she had been in touch with my father, and that he had given permission for Françoise to come and get me and take me to Mother.

All I remember is a feeling of great embarrassment, the kind that children experience when they have to stay at the bedside of a sick person who can hardly speak. There I was, sitting on Mother's left, not knowing what to say, feeling that I was taking up vital space, breathing the air she needed, tiring her out. I remember saying something that made her laugh, which started her coughing. Grandmother made a little sign, Françoise and I got up and went out. The visit had only lasted half an hour, and the proof that I still hadn't understood the gravity of the situation is that I remember so little about it. If I had known, when I was living it, that it was to be the last, it seems to me that I would be able to describe it second by second.

*   *   *

I had all the rest of the afternoon off. What were we going to do now? We decided to go and see Aunt Berthe, the wife of Mother's brother, a thing we were almost never allowed to do, and also that we would use this occasion to announce to her that for some time now we had been smoking cigarettes. At first sight, this mission might seem to betray a certain callousness of heart. But I think that Françoise was as full of illusions about the state of Mother's health as I was. I can remember her talking to me about her getting better and coming back to us.

My sisters and I had begun to smoke during the Christmas holidays. In secret, of course, for if my father had caught us he would have sent us to the girls' reformatory. Essentially, it wasn't the smoking that was so important. It was the beginning of our liberation. The first step. Dine and Françoise had begun without me and then had admitted me to the clan the day I discovered them, cigarette in hand.

"Promise not to tell?"

"Never!"

On the strength of that oath, they had given me a cigarette, which made me good and sick. After this new experience, all three of us had the distinct impression that we were in the process of throwing off our father's tyranny in a most effective way. The first step. We saw ourselves, as one thing led to another, free of our cage, married to real swells who would like to travel, who would take us dancing and to the theatre, and would let us wear décolleté evening gowns. We talked about it hours on end, and dreamed of letting Uncle Eugène and Aunt Berthe in on the secret of our evolution. They were young, they were fashionable, and we were sure we would get their full support. When my sisters came to see me on visiting days, we held passionate palavers about those silly cigarettes, and how urgent it was to let our uncle and aunt know we weren't bumpkins any longer. But since we scarcely ever saw them, that was difficult. So when Françoise and I found ourselves outside, it immediately seemed that the time was ripe for action.

In the streetcar we kept repeating to each other:

"I only hope she's there!"

"Won't she be surprised!"

"And how! She thinks we're still convent prigs."

We knocked at her door with fluttering hearts.

After half a second we were ready to give up.

"Let's wait a little longer."

At last the door opened. Aunt Berthe showed us in, but wasn't able to hide that she was a little put out. That didn't bother us a bit, the revelation we had to make was the very thing to dispel her embarrassment. She seated us in her little boudoir, which I remember as being very, very 1925, in what was called flapper style: dark as the devil's den, hung with navy blue wallpaper brightened a little by a sparse orange design, choked with cushions without a traditional colour among them and strewn with odd bric-a-brac. Tiny Aunt Berthe, with her chemise dress and her black hair plastered down on her small head, reigned supreme in the middle of this decor.

"I'm going to make you a cup of tea," she said suddenly.

Françoise saw the time had come to stop beating about the bush.

"Perhaps we could smoke a cigarette first."

Aunt Berthe almost choked.

"You smoke?"

And, as if the one thing never went without the other:

"In that case, instead of tea we'll have a glass of port."

During this exchange Françoise was struggling to get out her cigarettes, which she kept well hidden in the top of her stocking. Aunt Berthe protested and went off to get some of her own.

"Won't Uncle be surprised when he hears about this, eh Auntie? He'll never get over it."

I would have liked her to telephone him that very minute, to tell him the extraordinary things that were going on under his roof. But my aunt's surprise didn't go quite that far.

Soon it was time to go. We parted and went our respective ways, one back to the house, the other back to the convent. My whole destiny seemed altered. I had the feeling I had won a victory over my father that would be followed by many others.

In telling about these things, I realize what a sharp memory I have of some things, and a what a blank there is for others. I don't feel guilty. I know that this came, not from my heart, but from circumstances.

My father came to the parlour the next Sunday.

"Did you know it was the Superior who telephoned me to suggest that you should go to see your mother?" he asked immediately. "What's going on here? Was it you who asked her to telephone?"

"No. It was a little girl whose father is sick. She goes to see him every week and — "

"You tell her to mind her own business," my father interrupted. "When I want you to see your mother, I'll decide that myself."

And so I never saw Mother alive again.

*   *   *

It happened on the thirteenth of March, 1927. The murmur that memory makes around this first irreparable loss will never be stilled. After breakfast, I was called to the Mother Superior's office. Mother Saint-Fortunat was there too. They made me sit down between them.

"Is it long since you last saw your mother?" asked the Superior.

I thought she wanted to send me back to see her again and I didn't know what to say. I would rather have died than repeat my father's orders, or admit what kind of a father I had.

"A month," I stammered.

They both seemed very sad, and very understanding, but, hypnotized by the fear that I would have to confess my father's interdiction, I didn't notice anything else.

"Now you must be very brave," said Mother Saint-Fortunat.

"Yes — your Mother died this morning."

Then, oh, I don't know. First that feeling of disbelief that helps you get over the first few seconds, then the sobs and tears and all the intemperate excesses of innocent despair, and then, but vaguer still, the sensation of the white starched cloth of the nun's wimple under my head, of something hot and spicy to drink, of the sweat that wet my hair.

Though I had been to low mass already, my father had decided that I should go to high mass, too. The Mother Superior, a big adorable woman, wonderfully human and just, seemed to think that it was too much to ask. But since my father had ordered it, both nuns pretended to believe that such an exercise of piety was just the thing, and that a child who has just lost her mother couldn't do better than go to church and pray.

"After mass I'll send you home in a cab," said the Superior. "Your father asks you to bring the black hat that Françoise left behind."

I wasn't very good at praying, and what had just happened wasn't calculated to improve me. I spent the whole of the high mass cursing fate, cursing my father, and wishing I could die. When I came out of church, I saw the cabbie waiting for me with his sleigh at the convent gate. I went and got my sister's hat, said goodbye to Mother Saint-Fortunat, and left. When we came near our farmer's house, Pit ran out on the road and shouted that everybody had gone to town, and that I was supposed to go to my paternal grandmother's. I didn't know what was going on. No one had told me that Mother was to be laid out at her parents' home, no one had told me what time the rest of the family were going to leave for town. Besides that, I didn't know the part of the city where my paternal grandparents lived now, and didn't know how to get there. Grumbling and cursing, the driver turned the sleigh around, and took me back to the little station where there would be a train to take me to Quebec, God only knew when. I didn't have enough money to pay for the sleigh, and I had a terrible time making the driver understand that he could go and get paid at the convent. And then I waited. It was cold. I waited almost an hour. Finally I reached town and, after having asked my way I don't know how many times and thinking I was lost a dozen times more, I rang the bell at my paternal grandmother's house. My aunt opened the door. Behind her loomed my father.

"Well, can you tell me what you've been up to? Do you think I've got nothing better to do than wait for you? Did you bring your sister's hat?"

Yes, I had the hat. I handed it to Françoise and almost burst out laughing to see how she was got up. And Dine looked the same. It was my aunt who, during the past week, had taken charge of getting my sisters' mourning clothes ready. She shared my father's hatred of garments that gave the least hint of the body underneath. So she had bought dresses twice as large as necessary. Not only was it impossible to make out the breasts — which were the first things to hide — you couldn't even distinguish the shoulders. The girls looked like a couple of scrawny waifs wearing hand-me-downs from some portly matron.

"All right, let's go," said my father.

"Claire hasn't eaten yet," said Dine timidly.

"She'll eat tonight."

Aunt Maria slipped me an apple, and off we went, all eight of us, my father in front, and the seven children behind. We headed for the streetcar. My father had harsh words with the conductor. Children six and under rode free, and he tried to pass us all off as about six years old. In fact, even the youngest, Thérèse, hadn't qualified for free rides since January. I was disgusted. He came and sat beside me and made me tell him what I had done since he had telephoned. When he heard about the cab he flew into a rage.

"Do you realize that I'm going to have to pay that cab for nothing? And, of course, I'd be surprised to hear you were bright enough to think about using the chance to bring home the things Françoise left behind at the convent."

True enough, I hadn't been that farsighted. He knew it perfectly well. His pretending to think I might have made better use of the trip was a way of denying me the right to grief, a way of implying that nothing that had happened really warranted losing sight of life's little daily problems. He spoke very loud. Everyone looked around at this family in mourning. Everyone heard the story of the cab that could have been better used. When you've lived through something like that, you know it's not possible to die of shame.

At last we arrived at Grandmother's. Under my father's watchful eye, she kissed each of us in turn. Seven little puppets, frozen stiff by the fear of showing some weakness they would be called upon to account for later on. Throughout the two days that Mother lay there, he never took his eyes off us for an instant, and his face was heavy with barely suppressed anger, ready to break out the minute one of us dared to show his sorrow. It was a terrible spectacle to see those seven children seated around their mother's coffin, dry-eyed.

The coffin was set at one end of the living room. Under the glass, her face wasn't peaceful. It was the very image of distress, with knotted eyebrows, and a drawn mouth. Long afterwards, I learned that she had spent her last days tormenting herself about what would become of us all, but especially me.

"She's the one who loves her father least," she kept repeating.

Loves least was hardly the right way to put it, but on one's deathbed, questions of terminology —

At last my father left for the presbytery at Beauport where he had arranged for the funeral service, and that gave us an hour's grace during which we could give way to grief as if it were a normal emotion. Then he came back.

"I've ordered a second-class funeral," he announced in his trumpeting voice.

As he spoke, he looked at Grandmother with an arrogant smile. Then he thought to add:

"That should be good enough."

"Why, certainly," Grandmother murmured.

Later, since the dining room was full of visitors — an overflow from the living room — she gave us something to eat, two or three at a time, at the little table in the kitchen. I was ravenous. I couldn't help it, I just was.

I watched my sisters, who seemed to have a hard time nibbling a mouthful or two, and wished I wasn't any hungrier than they were. But it was a day of shame, and I would have to play my part to the full.

About eight o'clock, my father decided that was enough. He took us back to our house, and after prayers we went straight to bed. At that time everyone slept on the first floor except me. I had one of the little rooms that my father had originally put in for the servants. In the winter, when I was at the convent, a large trap door placed at the top of the staircase closed this floor off from the rest of the house, in order to save heat. So it was almost as cold up there as it was outside. Because of this, Dine wanted to share her bed with me. My father, who was behindhand in his anger that day, because he had been in someone else's house where it's always more difficult to fly into a rage, now seized this opportunity to explode.

"What's all this about? Why exactly do you want to sleep in the same bed? Haven't you got any decent instincts?"

Filled with disgust once again, I climbed up to my icebox. I have never had, and know that in my whole life I never will have, a night like that with suffering and despair outdoing one another. If it had only been the cold, I might have slept and forgotten, but I didn't sleep for a second. There was only one compensation: since I was alone on that floor, I could weep in peace. "In peace," is a curious expression to use in the circumstances. For as long as I could remember, I hadn't ever had much peace, but I realized that night that I wouldn't have any at all for a long time to come. Mixed up with my feelings of love and grief, was the very well-founded feeling of dread that the future inspired in me. And all that scorn and hatred, and that cruel cold which never relaxed its grip. It seemed impossible to me that my father should long escape some kind of retributive misfortune, which would deliver us from him. But how long would it be? How many months or years? Though the night had been filled with distress, it was nothing to the terror I felt when I saw that dawn had come. Where would I find the strength to live through the day to come?

We spent the morning at our house, and didn't return to Grandmother's until after lunch. Everything happened the same as the day before. Instinctively on our guard against showing either sorrow or tenderness to our grandparents, we slunk around like seven scared little wild animals. I remember each face, because I scanned them all constantly, trying to find a model for my own, a sort of average pattern to follow, for I was completely terrified by my father's expression: Marguerite and Thérèse were the only ones who looked halfway normal, which is to say profoundly bored, as little children do in the presence of the mystery of death.

In the afternoon, the priest who had attended Mother came to pay his respects. He said one short prayer and then explained to my father that Mother certainly wouldn't need very much praying for.

"In all my years as a priest, I have never met a soul so close to sanctity. I don't believe she will experience the flames of purgatory."

The good man kept his eyes lowered as he spoke. In this he must have been divinely inspired, for my father's face was frightful to see. I think that if he had been alone with his visitor, he would have leapt at him and strangled him. To make matters worse, there we all were standing around listening to these pious words, which contradicted everything we were supposed to believe. Wasn't it understood that he was the candidate for canonization? After a time, when the priest got no response, he lost countenance and left.

Mother was to be buried the next morning. Before we left that last night, we all went to have what could only rightly be called a last glance at her. No question of storing up memories to last a lifetime. It was hurry, hurry. But a child's last look at her mother doesn't have to be a long one. She takes in everything instantaneously, and this memory is a treasure she can never be parted from.

Grandfather and Grandmother kissed us, and we went downstairs in single file. I left the house in blissful ignorance of the future: I was never to go back there again.

My father's house was frigid as usual, and we said our prayers kneeling in the usual draught. Then, as he got to his feet:

"You will all go to your mother's funeral," said my father.

In those days, only the men of the family used to go to the church for the ceremony, but my father had decided otherwise. With a voice that was slightly hesitant, even for him, he added:

"You mustn't believe everything people say — that priest is probably a good priest, but he could be mistaken. Personally, I'm not at all sure that what he said was true."

By now every last one of us had stopped breathing.

"I may as well speak my mind," he went on. "I don't think your mother will be saved."

There followed a few garbled statements in which he tried to explain his reasons for this conviction. He didn't dare say that he had this by revelation — there are, after all, limits to the ridiculous — but that is what he tried to imply, and as subtlety wasn't his forte, even the little ones got the point. Only, not one of us believed a word he said. But there again he was short on subtlety. In his sad vanity, he thought that he had only to speak to convince us while, on the contrary, he had only to say the most commonplace thing and we would immediately say to ourselves: yes, and that's something else that isn't true.

I listened to his awkward speech with a kind of ugly satisfaction. It didn't displease me to find this man even more despicable than I had thought. And as for my love for Mother, every word he spoke embedded it deeper.

The trap door had been left open. Dine had prepared me a hot water bottle. I was able to sleep. The next day my father left early with the boys. We girls went directly to the church. We sat a little off to one side where we could cry quietly. The coffin was carried in, followed first by my two brothers, then by my father, then Grandfather and Uncles Eugène and Lorenzo. Of all the men, I looked only at Grandfather. I don't know why, but I was amazed to see him walk up the centre aisle of this church where I came every day, and where I had never thought to see him. When, many years later, I walked up that same aisle on my father's arm on my wedding day, that half-buried memory came brusquely back to me. And it was Grandfather, with his little goatee that prickled your cheeks, the only man I felt a daughter's love for and without whom I would never have known it, it was Grandfather, it seemed to me, who was walking me up the main aisle to give me away.

At the end of the funeral service, the tenor sang the hymn: "I'll see her one day in Heaven, My soul's true home." I couldn't help finding a note of irony in such a choice, and craned my neck to see how my father was taking it. He was walking heavily behind the coffin with a surly look on his face.

As soon as we got back to the house, he set about showing us that it was just an ordinary day by assigning us all sorts of jobs to do. If one of us seemed a little absent, he acted as though he really didn't see any good reason for that.

"What's this? Mooning around again? What in the world's got into you to make you look so vacant?"

"Oh nothing," was all we dared reply.

VOLUME 2

The Right Cheek

*P*erhaps I haven't mentioned that after my sister Françoise left the convent, I took her place in Mother Saint-Fortunat's perennially half-opened little heart. Although I was permitted by the convent regulations to spend a week with my family after my bereavement, she telephoned me on Thursday morning, four days afterwards, to ask me to come back. Time dragged without me, she said. Only too happy to leave the house where the poisonous atmosphere was suffocating, I went off to the convent without delay. When I got there, the girls seemed so different from what I had become that I found it really maddening.

"And of course it must be the saddest for your father," they kept on saying. "He must be disconsolate."

"Disconsolate. Yes, that's it."

"I thought he was very brave. He didn't cry at the funeral."

"Oh yes, he's very brave."

But wasn't there a single one in the whole bunch who came from a family like mine? And every day it would start all over again.

"My uncle had a heart made out of my aunt's wedding ring when she died. He always had it on him. And what about your father, what's he going to do with your mother's ring?"

"Well, uh — a heart too, naturally."

I sank into a complete torpor. My nights were filled with such nightmares that I tried to keep from going to sleep.

Luckily, very soon after I came back the sisters decided to mount a grand theatrical spectacle. It was to be *The Ray* by Reynès-Monlaur. (I haven't kept in very close touch with this highly respectable author since, and in fact to find his name I had to leaf through my old copy of that precious document, *Books to Read and Books to Shun* by Abbé Louis Bethléem. Of all the books in my library, I couldn't have chosen a better one to relieve me of the sadness stirred up by all the events I have just been relating.) I was to play the part of Suzanne, and my cousin Louise, the part of Christ. Once rehearsals began, the sisters gave them so much importance that bit by bit I got over my depression. They took up all my spare time. My role included interminable exchanges (if you can say that of monologues, three or four pages long) in which Suzanne, in incandescent rhetoric, poured out her soul in the Saviour's ear. It was a lot of work.

Contrary to anything I had known in my first convent, plays here were usually presented in the stupidest way possible. For instance, one of our plays featured a certain Marquise de Verneuil (strangely enough, in these convent plays every marquise, and God knows there were plenty of them, was a Verneuil), and although all of the cast were dressed in clothes borrowed from mothers or big sisters, it was thought proper to put the marquise into an enormous crinoline and top her off with a pointed mediaeval headdress. That got my goat. I tried to hint, in vain, that pointed coiffes and crinolines didn't belong in the same period, and that it was only when all women of a certain social rank began to dress like marquises that marquises themselves started to dress like marquises. It was no use.

The only result was that I was accused of jealousy, supposedly because I was only playing the part of a simple bourgeoise. I finally understood that for these nuns the title of marquise meant nothing more than dressing up in wide skirts and a pointed hat.

But this time things were done seriously. And in this case there was no cause to worry about the costumes. With all those picture calendars we got every year from the four corners of Quebec, correct biblical attire was pretty well fixed in the mind's eye. Rehearsals took up all my recesses and I was glad of it, because I could be sure that Mother Saint-Alexis, who was directing the play, wouldn't ask any irritating questions about my grief-stricken father. She was a darling woman, intelligent, lively and gay. She was tiny and dark-complexioned, and reminded one of a little black cat. In the whole convent she had nothing but friends.

When the big day arrived, everything was ready. I don't know which calendar my costume was modelled on. One from some dry-goods retailer, probably. I had on so many tunics, surcoats, draperies and veils of all sorts, that I made quite a scandalously plump Suzanne. Kneeling at the feet of my cousin Louise who personified a stripling Christ, my physical magnitude was almost sacrilegious. When she told me that she would have to die, tears came to my eyes, and on this score everyone praised my talents as an actress, never thinking they were just the tears of a motherless child.

The last months of the school year went by one after another without any lessening of my grief, despite the fact that Mother Saint-Fortunat had transferred to me all the passion that had drawn her to my sister Françoise. She lavished the grandest favours on me. In June she permitted Grandfather, Grandmother, Uncle Eugène and Aunt Berthe to come and spend an evening with me while the other boarders went on with their studies. She came herself to welcome them in the parlour. She told them about the part I had played in the production of *The Ray* and invited me to recite my purple patch for them, the speech four pages long. Standing up there in the middle of the room, I did my bit, gestures and all. Not overfamiliar, I imagine, with Reynès-Monlaur, Uncle Eugène hid behind a hand crooked in a meditative attitude an insistent little itch to laugh.

When I had done, Grandfather declared that decidedly a performance like that called for the hat to be passed around, and said he was going to put in five dollars. Grandmother gave five too, and so did my uncle. I had never had such a sum all to myself before, and several years were to pass before I did again. I was quite dazzled. Mother Saint-Fortunat, who had a healthy respect for money, seemed to be even more dazzled than I was and on the strength of it left us discreetly, advising us that we could stay together until nine o'clock. By nine all the girls were in bed, which just goes to show how good my credit was. After the parlour door had closed and we were alone, I went over and sat on Grandfather's knee until he had to beg for mercy, which didn't take long, for at thirteen I had already reached my adult size.

"How heavy you're getting, Ti-Claire!"

I went back to my chair, but never for long. I just couldn't tear myself away from him, and if it hadn't been for the black clothes we were all wearing, which in a way was like the presence of Mother amongst us, I would have been happier than I ever had a chance to be that year.

"See you soon!"

"See you soon!"

Soon? Never. I went up to the dormitory on tiptoe with a heart full of love and not a single foreboding.

*   *   *

Then June came, the final lessons in domestic science, and finally prize day. Parents were invited. From our seats we watched them coming in. When the ceremony began, there was nobody from my family. I was first in my class that year, and a pile of thick books with gilt-edged pages accumulated in my lap. Besides, since Mother Saint-Fortunat had a real talent for soliciting gifts from various benefactors, there were all sorts of special prizes: for diction, good manners, academic zeal and so on. As teacher's pet number one, I raked in a good many of these too. My neighbours eyed me enviously. For my part, I was quite distressed. How was I ever going to get home with such a load? It was a good three-quarters of an hour's walk under ordinary circumstances. I'd have a terrible time getting there, exhausted as I was by my inevitable end-of-term diarrhoea.

Anyway, off I went, my pile of books beginning at arms' length and ending up just under my chin. Since I couldn't see where my feet were going, I fell several times. It was a real calvary. Saint's lives scattered in every direction and got covered with dust. I had to brush them off, get the pile back into balance and start off again, my feet dragging a little more each time. At least ten different people stopped and offered to drive me home, but I didn't dare accept. If my father had happened to be there when I got back, he would have considered it very suspect, even though I was just a schoolgirl, to see me arrive in a stranger's car. To make the journey perfectly wretched, it was dreadfully hot, and getting hotter as noon approached. By way of consolation all I could do was curse my sisters for not coming to the prize giving, and Mother Saint-Fortunat for liking me too well. She was really killing me with kindness.

At last I reached the house. I was in tears. Because of all the stops I had had to make, I had been an hour and a half on the road.

"Why didn't you come?" I asked my sisters.

"Father's away on a trip. When he left he told us we weren't to leave the house for any reason."

I was suffocated with anger, one of those real rages generated by the bad half of my chromosomes. I started shouting:

"And what if the house caught fire, you couldn't leave it then, eh?"

The fact is that, if it hadn't been for this possibility, my father would have locked the doors and taken away the keys. I'm not exaggerating. As though it was self-evident, he had mentioned this with his parting instructions, and had ordered my sisters to "act as though all the doors were bolted." Now that he was at last rid of the bothersome presence of another adult, he could give himself over completely to his vocation as child-torturer. This was just the beginning.

That first year without Mother we were frightened and timorous. It wasn't to last long. For the time being, we settled for smoking when he wasn't there, but he forbade us so many things, one after another, that disobedience soon became an obsessive occupation.

We were restrained, too, by the presence of the two youngest ones, the little girls. They didn't belong to our clan and were not to be trusted. My father's predilection for them was still strong and, quite normally for that age, this resulted in a lot of tattle-taling. Thérèse was particularly dangerous. She was only six. My father was not the man to draw back before that minor family crime which consists in setting off children one against another in order to rule more effectively, and if we still love one another tenderly today it's no thanks to him. He used to shut himself up in his study with little Thérèse, take her on his knee, stroke her hair and then question her. The more she had to tell him, the sweeter he got. So, naturally, when she had run through the true things, she began to invent:

"I heard Claire talking out loud to herself last night."

People do talk in their sleep. I might have too. But to hear me, Thérèse would have had to stay awake herself. The fact of the matter is that between eight at night and six in the morning a cannon wouldn't have wakened her. Besides, as far as my father was concerned, that story wasn't good enough. The most urgent desire in the world could hardly have made a scandal out of that. He preferred to imagine that I had had my brother up in my room. That was to credit André with a great deal of courage and boldness: to reach me he would have had to go down a long corridor, pass in front of my father's open door, climb a staircase with very noisy treads, having reached my floor go along another corridor that corresponded to the one below, open my door, and then make his way into my room which was directly over my father's. And then do it all over again in reverse order. But that didn't matter! When you've got the essential ingredients for such a good novel, you hang on to them just as long as possible. All summer long André and I were subjected to narrow scrutiny. It was so rigorous that in front of my father we didn't even dare say, "Pass the salt," to each other.

*　　*　　*

That summer I don't think Grandmother came to see us more than once. At any rate I can only remember the visit she made in company with our cousins from Sorel. As for us, we didn't go to see her, for we were forbidden to set foot outside the house except for mass. However, when my father wasn't off on a trip, he used to take us out on Sundays after lunch. It was our weekly entertainment. An entertainment as only my father knew how to concoct them, that is to say, a dreadful chore that we would have gladly exchanged for waxing floors or collecting potato beetles. Our car was about the size of Noah's ark. All eight of us fit inside quite easily, my father and the seven children. The male contingent took over the front seat, and the female shared the back and the folding seats. There again we didn't mix sexes. The day my sister Dine innocently suggested switching one of the boys with one of the girls, she was accused of the worst perversities imaginable.

Once all questions of morality were settled, off we went. In perfect silence. Adjusting the rear-view mirror, not to see the road but to keep an eye on his daughters, my father would drive along, smoking cigars one after another. He drove very badly. He believed you used less gas if you only trod on the accelerator in little spurts. I don't know how well this method works for saving gas, but for inducing carsickness, if you add in the smell of cigar, there's nothing like it. Sitting there pale, tight-lipped, eyes closed, nursing our nausea, we would wait till the outing was over; and no matter how sick we felt, we must never forget to thank our father warmly for the delightful drive.

Sometimes he made us take a snack along, which we always ate too soon, without appetite, our sinuses still clogged with cigar smoke. Never under any circumstances would we eat our sandwiches on the grass. In obedience to some strange prompting — it must have had something to do with skirts and the bit of leg or knee they sometimes fail to cover when you are sitting on the ground — my father had outlawed outdoor picnics. We had to eat in the car. In silence and as quickly as possible, as if discharging some odious duty.

More often than not, towards the end of the day these drives would land us at our paternal grandmother's. My father would install himself in his own special chair and the rest of us would sit where we could. The living room was too small for ten people, we were all on top of one another and the cigar smoke issuing from the paternal mouth went straight up our nostrils.

"It's a nice day," my aunt would say.

"Yes, it is nice."

"But a little cooler."

"Yes, cooler."

"Yesterday was warmer."

"Yes, it was warmer."

This conversation was invariable, unless the terms changed to fit the bad weather. Thereupon a long silence settled in, relieved only by the "puh, puh," of my father puffing on his cigar, and noisy breathing of my brother André who was afflicted with a respiratory system like a wheezy bellows. Sometimes the canary in his cage, wanting to cheer up this family reunion, would let out a few chirps. Sheeplike, we would all turn our heads in his direction.

"Just look at that, the canary is glad to see you," my aunt would simper.

"Yes."

And on and on it dragged. Embarrassment and boredom deformed every face except my father's. He seemed to think that this was the way a visit should be. At the end of an hour:

"Well, it's time to go home."

"There's no hurry."

Up we'd get, all eight of us, and out we'd file. On the way back my father always found something to grumble about. No matter how thin the conversation had been, he always discovered, on reflection, hidden meanings and treacherous innuendos in my aunt's remarks. So he would swear he would never set foot in that house again, once our grandmother had passed on. Yet, in addition to our Sunday visits, he used to go there every day after lunch. Sometimes dreadful scenes took place, which we only heard about much later when my father got too old to keep his secrets.

"That was the time I hit my mother," he said one day in conclusion to the long rehearsal of old grudges.

You can imagine the stunned silence that greeted this revelation.

"It was my sister I wanted to hit, but mother got in between us."

He shrugged his shoulders fatalistically, like someone who has tried to act for the best but sees his good intentions turn against him. After all, there is nothing so very surprising in this story. My poor father, right up to the brink of old age, never thought of anything but that: blows, blows and blows. It's like writing thousands of letters — there's always one that will turn up at the wrong address.

At any rate, even the most interminable Sundays had to come to an end. We would dine in silence, say our evening prayers and go up to bed. It was still so early that we could read in our beds without turning on the light. We didn't complain. We were all passionate readers and we were forbidden to gratify that passion in the open. What did we read? I really wonder. The prizes we got at the convent, books that were sometimes handed out to civil servants from the Secretary of State's office and which my father would bring back to the house — but not before he had sifted them very carefully — and serial novels from *l'Action catholique*, cut out and stitched together (always with an episode or two missing, for when he suspected us of following the serial, my father would buy another paper). Besides that there were a hundred or so old tomes in the library. The only reason they were there, I think, was because they were so utterly boring. I suppose we must have read the same things over and over. For my part, I would gladly have read the want ads for lack of something better to read.

When the sun set, we would slip the forbidden fruit under our mattresses. One more Sunday gone! Next day our father would leave at eight-thirty. At last we could start to breathe.

Sometimes on weekdays Thérèse would telephone my father and ask him to bring some candies back with him. Such audacity always stunned me. And he would bring them back, which was equally astonishing. Another source of endless scenes. Thérèse kept miserly track of her goodies but in the end would always get mixed up in her accounts.

"One of my candies is missing."

"Who stole that candy?" my father would shout.

That started interminable inquiries. We were all subjected to wrathful interrogations and punished in succession, five or six for the same candy. And if one of us decided not to risk accepting another one, just to avoid this kind of trouble, he would be accused of holding a grudge and, who knows, perhaps even of acting out of a guilty conscience. We were all accused of ingratitude. Of the blackest hue, naturally. My father was quick to label this as our characteristic way of acknowledging his kindness. For that matter, we recognized his behaviour as his own characteristic way of poisoning the least treat.

It's true that at this time we all held a kind of grudge against Thérèse. Even Marguerite, though she shared paternal favour with her, began to look towards the clan and wonder if moral comfort didn't really lie there. Margot only held second place in her father's eye; when both were at fault Thérèse always got the benefit of the doubt, and Marguerite the handicap of the certitude. Yet it turned out that although Thérèse always remained my father's favourite, my father didn't long remain hers. Children are born just, and certain kinds of favouritism humiliate much more than they satisfy. When they are small, children try to work their advantage to the limit, until the day they learn what ugliness is.

*   *   *

One evening, just before the end of the holidays, we had a visit from a contractor who specialized in carpentry and odd jobs. My father had called him in without breathing a word to us about it, and never mentioned it afterwards. A few chance remarks were the only warning we had that our house was to undergo serious alterations. Then it was the beginning of term, not only for Marguerite and me this time, but for little Thérèse, too.

As soon as we had gone, the work began. And it lasted for ages, because in this matter, as in all others, my father had his own special way of going about things: he usually began at the end. This time he first had all the downstairs floors done over in blond maple, almost white, then he had the plaster patched and the walls painted. The contractor protested, but my father stuck to his guns. The workmen were then invited to move upstairs where they knocked down walls and put in another bathroom. (I must say that my father never skimped on bathrooms. A little later he had one put in downstairs too, so that you could wash your hands in any corner of the house — if only the water in this benighted place hadn't been so rusty it looked like tomato ketchup.) After the bathroom, they repainted the upstairs. You can guess what a threat all that was to the blond maple. But my father kept a sharp eye on things. My sisters were made responsible for picking up the least little flake of plaster. Every night, after the workmen had left, they had to clean the floors with varsol and rewax the living room, the dining room, the study, the hallway and even the kitchen — where my father, unable to resist his passion for pale maple, had refused to have tiles laid — and they were all rooms of vast dimensions. It wasn't the first time he undertook to turn everything inside out and it wasn't to be the last. I never saw him proceed in any other fashion, despite the fact that he had to begin all over again at the end what he had done to start with. That was due, I think, to the extraordinary impatience that possessed him, which he obeyed like a slave. If hardwood floors were to be the main item of renovation, then he wanted them right away. The downstairs work would be seen much more than the upstairs changes, therefore he wanted to see it immediately. It was in response to the same impatience that he used to pick strawberries when they were still green, open flowers with his fingers and wear a spring coat the very day he got it, a frigid day in late February.

While the work was still in progress Grandmother came to spend a day with my elder sisters.

"Is that the way you're doing it?" she innocently asked one of the workmen. "In my day they did things differently."

There wasn't any malice in her remark, and I think the carpenter wouldn't have paid much attention if my father hadn't questioned him the next day.

"My mother-in-law was here yesterday. I suppose she found fault with everything?"

The men were afraid of my father. Since the day work began he had, on various occasions, fired several of them. The ones that were left looked only to humour him. There was a full winter's work there.

"She said that in her day they didn't go about things that way."

At long last! This was the opportunity he had been dreaming of since Mother's death. He flew into a rage a good half of which must have been entirely artificial — he had been seeking an outlet for so long — and left for the office howling that this wasn't the last we would hear of it. Indeed it wasn't. The next day, Grandmother received a frightful letter from him. He forbade her ever to see us again. Grandfather, Uncle Eugène and Aunt Berthe fell under the same interdiction, naturally. Grandmother was crushed and reproached herself bitterly for her innocent remark.

My father often lacked the nerve to tell us about his wicked deeds. It seemed almost as though he was overcome with shame and couldn't manage to find the right words to set forth the pious side of the thing. This time it took him several days to tell my elder sisters of his feat. As for the rest of us, he never spoke to us about it. Except once, to me. I'll tell about that later.

At the time, I got the news from Dine one Thursday in the convent parlour. She whispered it to me before the little ones came in. The shock of it left me bewildered. As well as I knew my father, as clearly as I had seen at Mother's death how far his cruelty could go, as certain as I was, instinctively, that he was just waiting for a chance to separate us from our grandparents, I was still bewildered. The little girls came in and we had to listen to their prattle and answer it. Neither Dine nor I felt really up to scratch.

During the study period that followed, I started a despairing letter to Grandmother, but fear prevented me from finishing it. Not fear that the letter would get into my father's hands — that is, that it would be confiscated and passed on to him — but that one of the nuns might read it and the whole convent might learn about the horrors that went on at home. I knew my nuns, and I knew that for them all unhappiness was laughable. I knew how indiscreet they were and knew that, from nun to pet, such a juicy piece of gossip would quickly do the rounds from every mouth to every ear. I already had enough to bear during those parlour sessions that used to leave me so full of shame. I didn't have the courage to risk more, and Grandmother never knew all the pain, resentment and despondency our separation cost me. For weeks I mulled over my grief and my memories. I gave up studying. All my efforts were trained on remembering every last detail, even the minutest, of a period in my life that was as irrevocably over as if Grandfather and Grandmother had been dead. I began writing down endless notes and in so doing perceived, even then, that my childhood could be told as a story. So much so, in fact, that at the end of this book I could accurately write: *Beauport, 1927–Ottawa, 1966*.

When I had cried for months over the past and over the present, I suddenly found myself as dried up as if I had reached an arid old age. And all the other sorrows that lay in store for me found me, ashamed as I would have been to admit it, incapable of shedding so much as a single tear.

To make matters worse, it was just at this time that I fell out of favour with Mother Saint-Fortunat. The summer holidays had worked against me. As soon as school began again I perceived, by a certain coldness, that to be out of my Doña Juanita's sight had put me out of her mind too. I hadn't been replaced yet, we had only just got back, but I was about to be. To be certain of that, you had only to see the way she acted, like an unattached person playing the field. There were any number of candidates. She found all sorts of unworthy rivals for me, at whose hands I was to go down to inglorious defeat. There was even, among others, a brassy, vulgar little blonde who came from the small girls' division, which was really the limit.

Oh that Ninon! This passion lasted all of two weeks, during which she let herself be treated with incredible effrontery by that little blondie, who didn't have the slightest hesitation in tutoying her loudly. Later on, I saw cynical young women using the same tone to reply to bashful old beaux, and I recognized the style immediately. The little blonde was replaced by another of the same species. I was humiliated, but that was still nothing. I was soon to be deeply embittered. As I've already said, Mother Saint-Fortunat's passion knew neither let nor stay. She stepped out of love to charge hotly into hate. Passion was her province. The odd thing was that she brought to her hatred a constancy that love never required of her. As a result I was to remain her chosen scapegoat until she was moved to another convent two long years later.

There were holidays at All Saints that year. I don't know if this was an innovation, but those were the first I remember, and if I remember them at all it is because all our holidays now could be classed under the heading: "Cod Liver Oil." Ever since Mother had died we had been forced, summer and winter, to choke down enormous quantities of the stuff. The Easter holidays had come right after her death, then the summer ones and now All Saints. And spread over them all was a thick layer of cod liver oil. My father's dangerous hand would ladle it out to us morning and night. He bought it in big demijohns, the cheapest kind and the worst tasting. If we showed any signs of aversion, he would explain that tuberculosis is an expensive illness, that he had already spent enough on Mother and that he had decided to cut back on costs. More often than not, we would go and vomit it up in the toilet or the sink, and there was always a lot of competition for the john amongst us kids at vitamin time.

Christmas holidays were no different. It was our first Christmas without Mother. She was never mentioned. On the rare occasion when father remembered her, it was to tell us over again about the revelation he had had. Otherwise it was as though we had never had a mother. Except for the cod liver oil.

New Year's Day held a nasty surprise for us. My father had concocted a new ritual for the paternal blessing he used to give us on that day. Previously the ceremony had run this way: we all knelt down around my father who remained standing in the midst of us as solemn as a patriarch, and it was Mother who asked for the general blessing. This way it went off without too much digging into old misdeeds of the past year, which was a pity, because with a little know-how the proceedings could have been made quite fruitful. So on December 31, 1927, my father warned us that from then on we would have to ask for the blessing one by one, every man for himself.

The next day we had to comply with the new order. Only, when the boldest of us tried to find my father in his study which he had just been seen to enter, he found the room empty. My father had gone out by the other door, had rapidly crossed the hall and was now stationed in the living room. The unlucky candidate for benediction rushed in there, only to find the dispenser of blessings making for the kitchen by way of the dining room, and ready to move off from there on the hall-study-hall-living room-dining room circuit again, unless the pursuer gave up and started to back track, which would oblige my father to do the same. From then on, every year it was the same thing and when you consider that there were seven children you can imagine the kind of madcap minuet it was.

"It's ten o'clock already," my father would exclaim suddenly, "and there are still some who haven't been blessed."

Overcome with discouragement, one or another of us would sometimes quickly kneel on the kitchen floor right in the midst of the preparations for dinner, which my father used to come in to supervise every fifteen minutes or so. He would pull the little kneeler up with a jerk.

"You'll ask for the blessing when we're alone."

The chase continued. Sometimes we were lucky enough to trap him coming out of the toilet, a room we could besiege because it only had one door — the only one on the ground floor so equipped! I don't know how to explain all this coming and going, unless by the sadistic pleasure he took in seeing us whirling around from one room to another. But the explanation for the solo benediction is quite evident. It was the ideal occasion for a general review of the year's scoldings. And since, to top it off, he had a bad memory, he would often remember the misdeed without knowing who had committed it, and collar the innocent instead of the guilty. When it was all over he was supposed to give us two dollars as a New Year's gift. The days of Grandmother's beribboned packages were past. Two dollars each, from hand to hand, and no ribbons. If only you could always be sure of that.

"You don't deserve any present this year," was all we sometimes got.

After all that galloping around, and considering that with our birthday dollar that was the sum total of the year's spending money, it was a bit thick.

Of all the nightmares we dragged from one Happy New Year to the next, this was the most irritating and the most deadly. The longest lasting too. Believe it or not, for years after my marriage, my father used to telephone from Quebec to Ottawa to give me a chance to ask his blessing. He didn't offer it. After the usual New

Year's greetings he would stop talking, and wait for me to think of it. It was a telephonic transposition of his old open-door policy. The first time, I didn't catch on right away. I talked and talked, about the weather and all that, with never a sound from the other end, just a brooding silence. That finally reminded me, just in time, of the New Year's blessing. The most moving of our French-Canadian traditions, so they say. It wasn't until my father had reached extreme old age that we were spared that particular emotion.

*   *   *

A little before the Christmas holidays, my half-brother Gérard had to stop work and take to his bed. Then in January he requested — and I will never know what aberration prompted him — to be sent back to us to die. Since his marriage he had been working in a city in the south of the province where he lived with his young wife, Yvonne. Her family, like ours, lived in the outskirts of Quebec. I suppose that, feeling his time was short, he didn't wish to deprive his wife, whom he loved dearly, of the consolation of her family. Something like that might be a plausible explanation for his return.

*   *   *

If I have not spoken of Gérard until now, or rather so infrequently, it is because I don't know very well where to place him in these reminiscences. I remember him perfectly, but I can't say exactly how. He was eleven years older than me. So when I began to remember things he was at school, probably a boarder as we all were. Then he got sick and spent quite a long time at the sanatorium at Lac Edouard. After that he started working and got married. I recall that my father was hardly any gentler with him than he was with the rest of us and that, even when he was big, Gérard was often beaten. As a result, he used to run away for weeks, sometimes months at a time, as my two other brothers did later. My father always treated such rebelliousness as pure folly. Apparently it never occurred to him, out of a total of a good dozen times, that if the boys ran away, they were trying to run away from something. He preferred to believe that they fled to be in a better position to satisfy certain criminal instincts. He would devour the newspapers, and as soon as he found a paragraph on the arrest of some rascal whose name was withheld but whose age corresponded, however roughly, with our fugitive, he would decide that it must be him. He would get up heavily out of his armchair and, clenching the newspaper in his fist would put on his "best tragic actor" face and voice:

"My poor children, your brother is in prison."

Although we always knew their hideout — they kept in touch with us, we washed their things and helped them get through these periods of liberty — we had to pretend to believe the sad news, so we put on our tragic faces too. The fact that this had never been true for the previous flights didn't change a thing; each time we had to play out the comedy anew. At first sight it might seem that there is an element of plausibility in all this, that in families like ours delinquency is likely to run rampant. I've got my own theory about that. I believe that the delinquent child wants to punish his parents, wants to be a living reproach to them. As far as we were concerned, we all sensed very strongly that my father's pride would always prevent him from feeling that he was the one who was being punished. We might have killed, stolen, pillaged, he would never have begun to think that he had failed in some fashion, or that he hadn't given us everything a father ought to give his children. He would just have said that we didn't get that from him.

I know that Gérard ran away a number of times, but I only remember one of them. I was quite small. It was Uncle Eugène, Mother's brother, who was sent to bring him back, and I remember the consultations that took place beforehand. At last my father was made to understand that it was wiser to send a human emissary than to go himself. He said with great simplicity:

"It would be better for you to go, Eugène, he's not afraid of you."

Even at that, Gérard enjoyed preferential treatment, for my father never sent anyone to look for Mother's sons. He just waited for the pinch to bring them back.

So in January Gérard was transported to my father's house. He was put into Mother's old room where a small bed was also set up for Yvonne. I don't think either of them was long in regretting their decision. Any arrangement would have been better than that. Every morning before he left for work, and every evening when he came back, my father would go in to chat with Gérard. Chat! Every time it was the same thing. He would begin by asking him how he felt and by giving him medical advice. Then he would build up steam. "If you had listened to me you wouldn't be lying there now, but you were always too headstrong. I told you as much. That's what happens when you won't listen to your father — the good Lord punishes you." As one thing led to another, the paternal volume rose. Gérard would start to cough, but that was of no consequence, my father could talk louder than Gérard could cough. The sick call would always finish the same way.

"It's your own fault you're dying. Admit it. Admit that it's your own fault you're dying."

He would shake Gérard and wouldn't leave him until, finally, he had admitted that it was his own fault he was dying. In the midst of this madness, Yvonne didn't know which way to turn. It lasted until the very last day. Gérard died on the fifth of April, 1928. On the fourth, when he was in a state of semi-coma, he had to go through the same torture.

"Admit that it's your own fault you're dying. Answer me!"

And the poor boy interrupted his agony to whisper:

"Yes, yes."

The last day, when my father left for work, he ordered my sisters to telephone him immediately if the end seemed near. Early in the afternoon it became apparent that the time had come. Although they were very fond of Yvonne, my sisters were not close enough to her to exchange confidences. Just the same, without mentioning their disobedience to my father's orders, no one suggested calling him. He usually came back from the office about a quarter past five. At five past, Gérard decided to wait no longer. He hastened to die while he could still do so in peace.

For months afterwards, at the drop of a hat, my father would question us to know if Gérard hadn't asked for him at the last moment, if he hadn't seemed to have something to say to him just before he passed away. The dear man had got it into his head that his son wouldn't have wanted to leave this life without asking for his paternal absolution. And why? For all and for nothing. My father always believed that he was the one who held the keys to heaven.

*　*　*

Yvonne, poor thing, stayed with us until summer. You would have said that she, too, was so afraid of my father that she didn't dare move. The most incredible thing of all was that after a very few weeks of widowhood, she received a proposal of marriage. From my father. He had decided that would suit everybody. Besides, since Yvonne hadn't borne Gérard any children, it was unlikely that she would bear him any. On this score my father had already fulfilled his duty as a Christian. A man who has begot nine children has a right to a sterile wife. (Nine children: Gérard had had a little sister, Andrée, who died at eighteen months.) Yvonne, however, didn't seem to think this was sufficient motive to marry an old Torquemada of fifty-four when she was only twenty-five. What's more, it just so happened that she wanted children. Later she remarried and adopted two.

That wasn't the only time my father showed considerable originality in his offers of marriage, far from it. Until our paternal grandmother fell ill for the first time — when in return for her cure he promised never to marry again, a vow which he got out of with double indemnity later on — he never gave up trying. As soon as he met a widow or a spinster, he made up his mind to marry her. He would ask her on the spot, at the first encounter, and would declare his intention to lead her to the altar within two weeks. He realized that he had been a bad husband twice already, and he was afraid of gossip. Only, his very haste put a flea in the ear of his intended. Why such speed? Do you know him? Do you know someone who does? In those days it wasn't much of a problem to find someone in Quebec who knew someone else, and the interested party always managed to dig up some unsettling information. My father would be shown the door. From one source or another, we always heard the story, but we had already guessed the gist of it by the unspeakable temper that the jilted suitor brought back from those bouts.

Among the besieged were a widow from Lachute, an old maid who lived near Beauport, at Giffard, I think, and a salesgirl in a department store of whom he had heard it said that she wouldn't turn down a good husband, which prompted him to go and buy a dressing gown for my eldest sister. At the time, not knowing his intentions, and seeing him come in with a big cardboard box under his arm, we nearly fainted with astonishment. That was nothing. Three days later he turned up with a second one — that couldn't be helped, the girl worked in the dressing gown department — and we suddenly realized what we owed these surprises to. Now that my two elder sisters were looked after, I thought it would be my turn next. It was at this point that the salesgirl opened a brief inquiry.

Result: right up until my sister Françoise's marriage, she had to share her dressing gown with me.

These attempted conquests were just a modest beginning. As time went by, the stories got richer. In the convent where we were boarders, there was a particular sister, tall, strong and ruddy, who often greeted parents at the door of the parlour on a Sunday. My father spotted her, found her to have that robust look that suggests a future centenarian, and inquired of us if Mother Saint-Frumence had taken her final vows. No, she hadn't, since she didn't wear the big rosary at her side yet. Then she was free to relinquish the habit? Yes, she was. This time it was a delicate proposition, tricky to handle. Unluckily, the first consequence of this new scheme was that instead of getting more dressing gowns, we got more visits. From then on my father never missed a single one.

After several weeks of hesitation, and on the eve of one of his long trips, he decided to put an end to his painful incertitude. Just before leaving, he sat down at his desk and wrote a letter, then a better one, then, with more and more persuasive arguments flooding in on all sides, a better one yet. Then he began to get fidgety. In the end he sealed an envelope and gave it to Dine whose mission it was to give it to Mother Saint-Frumence. And off he went, sure that he would come back an engaged man.

That was on Wednesday. The next day, just as she was about to go to the parlour, Dine got out the envelope and, discovering that it seemed thin and flimsy, held it up to the light. It was empty. In his agitation, and especially in his concern to destroy the letters he judged inadequate, he had torn them all up.

"Did you deliver my letter?" was the first question he asked on his return.

Dine explained as well as she could what had happened, but my father wouldn't believe her. He examined the envelope, declared that it had been opened and resealed, and beat my two sisters black and blue. Then he jumped in the car and went over to ask for his sweetheart's hand from the parish priest.

Knowing how embarrassed I would be by the behaviour of this new Noël de Chamilly (appropriately, the nun's given name was Marianna: one couldn't have invented a better joke),[1] Dine and Françoise never mentioned it to me.

"Does your father intend to marry again?" the sisters asked me on the slightest pretext, one after another.

And exchanged ironic smiles. I began to wonder if gossip about my family had begun to reach the convent. There was nothing I dreaded more.

"Oh no! My father was much too sad when Mother died."

To make a long story short, my father was refused. He developed a terrible grudge against Mother Saint-Frumence, all the more virulent, I imagine, because he felt how ridiculous the whole business had been.

"She's certainly grown ugly," he would remark. "She's got bags under her eyes."

And he would shrug his shoulders in a pitying way. He came close to thinking that this disgrace had befallen the poor girl as a punishment for having turned him down. In conclusion, he pronounced his habitual anathema on her:

"She looks constipated."

We didn't care two hoots about Mother Saint-Frumence's intestines. All we wished was that my father wouldn't spend all his Sunday afternoons in the parlour, and that he would take up going to lay brothers' services, Vespers, Rogation parades and Father Lelièvre's processions, which is exactly what happened after he got over what I can only inappropriately call his broken heart.

For that matter, my father never knew anything about love. Since he was a widower, he wanted to remarry. Who? A woman. From the first minute of a new encounter, or even long before that if it was a meeting arranged beforehand, he fell madly in love. Rejected, he would choke with anger for a couple of days, and then be ready to start all over again. For him, love was like an object that you hang around a woman's neck. If she will have none of it, then that proves that you were sadly mistaken concerning the wisdom of the person in question; so you take the object and hang it around some other neck.

When our paternal grandmother was sick and in danger of dying in the autumn of 1929, she was saved from asphyxiation by her doctor son, my Uncle Lorenzo. Like many people in a coma, she was strangled by her own tongue. Using a spatula to hold her tongue down for I don't know how long, my uncle saved her from suffocating, and indeed, she lived on a great many years after this alarm. To all appearances it was thanks to Uncle Lorenzo that she was saved. At least that's what we believed in the family. When there were emotional conversations on this subject, my father used to pull atrocious faces, the vinegary grimaces of someone unjustly overlooked. Then one day, he announced that it was he who had obtained her cure, in exchange for a vow never to remarry. He made no allusion to the five or six refusals that had kept him single better than any vow. But logic and my father —

Let's finish the story of this vow. Several years later, the women on my father's side of the family took it into their heads to marry him off. I have never been able to understand why. Out of spite, most probably. They claimed that it was with an eye to our future — that a stepmother would find us husbands — and cast their choice on a shrew who didn't know a soul. Still, to marry her my father had to be freed from his vow. He went to see his confessor, who bargained to release him if he would say three rosaries a day. For life. We already said one set of the beads a night for family devotions. From then on we said three, linked despite ourselves with this swap of his which never brought enough advantages to us to make up for all the surplus prayers. And over the years events took an even more incredible turn. After he had buried his third wife, my father took a fourth, with whom he always said his daily rosary. Though it remains a mystery whether she agreed to pay off the old debt contracted because of her deceased predecessor, or whether she simply said the responses without knowing the origins of this practice.

*   *   *

But we were talking about his proposal to Yvonne. Once she had given her reply, she took the first opportunity, during one of his business trips, to return speedily to her own family. As soon as we were alone, our first move was to telephone Uncle Eugène and Aunt Berthe and invite them to come over and spend the evening with us. There wasn't any question of inviting Grandfather and Grandmother, they had been gone from Quebec since the month of May.

After so many hard blows, they had only one thought, to leave, to get away. Then too, all those worries had aged them both considerably in a very few months. Grandfather couldn't manage the pharmacy any more. It was beyond his strength now. He found a buyer and, during the negotiations, he was offered a job in Chicoutimi. So now we would be so far from one another that it would be impossible for them to see their grandchildren under any circumstances. That was less cruel than to live almost within the same city and scarcely even get to speak to each other on the telephone.

From Chicoutimi Grandmother had written me a short letter and a very discreet one. In those days — and perhaps still today — letters were usually opened in convents and a good many people could read them before we did. She gave me her address and asked me to write her from time to time, if I could. She had written her name on the back of the envelope, and thanks to this the Mother Superior had given it to me unopened. I suppose that she alone possessed "the right of the paper knife."

"There's a letter for you," said Mother Saint-Fortunat. "Mother Superior hasn't unsealed it."

She couldn't make up her mind to give it to me. Looking puzzled, she turned it over.

"It's from your grandmother. I'm going to ask if there hasn't been some mistake."

That Superior was really a good woman. She was deeply imbued with a sense of justice, and I would often have occasion to thank my stars for that. She must have thought to herself that there was something indecent in reading letters from a grandmother to her granddaughter, that there couldn't be anything really reprehensible in them and that this wasn't the time to use the paper knife. Mother Saint-Fortunat's insistence stopped her perhaps from automatically and thoughtlessly using the same right many other times. Moreover, she knew very well that I replied to grandmother. But I always entrusted my letters to day-girls, though this was a breach of the rules, and I was never worried on that score.

This correspondence continued till Grandmother's death. During the holidays it would have been too dangerous for her to answer my letters, but on my side I could write to her every week. Thinking that she and Grandfather must suffer from being completely cut off from their youngest grandchildren, one day I asked Marguerite and Thérèse to write their names at the bottom of the page.

"I know who for," Marguerite said to me in a whisper.

And seeing how terrified I looked, she added:

"Don't worry, I won't say a thing."

Grandmother was deeply touched by these poor scribbles, and there was seldom a letter thereafter that failed to mention them.

She never got over not seeing them grow up, and spoke about these last grandchildren that her daughter had given her as though they were amputated limbs.

*　*　*

So when we were all together again, after Yvonne had gone back to her family, we used to invite my uncle and aunt over as soon as my father left on one of his trips. They would turn up with their pockets full of cigarettes, my uncle taught us to dance, my aunt told us all the latest Quebec gossip — in short, they civilized us a little. We certainly needed it, for our idea of the gay world and its frivolities wasn't any too clear. The only thing was, we had to hide these visits from the two little girls. This procedure began in the morning. We put the clocks on. At eleven we would tell them it was one o'clock already, that time was flying, and that they had to come in for lunch. Benoît was in on the scheme, and it was his job to keep his sisters running and jumping around all day long. While this was going on we would move the clocks ahead again.

By half past four we were ready to call out: "Come on in children, it's dinner time."

We pretended to nibble away with them, then we started to put them to bed.

"But it's still light outside," they protested.

"That's because these are the longest days of the year."

By the time our visitors arrived, they had been in bed for so long and were so tired out with all their playing that they were as sound asleep as if it had been midnight. We had to pay for it next morning. They were up and around at five.

This system only worked for one summer. Next holidays when we tried to start it up again, Marguerite and Thérèse stated flatly that they weren't babies, that they knew very well why we wanted to put them to bed so early and that they could keep a secret as well as the big ones.

From then on, we all belonged to the same clan. My father could hold all the inquiries he liked, he never again got anyone to talk. And I sometimes find myself pitying the solitude of this man who lived cut off from us by as total a lack of understanding as if he had come from Venus or Mars, and even more so, because he didn't even excite our curiosity. But I'm sure he wasn't aware of his own solitude and never questioned himself about it. The man had never had a real friend, no one ever came to see him, except at the end of his life when he wasn't himself any more and some neighbour might drop over. He never knew what it felt like to be attached to some-one, an old friend he could go over and take a cup of coffee with or smoke a pipe with in the evening. He was inhuman in everything. Perhaps he was afraid of being sidetracked from the strict exercise of his tyranny. Or, if he invited people in, of possibly having to face their attempts to dissuade him from it. Or of letting some of our allies inside the walls. That was a superfluous precaution. We already had our own accomplices. As the years passed, our resist-ance became better and better organized. We had always deceived him every time we had to save our own skins. But from that sum-mer on, it was a different matter. From then on, as self-satisfied and oblivious to what was going on around him as ever, our father was to live at the centre of a permanent, well-articulated plot, one which, from this time on, was to be unanimous. When you came right down to it, we really only had two preoccupations: to lie to him when he was there, and to disobey him when he wasn't. To my way of looking at it, two eminently moral preoccupations!

To belong to the clan meant a lot more than just knowing how to hold your tongue, smoke and receive clandestine visitors. Just con-sider what was forbidden in the category of clothes and cosmetics alone. We weren't allowed to cut our hair, to wear dresses in the least décolleté or which revealed either calf or upper arm, to wear sheer stockings or high heels, to use powder or rouge or perfume, to have long nails, let alone painted ones — and I scarcely know where to stop this list because I had forgotten bright colours, brassieres that bore some relation to the human form, and shaved legs or armpits. When you think of all those *verboten* things, plus all the others that devolved from all the other categories, you can well imagine that to belong to the clan — that is, to break the rules — was a full-time occupation.

For example, we needed up-to-date clothes. The ones we wore for my father's benefit would hardly serve that purpose. They were a kind of sack that drooped down all around and that for some reason we used to call "chapels." To add insult to injury, we had to make them ourselves, and I don't know anything more frustrating than to take pains in making a garment that can never be anything but horrible. If, by some extraordinary fluke, my father did buy us something ready-made, it came from Eaton's, by way of the catalogue. We were the ones who wrote out the orders, but he was the one who mailed them, after revising them according to his lights, which meant increasing the sizes by three or four, always with the same intention — to see our busts swamped in floods of cloth. I remember one coat whose armholes came down to my elbows and the rest in equal disproportion. It had to be taken apart completely in secret and be done all over at top speed, because Christmas was coming and I didn't have anything else to wear.

But I don't hold anything against Eaton's. Thanks to them and their catalogue, we managed to recoup a few dollars that we used to buy clan clothes with. My father didn't like to spend money on heating the house and he had dreamt up a system that seemed more economical to him. From October to May he made us wear frightful shaggy underwear that covered us from neck to ankle and curled up under our stockings. Every morning before he left for work he would check under our skirts. The long johns were on. But as soon as he stepped out the door, we began to take them off. They never wore out, though to hear us talking you would have thought they were as fragile as cobwebs.

"They're really not very durable," we would say in sorrowful voices. "Perhaps we should ask for the next best quality."

From next best to better still, we wound up ordering pretty expensive underwear. But my father always approved this kind of purchase just as he did the girdles — I should say the invincible armour — that he made us wear. When the packages arrived we would undo them just enough to stir up their contents a little and then return them and ask for a refund. When the money came we would buy as many pieces of cloth as we were girls. As might be expected we cut out dresses for ourselves that didn't have a hint of a sleeve, that weren't overlong in the skirt and that were a great deal more décolleté than necessary. It was an entirely normal reaction and besides it took less material. In addition to this, our Aunt Berthe gave us her old dresses and sometimes some of her friends'. We were in no position to stand on pride. Even the sorriest old hand-me-down could be made into a blouse here or a skirt there. Our "chapels" we saved for going to mass in. Well, we won't labour the point.

As for my father, he was never pushed to such extremes. Come rain or shine, his wardrobe was always hung with a dozen expensive suits and as many pairs of shoes. He frequently repeated that there wasn't any sense in buying things that weren't of the best quality, but that was a principle he reserved exclusively for his own use. If he thought he had been extravagant, he tried to make us believe that he had "got that for a song," which was curious, because, as I need hardly say, he wasn't prompted by any fear of our reproaches. I remember one day after he had refused us a few dollars for some essential items in the morning, he came back the same evening laden down with boxes. He had bought himself, at one fell swoop, four superb summer suits which he poked at with a disdainful finger as if they had been dirty old rags.

"They're bargain stuff. The tailor absolutely had to get rid of them. At any price. He said to me, 'Just give me whatever you want.'"

As if by some miracle, the bargain articles fit him like a glove, like a fine kid glove.

"What a stroke of luck," we gurgled in various registers. "They couldn't fit you better if they'd been made to measure."

"Bah. They'll last for a while."

And to show his indifference he tossed all the suits in a pile on one of the chairs, saying it wasn't worth his trouble to hang them up right away.

This story amused us so much that we sometimes acted it out between ourselves like a little play: "The tailor threw himself down on his knees and said to me. . . ."

Another nice little farce came from the rigmarole about shoes. When we asked for a pair, all we normally got was our old ones resoled for the second or third time. When this happened, my father would exhume an old pair of his own which he would take to the shoemaker at the same time. Like practising what you preach. Afterwards he would walk around like a hero — for one whole day. Then he'd never wear those shoes again.

*   *   *

Grandfather died soon after school opened. Beginning in September, Grandmother had begun to write me again every week. At the end of the month, she told me that Grandfather was not well, that he hadn't been able to get over his sorrows and that his health was failing fast. Then there was one letter that was a little more optimistic, then another in which she said he had had a bad case of boils on his neck. I didn't know what diabetic anthrax was and wasn't unduly concerned. I wrote to Grandfather, enumerating all the cures the nuns used for boils. A few more days went by, and then one evening during the recess the Mother Superior called me in.

"Your aunt wants to speak to you on the telephone," she said.

I ran to the little room the telephone was in. Picking up the receiver, even before I could say hello, I heard someone crying.

"It's Aunt Berthe. Your grandfather is dead."

I couldn't find anything to say.

"I'm sorry," she said, "I wish I'd been able to break it more gently. I just couldn't."

Then she added:

"Don't cry, dear."

I wasn't crying. I was struck by a kind of horrible anger that didn't call for tears. My aunt explained that Grandfather would be laid out at her house in Quebec and that I should try to get permission from the nuns to go there.

Mother Superior was in her office right next door. I went to speak to her, and even without my asking — that was the kind of person she was — she said I could go to my aunt's as soon as Grandfather's body had arrived there. Before I went to bed I wrote a long letter to Grandmother. Today, thirty-five years afterwards, I have tears in my eyes as I write this page. That night I wrote three or four, and my eyes were as dry as an ancient desert.

Two days later Dine telephoned, we fixed a rendezvous and went to my aunt's house together. We were worried. What we were doing might cost us plenty, and once again I felt how much harder unhappiness is to bear when one can't abandon oneself to it completely but must keep part of oneself on guard against other dangers. In the kind of existence imposed on us, we were robbed of everything, pain and joy alike. But all I could do to get my own back was imagine incredible acts of vengeance, none of which came to fruition and which, for that matter, I gave up hoping for quite early in life.

So for the second time in the space of a few months I found myself in a room darkened by black drapes and, there in a coffin, one of the three people in the world for whom I felt a deep filial affection. Unlike Mother's, Grandfather's face was peaceful. Too peaceful, this calm didn't suit him at all. His grave expression seemed borrowed, and I couldn't recognize the joyful Grandfather I loved so well. It's true I hadn't seen him for eighteen months, since his visit to the convent. Grandmother arrived and took Dine and me into her arms. Both of them were crying and, because it was catching, I cried a little too. But my tears dried up right away. I was still in the clutches of a kind of dry fury.

Visitors began to arrive. I spoke to one lady — I won't forget her — by the name of Larivière. Dine had to leave at four, so she would be back at the house by the time my father came in. I stayed till seven, and my uncle drove me back to the convent.

I spent those last three hours almost alone with Grandmother who had grown tired of receiving so many people and had left this duty to my uncle and aunt. We sat together in a little room out of the main stream of traffic. She told me about Grandfather's last days. From the very start of the anthrax he had said, "I know this is the end," and for a week he had watched himself drawing closer and closer to it. The day before he died he had undergone surgery, and he never regained consciousness. And she told me everything he had said about me during those last days.

"You were the last person to make him laugh — with your recipes for poultices."

I was a little ashamed to have written jokes to a dying man, and it seemed to me that Grandmother should have been angry with me. I tried to excuse myself.

"Don't be sorry. It was so essential for him to be gay, and he hadn't laughed for months. He died of unhappiness. And he was only sixty-three."

We never mentioned the assassin's name. Grandmother had always forbidden me to judge him openly in her presence. But no one in the world could prevent me from judging him privately. After a painful silence, Grandmother began to go over in review all the memories that were so dear to us. Then, timidly, without much hope, I began to talk about the future.

"In seven years I'll be twenty-one. I'll get a job and come and live with you. Until then we'll see each other from time to time. When he's away on his trips in the summer holidays, I'll come to see you because you'll be back in Quebec. And for seven years I'll write to you every week."

Write every week — that's the only one of those projects I was able to fulfill. Before I left, I hugged and kissed her as though I was never going to stop. It was a good thing I did. I was never to see her again, living or dead.

A few days after these events, I got a frantic telephone call from Dine. Madame Larivière knew my father — she worked in the same ministry — and she had told him everything. Luckily, the old busybody hadn't noticed that Dine was there too. Otherwise, I don't know how we could have gotten out of it.

"You'll have to cook up a story. If you told Mother Sainte-Sylvie, maybe she could help you."

Dine unveiled her plan. I was shaking so my teeth chattered and I could hardly reply. In a few seconds' time, my face, my hair, my whole body, were as wet as if I had fallen into the water. I hung up and, completely shattered, made my way to the recreation room. Now I would have to reveal everything that I had been trying to hide for so long, and the thought of this did nothing to ease my terror.

At the time of the forced confidences I am speaking about I was Mother Sainte-Sylvie's pet. But afterwards all that ended. I knew that was what would happen, so I didn't let it bother me, for although I was attracted to her in a certain way I didn't really respect or admire her. Like Mother Saint-Fortunat she was passion's slave. She was in love and then out of love, and when she was out it was murder! She was a snob. Only the people who were rich and happy interested her.

When I came into the recreation room, she was surrounded by children. I asked to see her in private, the little ones left us, and we began to pace up and down the room. In silence.

"Well! I'm listening — "

So I wouldn't have time to think, I had rushed up to her when I came in and now I didn't know how to begin. I was unprepared and choked up. Over the next quarter of an hour I began I don't know how many sentences, and abandoned them all unfinished, because suddenly it seemed impossible to go on that way. So I would try another, only to discover that I couldn't work that one out either. Time passed.

"Come on, be brave," said Mother Sainte-Sylvie. "Recess will soon be over."

At last I managed to explain the gist of it and asked Mother Sainte-Sylvie to tell Mother Superior what had happened and beg her not to let me down if my father asked questions. I was counting on them to reply to the effect that they had read the obituary in the newspaper and, thinking to act for the best, had told me, "Your grandfather is dead, you must go."

"But your father will never believe that," Mother Sainte-Sylvie objected.

"Oh yes, if you know how to go about it, you can make him believe anything."

This rash reply scandalized the sister. But I had already been forced to say quite enough. I wasn't going to explain to her that my father's infernal pride would keep him from believing that any of us could ever really deceive him.

I never knew if the Mother Superior agreed to back up my lie. All I know is that the other nuns were informed of my family troubles. After that, I got nothing but icy stares and I often surprised excited conversations on the subject. One example occurred a few weeks later when I caught the flu and had to stay in bed. While pretending to be asleep — when we were sick it was just as well to feign sleep if the nuns came in, for they had a terrible propensity for pouring quarts of castor oil into us as soon as we opened an eye and this kind of treatment made me faint seven times in a row one flu-stricken day — well, pretending to be asleep I overheard the following conversation between two nuns:

"Her father is some kind of monster."

"What a little liar she is. She tries to let on that he's perfect. Did you know that her mother only had a second class funeral, and they say that he's quite rich. When the grandfather died. . . ."

The whole story I had had to confide to Mother Sainte-Sylvie was trotted out. Curled up under my sheets, I breathed like someone in a deep sleep and even snored a little from time to time. I wanted to hear everything. It wasn't very painful. What is dreadful is having to take that kind of insult openly and losing face and wishing you were dead rather than have to put up with it, when in spite of everything you are really very much alive and likely to remain so for a good long time.

When I was called into the parlour the next Sunday, I set out at a snail's pace. My father's face was twisted in fury.

"You disobeyed my orders," he began without even saying hello.

I could have said that he hadn't given me any orders in this matter. That would have been very bold, and I didn't have a speck of boldness in me.

"I forbade you to see your grandparents again. Why did you go there."

We were sitting near the Mother Superior's office. I could see her through the open door. She had her head turned a little in our direction and I was sure she could hear us. I told the lie I had got ready. I was afraid he would get up and go over to check my story. But he was much more courageous with us than with strangers. I knew that all along, but in my terror I had forgotten it.

He scolded me at length but quite low. When I realized that he wasn't going to do any of the things I dreaded he might, I stopped listening, just as we always did. I simply put on my glum look, which in my father's presence had become second nature in the family.

Marguerite and Thérèse listened without saying anything. For fear the facts might leak out, I hadn't dared tell them about grandfather's death. So that was the way they learned about it. When I had asked permission to go to my uncle's house there was no question of their coming along too. I can't remember why.

I discovered afterwards that my father had gone to Grandfather's funeral, as he was to go to Grandmother's later. The man was afraid of what people might say. At these ceremonies, he blatantly occupied the place due his relation as son-in-law. He had his name in the newspaper write-ups, as we saw in the clippings my uncle showed us; for my father pretended to have forgotten all about newspapers on those particular days.

All parlour sessions come to an end. I had lived on the strength of that faith for many years. After this one, I could breathe deeply for the first time in several days. For the first time, I could think about having lost my grandfather, instead of thinking ceaselessly about all the dangers that hung over me because of his death.

*　　*　　*

During the study period that followed, I was sharply rebuked by Mother Sainte-Sylvie. I wasn't much surprised. From the day I confided in her, she had grown increasingly cold. Bit by bit, it veered over to persecution.

This nun had come the year before, in the springtime. It had become urgent to replace poor Mother Saint-Léon who had suddenly turned quite wacky. For that matter, spring was a rough time for the nuns. When March and April came around, they were all on the verge of giving up. That's when the children got more and more difficult. Only the nuns who knew how to make themselves liked escaped this fate, and they were few and far between. Their example bore little fruit. For the most part the sisters sowed the wind all year long and folded up when the time came to reap the whirlwind. They were all convinced that love and authority were incompatible, and continued to believe so even when confronted by our vengeful intractability.

So all of a sudden, one spring morning, poor Mother Saint-Léon began to shout and bang her desk and stand up and shuffle around and sit down again and get up again, and in the end left the classroom at a dead run. Such an uproar followed in class that it reached the ears of the Mother Superior whose office was located two floors down. In spite of her asthma, she hurried up to see what was going on, restored order and set about looking for Mother Saint-Léon whom she found — one of us had been stationed to listen at the foot of the staircase — laughing, talking and gesticulating in the dormitory. The upshot of which was Mother Sainte-Sylvie.

I became her favourite on the very first day.

"What does 'insular' mean," she asked after reading a text in which the word appeared.

I was the only one to hold up a hand. I had dreamed of peaceful Pacific islands often enough the year I studied geography with Mother Marie-de-la-Trinité never to forget that word. I gave the definition, after which Mother Sainte-Sylvie asked in a cross voice:

"Why is this girl the only one who can answer? Aren't you all taking the same course?"

Whereupon a singular thing happened: all the little girls shouted out in chorus:

"She's not like us. She comes from a big convent."

Mother Sainte-Sylvie's loyalty to her own order brought the blood to her face. By dint of much shouting, she convinced us that her order was second to none. I was quite surprised by the whole affair. No one had ever spoken to me about my first convent, and all at once I discovered that if by chance I gave the right answer it was credited to the old school. Instead of being vexed, I felt wonderfully flattered and came closer to pardoning Mother Saint-Chérubin than ever before.

Like all convent girls the world over, every day at noon we went out for a walk, two by two, followed by one of the nuns.

"Won't you walk with me?" asked Mother Sainte-Sylvie.

She had pretty features, and if the convent rule had allowed her to use a little powder on her red complexion she would have been almost beautiful. Besides, she wasn't afflicted, as almost all the nuns were, with that horrible accent which I found so repulsive. She asked me many very pointed questions about my family, about my father's job — she suffered from extreme snobbery, money snobbery, the worst kind — and my replies must have seemed satisfactory, for I was accepted from that day on. When she discovered that on top of that I was cousin to the mayor, who was a Supreme Court judge, acceptance became a passion. As time went by, and particularly after she learned about my family's disgrace, she got the idea of transferring her affection directly to my cousins, the mayor's daughters, which left me with the impression that I had played the role of go-between.

I liked to be with her on our walks in the palmy days of our affair, although such occasions were often a source of embarrassment to me because of the subject of our conversations, which was almost always our families, their style of life, their social activities, their receptions, invitations and so on. But it was even more gruesome to have to walk with my schoolmates. Like me, they nearly all had big sisters. Theirs had begun to "go out with boys."

"Does your big sister go out with boys?"

I had to say yes. Otherwise no one would have ever said another word to me. I invented names, deliveries of flowers, fabulous dates. Once I got going, I didn't know where to stop. I went on and on. My sister's boyfriends were always built like young gods, and the bouquets they sent were never less than six dozen roses.

"Six dozen?"

"He's rich. He lives in Montreal."

At least it was hard to check up on a Montrealer.

"Did you do any entertaining over the Christmas holidays?"

"Yes. We had a huge ball."

"A ball? Even though you were in mourning?"

Whoops! I didn't know how to get out of that one. I embarked on tortuous explanations of how my father, torn between his bitter grief and his desire not to let our life become too sad, had decided, with a heavy heart, to think only of us.

"'One must live with the living,' he said, 'I have to think of your future.'"

Once again I didn't know where to stop, and moving sentiments gave way to pious thoughts, until I had brought my listeners to the verge of tears.

In September it was even worse. I don't know whether the other girls lied as much as I did, but at least they seemed to have travelled a little. I had never been farther than Sainte-Anne-de-Beaupré for our annual pilgrimage which was not, I can assure you, a pleasure trip. So I plunged into descriptions of outings that took me so far I didn't know how to get back. Why, I often asked myself, haven't I got the right to tell the truth? It isn't my fault I lead the life I do. But in my first convent I had known a little girl whose father was quite like mine. Like mine, he only came on visiting days to scold. That was humiliating enough. But Marie-Antoinette added to this the humiliation of frankness.

"My father treats us like dogs," she would say innocently. "My mother is a martyr."

After such revelations, the girls would go and play somewhere else, and I would be left the only one to share confidences I could have duplicated word for word myself. But I didn't dare linger, for Marie-Antoinette was the plague. Nonetheless I envied her a little. I thought her courageous. Maybe she was just naive.

I preferred lying. Inventing trips and balls was something I could do. But then one day I found myself making up film scenarios. That was harder.

Until Jeanne and Olivine arrived at the convent, there wasn't much talk of movies. Then came these two fans who spent all their holidays watching John Gilbert kissing Garbo on the mouth. Merciful heavens!

Film fever spread like measles. Soon I was the only one never to have set foot in a movie house. When I noticed that my friends were beginning to hold their noses in the air when they spoke to me, I decided the time had come for a major move.

"If you tell Mother Superior that I have to go to the dentist," I said to my sister Dine, "I could get out next Thursday and spend the afternoon with you. I never get out."

Everything went according to plan. I came back to the convent whispering that I had been to the movies. I had taken the name of the film and the names of the actors from the newspaper, and so I wouldn't get too far off the track, I had written a scenario, just the main events, leaving the rest to the inspiration of the moment. My story was such a tear-jerker that my listeners swore they were all going to see it if it was still on the next time they were free.

Having my cousins in the same convent didn't help things. On the one hand, I was constantly quaking for fear they would explode my stories of balls or excursions; and on the other, I was afraid my pretended passion for the cinema would become known at home. We didn't have much to do with them, my father was very anti-family and we didn't see any more of his cousins than of his brother, which is to say only when he needed a doctor, like him, or a notary or a lawyer like the others. We kept on strict business terms with our relations. But these cousins kept in relatively close touch with my aunt and my paternal grandmother. A perfectly innocent remark could plunge me into inextricable complications. And yet this threat didn't stop me from inventing tales that became more and more extraordinary. I was like a child who steals money to win friends by buying them presents. Only I gave them stories.

*   *   *

Grandmother continued to write me every week. This woman, who had lived so comfortably all her life, was now installed in a single room. Grandfather had left her a little money, but she was still young and might live a long time yet and she was afraid she might end her days in need. This kind of anxiety might have been spared her if we hadn't cost her so much. My grandparents had always spent a great deal of money on us. For three years they had put up Mother and her four children, then they had paid for Dine's schooling, and they had clothed us all as if we had been destitute. We weren't, and they knew it; yet they continued to give open-handedly. When I learned that she was living in a rented room, I was horrified and I wrote to her saying everything I have just written. She replied with a gay letter. She claimed she was happier like this:

"I've got fewer worries than I would have in an apartment, it's like being in a hotel, I've got nothing to do, I can go out whenever I want to," she said.

Go out? One day, a few months after Grandfather's death, she was forced to admit that she was too sick to go out; hearing her coughing, her landlady had taken fright and had asked her to leave the house. "The landlady is a bit touched," she wrote, "all I've got is a bad case of bronchitis." And she finished her letter by saying that she would have to find something else, and that she would write soon giving me her new address. Two weeks went by and at last I had a letter from her. On the back of the envelope she had written her return address: "Laval Hospital."

I knew that Laval was a sanatorium for TB. But, true to style, with that natural tendency I have to refuse to see troubles even when they're toppling down on me, I didn't understand. What earthly reason could Grandmother have for writing to me from this hospital? I tore open the envelope with great curiosity.

"My pretty little darling: Well, here I am at the sanatorium. I thought I had nothing more than a stubborn case of bronchitis, and I scarcely paid any attention to it. It took the insinuations of that land-lady, and the urgings of your Uncle Eugène, to get me to have a check up. It seems there are several shadows on my lungs. The doctor says I was weakened by too strict a regimen at the time I was taking care of your Mother, and I wasn't able to escape contagion. He could have added that I have lost all desire to live, and when that happens the microbes have an easy time of it. I cried a good deal the first few days, not because I am going to die soon, but because I know that now I'll never see you again, either you or the others. And, since that's the way things are, I would like to die as soon as possible."

I had to destroy this letter before I returned to my father's house, but up till then I read it every day, so many times that I would be surprised if there were more than three or four words changed. She only wrote me one other sad letter. That was when Aunt Maria decided to go to see her and took along snapshots of each of us. "You've all changed so much," she wrote, "that I can hardly recognize you. When I look at those photographs, I have the feeling that I've already been dead for a long time. I would rather have kept you in my memory the way you were. I suppose Maria thought she was acting for the best. The evening after her visit I had my first haemoptysis." All the other letters were amusing. At the San there was always something funny happening that she would comment on as though she were only there to laugh. Sometimes she would scold me a little if I revealed my grudges and rebelliousness to her. "You must offer all that up to God," she wrote, and at the time I replied, "I don't think that God gives a damn about me, and I might add that the feeling is mutual." I was served up a long sermon but nothing shocked about it. "It's unhappiness that makes you say that, and resignation isn't given to everyone."

I received the last letter from her in February 1930, towards the end of the month. She told me that she was getting worse and worse and expected the end from one day to the next. Young people are so stupid. Instead of answering the first things that came into my head, I started to hunt around for the kind of thing you could say to someone who is going to die, and to tear up copy after copy. I could never get it right. Days went by without my finding the right words.

* * *

"Mother Superior wants to speak to you," I was told one evening.

She was standing at the end of the hall with a newspaper in her hand.

"I thought it was my duty to tell you," she said, "someone has to. Your grandmother died yesterday."

I hung my head in shame.

"I think you had better not go this time."

Without raising my head, I mumbled, "Yes, yes."

"You loved one another very much, I know," the Mother Superior went on. "You wrote to each other often. As far as that's concerned, you can rely entirely on my discretion."

I wished myself a hundred miles from there, and she knew it.

"You mustn't be ashamed. Don't think of anything but your grandmother."

She was right. Unfortunately, I couldn't think of anything but my father. I turned and fled, full of tears that dried before they fell.

*　　*　　*

He came to the parlour the following Sunday. Marguerite and Thérèse were there, but he only spoke to me.

"Your Grandmother de la Chevrotière is dead. She had been at Laval Hospital for a long time."

"Oh, really?"

I was filled with a sort of sad pleasure to hear him tell me things that I knew better than he did. Once again I had cheated him well and truly.

"The good Lord has punished her too," he concluded. "I can't tell you to pray for her. In the place they are, none of those people ('those people' were Mother, Grandfather, and Grandmother) need our prayers. I don't think it's too bold a judgment to consider them all damned. And if I say that, it's because I've got my reasons."

More of those heaven-sent revelations. If he had dared, he would have told me that the Angel Gabriel came visiting him at night to keep him posted on the fate of the dead. What he didn't say, but what we learned afterwards, was that Grandmother had sent to ask if we might see her one last time, and he had refused.

The day after I learned of Grandmother's death, the Mother Superior asked the girls to remember her in their prayers. One after another, the girls came to ask me why I hadn't requested leave. I answered as best I could. Afterwards I saw them whispering together in corners, and gathered from this that everyone knew the whole story.

I don't suppose that Mother Sainte-Sylvie made much effort to restrain herself on the slippery slopes of indiscretion. After Grandfather's death and the secrets I had to share, in a very few weeks she had grown to hate me in a way that made my life rather uncomfortable. She beat me every time she could find an excuse. But there was one time I was the one to have the last word. That spring I was afflicted with frequent and copious nosebleeds. They made her wild, and she claimed I did it on purpose. How did I go about it? She didn't say that.

"May I go out?" I asked her one day in church, with my handkerchief soaked in blood.

Unmoved, she sent me back to my place, and I had to bleed into my scarf. Then, when we were all back in the playground, she accused me of having blown my nose.

"Well, I have to blow it once in a while," I replied.

In answer to that, she began to hit me in the face, a series of short right and left jabs, and my nose began to bleed again.

Passing close to Simone, who was the Superior's niece, I whispered:

"Ask permission to go and see your aunt, and tell her to call me in."

Five minutes later I was called to her office. In the meantime I had lost a lot of blood. I arrived at her door weak-kneed, hands and face very bloody. On the point of nervous collapse, I fell into a chair and burst out sobbing. The Mother Superior got a towel and basin of water and washed me. Then she made me take a little cognac which relaxed me immediately and I was able to tell her what had happened.

When she was angry, Mother Superior's voice swelled until it threatened to bring the walls down.

"Struck you? In the face? This is not permitted," she cried. "Not permitted. Go and bring her here at once."

And she was still shouting when I went out the door.

"Mother Superior wants you," I announced to Mother Sainte-Sylvie, who had lost all her colour.

When recess was over and we went into the convent, it was still going on.

"You're behaving in a disgraceful way. You have no respect for the habit you're wearing."

And on and on it went. For once I hadn't been slapped with impunity. It was the first and last time, so I have kept a very sharp memory of it.

If, after that, Mother Sainte-Sylvie restrained herself from striking me, her treatment wasn't exactly what you would call tender. It was useless for me to ask her for anything. Without letting me finish my sentence, she would burst out, "No, no," and there was nothing for me to do but go back to my place. That got her into more trouble. To celebrate some feast or other, we had prepared a sung mass. Three of us were soloists. This mass was so beautiful, it seems, that the nuns asked to have it repeated the following Sunday. The only thing was that Albertine was spending that Sunday with her family. Mother Saint-Pascal, who had rehearsed us, stopped by my bed the night before and whispered:

"You will sing Albertine's solo. Get dressed quickly tomorrow morning and come down and try it over before mass."

It was a very difficult solo and not in my register for, as strange as this might seem to those who know me, I was a soprano, while Albertine was a contralto. So I had a bad case of jitters. In the morning I got dressed in five minutes and went to ask Mother Sainte-Sylvie's permission to go down to the music room.

"No."

I returned to my place and went down to the chapel with the rest. Françoise sang her part. I sang the one that was originally mine. When Albertine's came up, I had completely forgotten what little I knew from hearing it over three or four times. Mother Saint-Pascal played the introduction and gave me the note with an insistent finger. Stare as I might at the words on the sheet, they didn't mean a thing to me. The piece began, I remember, with "O Lord, O Lord," but all I would have been capable of singing would have been the first "O" on the note that was drilling my ears. It really wasn't worth the trouble.

"Why didn't you come and rehearse it?" whispered Mother Saint-Pascal, who was beginning to panic.

I saw red.

"Mother Sainte-Sylvie wouldn't let me," I said out loud.

And so saying, I threw my music book with all my strength. Sheets landed all over the place. Every head was turned in my direction, and the vicar interrupted his *oremus*. Mother Saint-Pascal wept while playing a little improvised air which ended the mass.

Mother Superior occupied the *prie-Dieu* nearest the choir. She had heard my reply. She was waiting for us by the door.

"What is it this time?" she asked, bearing straight down on Mother Sainte-Sylvie, who began to stammer.

Mother Saint-Pascal was still weeping. Her elocution wasn't too good either. Anyway, Mother Sainte-Sylvie was summoned to present herself in the Superior's office after breakfast and the walls trembled again for a good while. After this incident, I had the feeling of being well protected against Mother Sainte-Sylvie, and even if Mother Superior couldn't save me from a host of petty vexations that weren't worth complaining about, at least I didn't have to put up with any more serious trouble.

* * *

It was about this time that Mother Saint-Pascal began to grow very fond of me. This left me more bored than pleased. I didn't feel like loving anyone any more. With a joy that should have moved me, she loaded me with presents she had begged from her brother. That didn't touch me. I had a heart of stone. It was years before I could make it a habitable place again. The living exasperated me, all of them, breathing and eating, while the only ones I loved were rotting away in the ground. There were my brothers and sisters, of course, but for a child the love of other children is not enough. And then, Mother Saint-Pascal was a nun. Another nun! Years had to go by and I had to write this book before I could perceive that from time to time one of them had crossed my path who wasn't a shrew, who, I would even have to admit, was a really fine person. I'm glad to say that. It warms my heart to discover that I wasn't always as unhappy as I remember myself being.

"What are you going to be when you grow up?" Mother Saint-Pascal would ask me.

"Certainly not a nun," I would answer.

The term "nun" was already insulting enough. I added a lash of scorn in my intonation. But she didn't seem to register the blow.

"You haven't got the vocation?"

"The vocation! Don't make me laugh. Is it the vocation that makes Mother Sainte-Sylvie hit me in the face?"

The poor girl would join her hands, sigh, and suggest that I offer all that up to God. I'd had a bellyful of that suggestion. I would just as soon have gone without the merits and graces earned by blows received. It's great to save one's soul, but there must be other ways of doing it, ways I was too busy getting beaten to have the leisure to worry about. Choosing the words most likely to horrify her, I would tell Mother Saint-Pascal my feelings on that subject.

"Don't try to play the wicked girl with me," she would reply. "You're really good underneath."

"I'm not interested in being good. I'd rather be beautiful any time."

"To you beauty seems preferable to goodness?" she would exclaim, mournfully. The poor sister was painfully ugly.

"A hundred times better," I would say aggressively.

A tear drooped in her eye, but I avoided noticing it. I had an inoffensive one in my clutches. I was going to push my advantage to the hilt, and make her pay for all the rest.

"For that matter, you're far from plain," she would say.

To which I would reply with remarks that seemed, at fifteen, the height of cynicism: "I'll put it to good use, you can be sure of that," and other inventions of this sort, which left Mother Saint-Pascal aghast.

As far as that was concerned, I didn't need her praises to make me think myself stunning. For the last few years my father had worked so hard to convince me that I was ugly and awkward, that I had naturally concluded the contrary, albeit a contrary out of all proportion with reality.

"Say what you like, mister, I've got eyes to see," I would say to myself every time he got off on that tack.

Convinced that he couldn't tell the truth in this matter more than in any other, I spent hours making faces in front of the mirror. He was right about my ankles, I would concede that. It was true they weren't as slim as they might be, but since this defect came from his side of the family and not Mother's where wrists and ankles are very slender, I judged that he should offer me apologies instead of criticism, and this grievance kept me from being too unhappy about my poor ankles. Common sense, and with it a just appreciation of my good features which have never surpassed an agreeably average norm, came back to me after adolescence.

When a girl in a convent is the favourite of a well-established sister who is in a position of authority and has the right to voice an opinion on most matters, she usually reaps some benefit from this situation — as long as it lasts. Sister Saint-Pascal didn't enjoy any authority. Compared to the others, her position was more like that of a whipped dog. Being the apple of her eye only won me a share in the general animosity that surrounded her. If I had loved her I might have experienced a sort of joy in sharing this. All I experienced was irritation, and I learned that there is no exasperation worse than the kind that comes from people who love us but whom we do not love in return. This was aggravated by my tendency of giving way to pity to the point of feigning love, by not knowing how to be constant in pity and, consequently, by being doubly irritated both by what I had given and what I had to take back.

After I left the convent she wrote me long letters which I didn't always answer. If I did reply, her letters became interminable since the dear thing had so much to say about every last word I had written. The day she sent me twenty-five closely written pages — and all in a thoroughly discouraging hand — I tossed the letter in the wastebasket without reading it, and never wrote to her again despite the heartbroken letters that followed. While I didn't give much thought to this business, still I was struck by the constancy — I would have said obstinacy — of Mother Saint-Pascal. Was it enough to make love last to answer it with indifference? The world of feelings seemed to me to be set up like a vast game organized by the clever and the insincere, a game you had to be pretty shrewd to play. And when I did fall in love the first few times, I quickly spoiled everything by my clumsy scheming.

However, I did learn one true thing, that love can perform miracles. It's not just hearsay. Mother Saint-Pascal accomplished the following miracle. She convinced my father that it was necessary for me to learn the piano. No, that's the wrong way to put it. He wasn't convinced at all. But she pressured him so, with such a gentle obstinacy, that finally, hypnotized by this innocent creature who continued untremblingly to plead for me after his first rebukes, he gave in. This miracle took place on Low Sunday. That year our Easter mass had been so brilliant that it was decided to do it over again for the parents at visiting time. We had got up a sort of oratorio in which I sang the role of Mary Magdalen. I began with a *"Raboni!"* that made the plaster statues in the chapel tremble on their pedestals.

"It must be a real cry," Mother Saint-Pascal had told me time and again during rehearsals.

With my lungs, I managed a shout that gave to little Françoise's reply, *"Noli me tangere,"* a real sense of urgency. That was what impressed my father, I think. Coming out of the chapel, he showered such effusive praise on me, the one who usually never did anything right and was expecting nothing better than the usual acid remarks, that I thought I must be dreaming. Mother Saint-Pascal took this opportunity to speak to him pathetically about "talent going to waste." In short, after half an hour's discussion, my father, back to the wall, gave his assent. The next morning I began my first scales. Mother Saint-Pascal was radiant.

My own secret wish was to become a singer, not a pianist. I wanted to learn how to read music, how to carry a melody, how to accompany myself just enough to study a piece. I already saw myself in a décolleté evening dress giving concerts. In my father's teeth. This is what the hero, Robert, did — less the evening dress — in my last novel. Like him, I always wanted to learn *solfeggio.* Alas! now I can't even distinguish a *do* from a *mi* in a clutch of notes. That shows how brief my musical training was. My ignorance in music has weighed on me all my life. To really understand something I have always had to verify its first premises, and to know music properly I would have had to learn to play. It has remained for me a joy half-possessed, a pleasure comparable to that sharp but primitive and inexplicable pleasure I take in the sound of cascading water, the wind, a harmonious voice, a lovely laugh. It's always the same backwoods situation. But my life is full of these regrets. It's the same thing for painting, I showed some talent in that direction. For the theatre too — I could have acted a little, I think. I would have liked to swim like a fish instead of sitting with my feet in the water on the edge of the pool. All I know is how to sew and cook. I am undeniably a product of that age when women always "knew too much."

*   *   *

That year we had a dazzling prize day, replete with songs and poems. Dazzling and interminable for the simple reason that there was a guest of honour who spoke at length. He made a little speech to every prize winner, with much shaking of hands, many bravos, and then bravissimos. All in all, it took quite a while. This guest was Monseigneur Camille Roy who, one of my friends tells me, was disrespectfully nicknamed Camomille by the students at Laval University because of his soporific qualities. That was pretty cocky when you consider that he was one of our leading literary lights. Some say that, like Abbé Casgrain, Monseigneur Camille Roy was a bit overrated. But that's spiteful gossip. Camille Roy was an extraordinary man. Perhaps not in literature but most certainly in jewellery. He produced some really priceless pearls. "Boileau's rod, now limp, now lashing, is manipulated by a diligent contributor who signs himself *The Quiet Spectator.*" That comes from page sixty-five of *Nos Origines littéraires*, and to write that I think you've got to be not quite like anyone else. It's not possible otherwise.

In honour of this hero, we recited Sully Prud'homme's *The Swan* to the music of "The Swan" by Saint-Saëns. I imagine it must have been frightfully sentimental, but we thought it very moving. I don't remember any hitches in that particular presentation.

But there was no scarcity of hitches in our convent shows. When my sisters and I begin to talk about them, they come back in floods. You should hear my eldest sister tell the story about the pilgrim. It was a play in verse. One little girl just had one line to say: "That pilgrim was indeed a saintly man." She was supposed to come in right after Dine. She had got that much straight. But Dine had several speeches. In her excitement, the little girl lost track of her cue, and as soon as my sister had finished her first speech, she burst out:

"That pilgrim was indeed a saintly man."

"Sh!"

The poor little thing, overcome with confusion, hid behind her companions and waited attentively until Dine spoke again.

"That pilgrim was indeed a saintly man."

"Oh, shut up. It's not your turn."

Alas! When her turn did come after two or three more unlucky interventions, she shut up like a clam. No amount of signalling that this was the right moment could persuade her to make her statement on the character of the saintly pilgrim. Her neighbour had to fill in for her in the midst of great general hilarity.

Everyone went wild too, the day Dine played the title role in a pious little piece called *Naïm's Widow's Son*. It was given in the large music room, and bless me if the large music room didn't hold all of three hundred people! Talk about intimidating. They got through the rehearsals without any horseplay, but the night of the performance when Dine stepped down to the forestage to declare: "I died and came to life again," the whole audience burst out laughing. The good old Gallic common sense had taken over. Ingloriously, they had to finish the play to a doubled-up house.

There was a better sense of humour in that convent than in the second one, where any blunder immediately took on an air of calamity. I remember one Sunday in particular.

That morning, before high mass, Mother Sainte-Jeanne came to tell me that it was the Superior's feast day and that a little celebration was being prepared for her. A programme of songs and poems had been drawn up which we would have to memorize during the day. My part was to recite a piece of verse by — I don't remember who, some cunning knave, a very witty fellow. It was called *The Church of the Madeleine*:

> The Church of the Madeleine
> Stands empty all week long,
> But Sundays, brilliant women
> In their finery there do throng.

I can't remember any more. At this late date, well, that's just too bad! The trouble was, the night of the celebration I couldn't get any farther than this modest beginning either. I have a slow memory. It has always taken me more than a day to learn a sonnet. I had warned Mother Sainte-Jeanne about this, and she immediately began to talk about bad will. Good or bad, that evening, try as I might — at one point the Mother Superior herself was prompting me — it was no go. I have neglected to say that I was first on the programme. After that, no one else could get through her number. Finally, the Mother Superior, worn out by our bungling, rose to thank us long before we had run through the programme. And Mother Sainte-Jeanne never spoke to me again. Not the least little word, right through to the end of the year. A real papal mule.

*   *   *

The holidays that followed this were very important — my eldest sister got a boyfriend. It was never difficult for us to get boyfriends. The hard thing was to keep them. We could only see them when my father was away on a trip, which meant about one week out of three during the summer and not at all in winter. Generally, spring found us quite low in suitors. Few boys could pass such a long endurance test. At the beginning of this hibernation of ours they would telephone a little, during my father's office hours. But that stopped soon enough. Besides, this state of affairs generated a kind of mistrust. We were obviously so miserable that we had to count on marriage to extricate us. Speaking personally, I would gladly have given away my eighteen years to the first lovesick dog disguised as a husband that came along. Now, in those days, girls on this continent weren't supposed to want to get married. Nothing scared boys off faster than girls who were thinking of marriage, even a little. So they all feigned a great detachment in this matter and let it be understood they would only resign themselves to that extremity if they met a man who was absolutely extraordinary. That didn't help much, because all boys think themselves extraordinary.

And yet, people got married, I don't know just how. Sometimes it was after several years, not of engagement, but of what was called "keeping company." After ten or twelve years of keeping company, one sometimes had the feeling that the boy gave in because he really couldn't drop a girl he had kept tied up for so long. (But some of them did find a way and, more especially, the courage to do this, and that set the town talking.) The Depression was often held responsible for this phenomenon. Responsible? An accomplice at the most! The Depression took the blame for everything. I claim that those boys only wanted to marry girls who had given long proof that they didn't want to marry. It's easy to see what various forms of mistrust led them to such an attitude.

* * *

Our boyfriends came to us by way of a few girlfriends, old convent schoolmates, the latter as clandestine as the former. Since my father forbade us either to go out or to have people in, we didn't have the right to have girlfriends any more than boyfriends. Three or four times in seven or eight years he granted us permission to go to tea at our cousins', the daughters of the judge and mayor.

"I trust Marie-Louise [she was the wife of the judge and mayor and my father's first cousin] won't let some young coxcomb sneak into her salon," he would say on giving his consent, after having hesitated for hours. "But if that should happen [poor Marie-Louise] you will get up and leave immediately."

As far as virtue was concerned, my father wouldn't trust any woman, not even cousin Marie-Louise who transpired decency at every pore. On this account it was just as well to hide from him girls who did not belong to the immediate family. That's what we had to do, literally, one day when he came back unexpectedly from a trip while a friend of ours, Aline, was in the house. We had to hide her in one of the icy rooms in the attic. She spent five or six hours there — we took her sandwiches from time to time — listening, despite herself, to my father vituperating flesh coloured stockings, which according to him were just as reprehensible as transparent ones. When he left, at last, Aline came out of hiding extremely alert to the fact that it wasn't for nothing stockings like that had been invented.

As I was saying, my sister got a boyfriend. It was the evening of August 9. I won't forget it. For my sisters and me that was the night of our first kiss. Because the boyfriend wasn't alone. He had a friend with him. We had met them at Annette's. They had driven us back in their car and before they let us get out the two boys had kissed my two sisters while I sat back in my corner like a chaperone.

"O.K., what about me?" I said in a haughty voice, for I found it a bit thick to be cast in such a role.

Without a word, the friend turned around and kissed me, too. So I had no complaints.

After which we found ourselves in the living room like three visitors. Quite perplexed visitors. Was it really the thing to do to kiss a girl the first time you saw her? Should we have refused? And if we had, would we have seemed perfect ninnies? And what about the boyfriend who had already asked if he could come back, wouldn't he be put off forever by a refusal if it was really the thing to do? Unable to solve all these problems, we had to lay them aside until the next morning.

Alone in my room, even though the midnight hour was very late for me, I thought it all over for a long time before going to sleep. The thing that struck me most about the whole business was the difference between what I felt and what my sisters said. I didn't feel the least inclination to call what we had done wicked or dangerous. The kisses seemed very important to me at the moment, but very trifling in the long run. On final analysis, my prevailing feeling after this experience was one of curiosity.

The next day something else turned up. Wasn't what we had done a sin? Wasn't it urgent to go and confess it? At the thought of it, I was all of a flutter. The more I pondered, the less I felt like giving up this project of going to confession. My sisters weren't quite so sure, but I threw all my weight against the wheel. As a rule my confessions were of two kinds, always the same and used alternatively: ones where I confessed three acts of disobedience and four lies, and ones where I confessed four acts of disobedience and three lies, to which I sometimes added lack of attention during prayers. So this time I wasn't going to give up a revelation as stunning as the one I had to make. And off we went, one of my sisters and I, the other having decided to wait for the vicar's verdict before going to all that trouble.

I entered the confessional in a high state of excitement. I was to come out aghast. What I learned in there, all at once, takes some telling. Here is approximately how it went:

"I did something, I don't know if — I don't know how to — "

"Do you want me to question you? Does it have to do with a young man?"

"Yes."

"Have you any reason to think you are pregnant?"

Well, hardly, and moreover I wasn't very sure what reasons would make you think you were. All that was far from clear in my own mind.

"Did he kiss you on the breasts or on your private parts?"

Parts? What parts? I hastily said no, even before I understood very well, but understanding dawned little by little. Well! Some people did funny things! It takes all kinds to make a world! I really looked silly with my poor little kiss on the mouth.

"Did he put his tongue into your mouth?"

Ugh! Well, no, if you must know, not even that. I felt my stomach turn. Once the questioning was finished — and at the point it should have begun — I was given three Aves penance, and absolution. My sister, who was waiting at the other side of the confessional, was only asked the last question. The vicar had grasped that it had all taken place communally, and that if she had done more than me, it couldn't be much more.

On the way back to the house, we exchanged impressions, but I was so horribly embarrassed that I couldn't bring myself to tell everything. Maybe my sister felt the same and for that reason only mentioned the question about the tongue in the mouth. Anyway, when my other sister heard about the three Aves penance, she decided that it wasn't a very serious matter and that she wasn't going to walk three-quarters of an hour in the August sun for so little. In this she was greatly mistaken. It wasn't so little. At any rate, as far as I was concerned, I was overwhelmed, and it gave me plenty to think about for years afterwards.

*   *   *

I went back to the convent very different to the girl who had come out in June. Previously I had always listened with total incomprehension to the confidences of girls who had fallen in love with their cousins or with the boy next door, but now I understood. There was no question of seeing Jean-Marie again (that was the boyfriend's friend's name), but since I was burning to tell my story — I had been the only one without a cousin for long enough — and since I could hardly admit that there hadn't been any follow-up, I began to invent an interminable novel. During the holidays I had seen him every day, and since we had come back I had heard from him by a letter my sister had brought to the parlour, or else, taking advantage of the Mother Superior's absence (her office was next to the little telephone room) I had been able to call him at his house and had first spoken to his sister, who was so pretty and who liked me so much, and on and on and on.

My sister had received a snapshot of her boyfriend in which his friend appeared too, so I got Jean-Marie's head for my locket in exchange, of course, for the pledge of my passionate love (the passion had come from talking about it so much), and equipped with a proof as tangible as a photograph, I came close to believing my own lies. I was in love, I was loved, I wasn't the prissy little prig I had been in the past. Soon I would leave the convent, find Jean-Marie, or another — more likely another, I knew that well enough after all — and I would be married in less time than it takes to dream it.

That year, on arriving at the convent, I found I don't know how many new nuns. A wind of change had swept the place as never before: a new Superior, a new music mistress, and several others. I think that Mother Sainte-Sylvie had left, I'm not sure; at any rate Mother Saint-Pascal had gone.

The nun who taught my class was called Mother Saint-Justinien. My God, but she was ugly and surly and spiteful. It wasn't a nose she had, it was a veritable insult to good manners. And those eyes! You would have said two little holes with some dirty water rolling around in them instead of irises. Positively discouraging.

Sometimes it was my chore — yes, chore — to be her partner on the school walk. She used to tell me over and over again about her hatred for the Daughters of Wisdom. She had a sister who had entered this order, where she had been martyrized and almost let die of appendicitis. In conjunction with this appendicitis there was a dreary story about a typewriter — in those days typewriters were as heavy as locomotives — which Mother Saint-Justinien's sister had been forced to carry around, an imposition that came jointly from all the Daughters of Wisdom it seemed, so completely was the resulting bitterness fixed on the entire community. I was treated to the retelling of this drama nearly as often as I had to walk with Mother Saint-Justinien, and always with the same show of anger: reddening of face, clenching of fists and maybe even grinding of teeth. It amused me to hear a nun rail against her own sisterhood. It was probably considered a pretty big sin, and nothing pleases children more than to catch people they don't like in error. At my age I still followed the law of the jungle. I didn't like Mother Saint-Justinien, I wouldn't have liked her sister, I was certain of that, and it didn't occur to me that these two poor girls loved each other and suffered from each other's unhappiness.

When she wasn't telling me the story of the typewriter, Mother Saint-Justinien used to talk to me about religious vocations. I don't know if they were offering a bounty for recruits that year, a double ration of dessert perhaps, but they were keen on finding "subjects." Whatever must be, must be. With my taste for dramatizing everything my inevitable response was to feign a lively interest. Out of the prop shop I got a large pair of ecstatic eyes, turned on my warmest voice, and was ready for an idle hour's humbug. This amused me for a month or so. Then I was ready for some other kind of fun. Sister Saint-Justinien never forgave me.

To be truthful, I must say that these conversations took a turn towards reciprocal confidences, doubtless quite sincere on her part, but once again, on my side, straight from the prop shop and embellished with stories of interventions which were probably celestial and at any rate perfectly decisive. To put it mildly, my retraction, when it came, was taken as an insult. I remember, for example, that she often spoke to me, with transparent innuendos, about the horror the idea of marriage inspired in her, and that my own replies on the subject had been served up in a sauce of "rather death than defilement."

All of a sudden, quite quickly, things began to spoil. Someone told on Simone, Olivine and me, saying we had been holding heretical conversations. First of all, we had said that the story of Jonah in the whale was all a hoax, and then that the one about Elisha having no less than forty-two children fed to the bears because they had laughed at his bald spot, was absolutely disgusting. We had lost the faith, that was quite evident, and it became an urgent matter to turn us out. I believe that about the first of December it was decided we would be kicked out at Christmas. From that time on, our copybooks came back with neither corrections nor marks, we were never asked any questions in class, and Mother Saint-Justinien let me read *The Road of Tears*.

This novel was one of a small gift of books from some unknown benefactor. It was kept on the library shelf, and no one was allowed to touch it.

"You can read it," Mother Saint-Justinien said to me one day, in the tone one would use in speaking to one of the damned, if one happened to meet him on the road to eternity.

"And what about me? Can I read it after?" one of my school-mates asked.

"No, not you. It might be bad for you."

"Then why can Claire read it?"

"Nothing can be too bad for her any more," Mother Saint-Justinien replied in oracular tones.

A charming woman!

I moved off with *The Road of Tears* under my arm. There was never a daring novel (daring in Mother Saint-Justinien's eyes) that more emphatically turned its reader towards inoffensive books. Spurred on by vanity, I couldn't make up my mind to stop reading it, and I was bored to death! If that was what daring was — There was a story about some village adultery in it (more like infidelity, for I never caught the guilty parties in bed) which seemed to me — and my innocence would have astounded Mother Saint-Justinien — to be the most ridiculous thing in the world. How dumb did you have to be to fall for another woman when you already had one at home? Can you imagine? I went on reading in the hope, always frustrated, of finding at least one paragraph where "things that couldn't hurt me any more" would be told. I found nothing but boredom and that wasn't, I think, the kind of evil the nun feared would pervert my schoolmates, for boredom was recognized as a saintly thing. As for what I imagined I might find there, I wouldn't be capable of saying what it was today. Very probably I expected the description of kisses — with the tongue in the mouth since that was the way it was done according to the vicar — exchanged between a girl and a boy and not between partners one of whom was already married. In the end, I understood less and less what could motivate these people who couldn't get married, and abandoned *The Road of Tears* halfway through.

"You've finished it already? I can see you simply devoured it," said the perfidious Mother Saint-Justinien.

"I only read half. It was too badly written."

Bam! This was said in a tone of disgusted superiority. Not at all displeased to let it be known that I might be so lost I could read daring novels without danger but I still required them to be well written, I went back to bury myself in my anthology of selected poems. Reading these fragments opened endless avenues of reverie for me: one day I would be free to read the whole poems from which these extracts seemed to have been chosen with the express intention of driving me wild with curiosity. I also owned an anthology which had a lot of Musset in it. I learned his *Lucie* by heart. I started to copy out poems and made my own anthology — a sampling of everything I came across.

*   *   *

Logically, when the Christmas holidays came around, Simone, Olivine and I should have received notice to take our things with us, for it was understood that we wouldn't be readmitted when school opened again in January. Nothing of the kind. I turned up at the house in a state of jitters. My father didn't seem to have been alerted. The days went by and I began to think it had all been nothing but empty threats when, on the last Sunday, my father got a telephone call from the Superior. He left the house about two o'clock.

At four he wasn't back yet, and I was more dead than alive. At last he arrived, and just to hear his headlong footsteps made the whole family quail. He went up to his room without saying anything. We heard him pacing back and forth for two or three minutes, then he called me.

"Shut the door."

Having said that, he threw himself on me and began to beat me with all his violent might, punching my face and kicking my legs.

There was nothing to do but wait. I was bleeding from the nose and mouth, and one eye was turning black, a colourful spectacle which I got a glimpse of from time to time as my head passed in front of the mirror like a ball being thrown up and caught again. At the end of the first round, I noticed that my stockings were covered with blood: my period, which wasn't due for two or three days yet, had been brought on early by fear and blows. So what! A little more or less at this stage in the game wouldn't make any difference.

My father went off to wash his hands which were sticky with blood, then he threw me a handkerchief. What I did with it still surprises me today. I see here the sign of a presence of mind that frightens me a little. While pretending to wipe my face, I managed, by running my finger around under the handkerchief, to spread the blood right up to the roots of my hair. He can't help but be ashamed in the end, I thought. But that man was shameproof.

I had been in his room perhaps a quarter of an hour already and nothing had been said yet. Not a word. Everything in its place, and so far we had been too busy, one giving, the other receiving, to waste any part of those precious moments in chitchat. After he had thrown me the handkerchief, he began to talk.

Of course I wasn't so stupid as to think that I had been unjustly accused. They had plenty of things to reproach me with at the convent. Not so much specific acts as general attitude. Since I breathed nothing but an atmosphere of hatred and scorn, it would have been surprising if that had been translated in my behaviour into gentleness, piety and docility. But I was astonished by all the things the sisters had thought up. To even the biggest child-liar, adults' lies (and what adults: these were nuns) seem really scandalous. For instance, one morning I had pretended to faint. The whole convent knew why. The evening before we had been deprived of recess and had been sent to study right after dinner. We had all begun to mutter that it was a health hazard, that people had been known to die of indigestion for a lot less than that, and that it wouldn't be at all surprising if some of us turned out to be awfully sick the next day or so. In short, we were all furious.

"I'm going to fake a fainting spell tomorrow morning," I whispered to my neighbours.

Once I had said it, there wasn't a chance of going back on something that was immediately considered to be a firm commitment. News of it spread like a seven-day wonder, and I'm sure that long before bedtime the sisters knew I was going to faint first thing on rising. Only, in telling my father of this mischief, they made it seem as damnable as possible. They didn't say a word about the punishment that had been given us (every time he spoke to the nuns my father insisted on the need of physical exercise, which made the premise of the whole affair difficult to explain) and they claimed I had pretended to faint to get out of going to mass, because I hated mass, hated the priests, the sisters, the chapel and the Church. The proof was that they had caught me reading a novel during my nocturnal adoration in the course of one of the "forty hours," and that on the second night of the "forty hours" I had refused to mend my sin by staying two hours instead of one.

Accusations bubbled up like a spring. The stream was swelled every now and then by a blow or two. When we got to the bit about Jonah and Elisha, hysteria set in again. Second round: punching bag, handkerchief and paternal washing of hands all over again.

"I went to see the curé about you," my father said finally.

This curé was a sinister creature. I had loathed him ever since our little maid had told my sisters and me that he had opposed her having a hysterectomy on the grounds that she was still of an age to procreate — curés had more to say about hysterectomies than doctors in those days. She had to be taken to the hospital in the dead of night, in secret, and as a consequence doctor, husband and wife had been threatened with hell fire. "But she would have died, and she has six children," the poor reprobates argued. "God didn't invent operations, and someone else could have brought up the children," replied the priest. At this point in the story, every time she told it, the poor woman would turn her head away and her eyes would swell with tears. Once again I could only tremble with fear at the thought of my female condition, and wish the curé was dead. But I wished so many people would die, and only the ones I loved did.

When I learned that my fate was in the hands of that man, I realized that this was just the beginning. He made the discovery that to be so wicked I must have been in a state of mortal sin all my life, and intimated to my father that I had most assuredly made a sacrilegious first communion and that I had been accursed since childhood. To judge from the way my father hit me, I could plainly see he believed it too.

"You will return to the convent," he continued. "The curé says you are full of devilish pride and that this pride must be broken. He has arranged everything with the Superior. When you get back to the convent you will beg the sisters' pardon, on your knees, in front of all the students. And no more piano lessons. The curé says that if you go on in music, you'll end up a Hollywood actress. Besides that, in future he wants you to go to confession to him and not to the little vicar."

Poor little vicar, he was so nice, and he would have been so hurt to know how scornfully his spiritual direction was being treated. I said "Yes, yes," to all these commands. I had reached a kind of indifference that even blows to the head couldn't shake, and all I did was take mental note of all the idiocies I was hearing — Hollywood!

At six o'clock my father washed his hands for the third time and went downstairs, instructing me to "go and get tidied up." I went to my room and started to look around, as if it was the simplest thing in the world, I may say, for something to hang myself with. From the time I was very young, I had always dreamt of procuring some exemplary punishment for my father. I was covered with bruises and blood. The inquest would show what I had suffered, and my father would be punished. In any case, he would at least be so frightened he would never begin again, and perhaps that would be the worst punishment of all. The others could live in peace. As for me, I didn't have enough patience to wait till I was of age. It was too long. As for any fear of what possibly lay on the other side of death, I had pretty well lost all belief in that in the course of the afternoon.

With the belt of my dress in my hand, I climbed on a chair and tested the strength of the ceiling fixture, but at the first jerk it sagged a little and a few flakes of plaster fell on my head. The curtain rod was too flimsy. Nothing had been provided in that damned room for a quick suicide. I would have to smother myself in my pillow, which wouldn't be easy. I had just settled myself on the bed and was making ready, with the help of a towel twisted diagonally, to tie the pillow to my face, when my father came in — without knocking, naturally. I don't know that he ever knocked at a single door in the whole house, not so much out of lack of politeness as from arrogance: "Me, knock at the door of a room in my own house? I'm master here, and I go wherever I choose," and our attempts to cure him of this arrogance by arranging to show him our fannies every time he came into the room remained ineffectual.

"Were you asleep? Come down and join the others."

He spoke in an ordinary voice — I can't say it was tender — but as if nothing had happened and he had just found me taking a nice little snooze. I got up and made as if to go down just the way I was.

"You're not cleaned up yet?" he asked, still in this conversational tone. "Come into the bathroom."

When we were there, he sat down on the radiator and watched me washing.

"Here," he said, "there," pointing out patches of dried blood.

Then, drawing attention to my stockings, he told me once more to tidy myself up and said that he would be waiting for me in his room. When I had finished, he met me in the hall.

"What are you pouting for? Are you mad at me?"

"I am not pouting, my mouth's swollen."

"What do you mean, your mouth's swollen?" he replied, as though I had just announced that I had been stricken with some extraordinary disease that made the mouth swell.

I didn't answer and undertook to go downstairs. It wasn't easy. I was limping in both legs and my arms and shoulders hurt me so much I couldn't hold the banister.

"Come on, come on," he said behind me.

"I can't go any faster."

"What do you mean?" he repeated.

Among many other singular habits of mind, my father possessed the faculty of believing that it was enough to turn your back on something to make it cease to exist. I could either say nothing, and what had happened would cease to exist, or I could reply that he had hurt me, and he would have thrown himself on me again to teach me better than to judge him. I chose to say nothing.

That's the main reason I hated him so, because of that terrified silence he reduced us to, that cowardice he plunged us into, just as deep and as long as he wanted to. And it's awful to say, but I must confess that my cowardice instead of diminishing with age only grew greater, for about the time I am talking about I got it into my head that first and foremost I should protect my face. If ever he disfigured me I would never be able to escape. So to avoid his blows there wasn't any trick I wouldn't have played. For all that, I don't have the impression I missed much, and in the long run it hurt me just as much to crawl before him.

My brothers and sisters just gave me a furtive glance. André brought a rounded hand up to his own face, meaning that my cheeks were very swollen, and his eyes grew red and clouded with tears. This surreptitious sympathy didn't move me. Nothing could move me now. I was dried up, completely callous. My father said grace and we sat down. Despite our request for God's blessing on the food we were going to receive, I didn't have much appetite.

For such moments, moments when, whether he liked it or not, he couldn't escape feeling a collective hatred prowling around him, my father had a special face, an arrogant, stupid look that served as a fortress.

As for my own face, it was becoming more and more painful, and it was getting harder and harder from one mouthful to the next to move my jaws.

"You're taking plenty of time to empty your plate. You're holding everybody up."

I swallowed the last mouthfuls in the midst of general immobility and silence, one eye lowered — the other was already shut. We said grace, and at last I could run off to the kitchen.

The first thing I did was get the previous night's paper. I tore out the page of classified ads and hid it in a drawer. Now that I was washed up it was too late for suicide. But I could still run away.

After my father had left for work next morning, I declared my intention of running away. The Depression was on. In the ads there was nothing but openings for maids, and few enough of them. But that didn't matter, I would wash dishes till my skin peeled off rather than live five more years in that house. My sisters had a very hard time dissuading me: I would be picked up right away, and perhaps locked up in a reformatory, my whole life would be ruined. In the end I let myself be convinced, but with such a strong feeling that I had accepted the easiest way out — for *it is easier to submit than to run away* — that I was disgusted with myself.

At last it was time to go back to school. What was waiting for me there wasn't very alluring, but I was glad to go because during the two or three days between that Sunday and the day we left my father had never ceased looking for an occasion to begin the *corrida* again, and, though it's painful enough to suffer blows on a sound face, on a swollen and bruised face it becomes unbearable.

Anyway, I had to take my swollen face with me to the convent.

"What's happened to you?" asked the Superior when I went into her office where it was decreed I should go to receive my orders.

I hesitated a long moment. I tried to find the courage to say that my father had beaten me and that she was the one I owed my pretty face to, but it wasn't one of my brave days.

"I fell skating," I answered in a jolly sporting voice (I had never had skates on in my life for at our place, naturally, skating, skiing, swimming, et cetera, were hobbies for prostitutes).

"What's wrong with you?" the girls asked, too, when I came into the recreation room.

I began my skating story over again but I didn't know the least thing about it, and when my companions said that they hadn't even been out, it had been so cold the last few days, I launched into a detailed description (for example, I had worn a pair of good warm shoes inside my skate boots), which made them say that I hadn't ever skated in my life. I stood there like an idiot without a single thing to add by way of explanation.

The next day there was confession. I went and knelt at the curé's feet with rage in my heart.

"Make a general confession," he ordered.

I had always thought that it was up to the penitent to decide whether to make a general confession or not. But here again I wasn't asked my opinion. Of course, what the man wanted was to see his theory confirmed. He was going to find out what mortal sin I had committed on crawling out of my cradle, and he was delighted at his own perspicacity. I should have told him the story about my bad word.

"I don't know what to say. I'm not prepared for a general confession."

"I will question you."

We began straight off with sins of the flesh, a girl as bad as I was couldn't be anything but lost as far as the flesh was concerned. We had a prelude of trifles, thoughts, words, then, all of a sudden:

"Have you committed the act of marriage with your brothers?"

I must say here that if I knew more or less, rather less than more, what the "act of marriage," as he called it, consisted in, it hadn't yet occurred to me that I would ever do such a thing myself. When I dreamed about getting married, I saw suitcases and not a bed. Only the first part of his sentence struck me at first. Then the second caught me, on the rebound, so to speak. Before I could stop them, tears streamed down my cheeks. I couldn't speak.

"Yes?" asked the curé.

"No, no."

He had a fat red face punctured with little pig's eyes, thick lips, and wide nostrils, a face that made you want to spit. We passed on to masturbation — I knew no more about the thing than I did about the word — then turned to less important items, faith and charity. Without even thinking, I replied "no, no, no," and to get "yes" out of me he had to go on to acts of disobedience and lies. In the end, the curé seemed to be really bothered about something. He said that perhaps I was more thoughtless than bad, he turned tender, he urged me to thank God for having protected me from the worst evils. Look who was talking. Personally, I judged that I hadn't been spared the worst, and I didn't feel like thanking God at all.

I came out of there so overwhelmed with anger and disgust that it seemed to me I would never be at peace again. For penance he had told me to say a rosary. I decided to do nothing of the kind, and that decision marked the end of an era for me.

The next day was Saturday and the marks were read out. When everyone was seated, the Superior began with a little sermon to the effect that one of us had been the cause of turmoil and had set a bad example in the convent, that it had first been decided to expel her, that in answer to her father's pleas she had been taken back, but that first she would have to ask forgiveness on her knees.

"Kneel down," said the Superior.

"Kiss the ground," said Mother Saint-Justinien.

I knelt down and kissed the ground. In the nuns' eyes, these kneelings and floor kissings were supposed to plunge us into the depths of humiliation. I didn't see anything humiliating in that. It seemed to me, rather, that the humiliation reverted to the people who ordered these childish gestures. In Mother Saint-Protais' time we spent a good part of each day kissing our thumbs, and that made some of the little girls cry, especially one of them who sucked hers almost non-stop but who refused to kiss it, which I found very funny.

So I kissed the ground, being careful just the same, beneath my monstrous head of hair that cascaded forward over my eyes, to keep my mouth a good inch from the dusty floor. Then I had to repeat word for word a short act of expiation that the Superior dictated to me. From time to time, Mother Saint-Justinien changed a word that seemed too feeble. If they had known my profound indifference in repeating all that claptrap, I don't suppose they would have kept me a minute longer. But they thought they had struck a mighty blow. Such a mighty one that a few days later Mother Saint-Justinien started off again on the subject of religious vocation. This time I didn't want to play. I had learned that Mother Saint-Justinien wasn't much of a sport. No sense of fair play.

"I'll think about it," I replied coldly.

"You know we accept repentant sinners," she said winningly.

She wouldn't have used another tone in speaking to *la duchesse de la Vallière.*[2]

A little while after all these events, I met my piano teacher near the private door that led from the staircase to her studio. This door was hardly ever used. There was another one, an ordinary one, that opened onto the recreation room.

"Come in," she said, "I want to speak to you." Mother Sainte-Aimée was the Mother Superior's sister. All in all, they were two charming women, and any trouble I had with the latter was due to Mother Saint-Justinien who must have been pretty hard to hold down "when the bile entered her pious heart" — according to the expression I had found in the pink pages of the *Larousse*, and which I found delightful.

When she was upset, Mother Sainte-Aimée made a little grimace that looked like a Hapsburg pout.

"So you're not going on with your piano lessons?"

"No."

"And I hear that your father also forbids you to be soloist in the chapel."

"Yes."

Mother Sainte-Aimée puckered the pout a little more, blushed delicately and stated:

"I don't like your father."

And went from delicate pink to scarlet.

"I don't like to see music mixed up in this. It's got nothing to do with it."

"You can go ahead and say you don't like my father if you like," I replied. "I hate him and I despise him. But about the music, it was the curé who had that good idea."

It wasn't customary to say anything but *"monsieur le curé."*

"Tut, tut — you mustn't speak that way. But who is going to sing in chapel in your place?"

"You know, Sister, as for the chapel and what goes on there, I don't give a hoot."

I thought that would make her jump, but it didn't.

"What's wrong with your face?"

"I was beaten until I was covered with blood. You can tell the others, it'll make them happy."

"You're revolted, and I understand," said Mother Sainte-Aimée. "I won't say a thing to anyone."

"Just as you like," I said dryly, and left as I had come, by the little door.

Not three weeks went by before I was soloist again. I don't know how that was arranged. All I know is that my father wasn't asked to give his permission. I like to think that Mother Sainte-Aimée, who was nothing but gentleness and good sense, was instigator of this little rebellion.

* * *

It was then that Grandmother's death occurred. I took this new blow like an insult. An insult that, it seemed to me, deserved a vengeance so horrible that decent words couldn't describe it. I reread Grandmother's letters and their resignation stirred my anger. "Resignation is a mug's game," I wrote in my notebook — or something like that — and I was delighted with my coinage. It seemed to me as just and as fine as a proverb. For several weeks I kept myself busy inventing these maxims. "It's the weak who create tyrants." I didn't know that all this had been written long ago, and I would have been crestfallen to hear it, for I got some consolation from this faculty of reducing my grievance to short pithy phrases that would certainly pass straight on to posterity. They'd see what fire ran in my veins.

In the meantime, I remained pretty chilly. My two friends, Olivine and Simone, for want of parents who took orders at the presbytery, hadn't been treated to any false suspension. I missed them a lot. One day I decided to write to Olivine. She had told me before leaving the convent that I could do it without risk. So I didn't spare the irony. All the nuns got theirs, one after another. I wallowed in their ugliness and their stupidity. I remember that there was a paragraph in there on Mother Saint-Justinien — a real shocker! Three or four days later I was called into the Mother Superior's office. Olivine's father had written me a very severe letter and, on top of that, had enclosed my own, which I recognized as soon as I came into the office. Mother Superior was holding all these papers by her fingertips, like dirty laundry.

"I don't know what to do with you," she said after she had read out the letter that was addressed to me. "What cruelty! I didn't know a child your age could be so cruel."

I didn't know it either. I was learning something new every day. Sometimes I was surprised that I didn't love anybody, but who was there to love?

"Cruelty is like a disease, it's catching."

I was right at home in aphorisms these days.

"I'm going to have to ask you to empty your pockets."

I obeyed, and the Sister immediately laid hands on my notebook. She began to read my jottings out loud.

"Is this really what you think of Christian resignation?"

Since my adventure with Jonah, I was on my guard. If I got into some doctrinal tangle again, it might take me a long way.

"It's not by me," I said. "I copied it out of a book."

"Oh? And who is it by, then?"

"By René Bazin," I replied with aplomb.

She couldn't suppress a smile.

"Why not Bossuet?"

Then she added:

"I think I should put all this into your father's hands."

I didn't say anything, but I must have turned very pale, because she asked me if I felt sick and made me sit down.

"When you came back you said you had fallen skating, but — "

"I'd rather not talk about those things."

"All right, I'm going to forgive you one more time."

The interview closed with some literary counselling. If I wanted to write, why didn't I compose poems to the glory of God and the Virgin?

"What about some lovely alexandrines? Wouldn't you like to do that?"

Moved by her own charity, she smiled at me tenderly.

Alexandrines? I had seen Mother Saint-Fortunat too often composing those things, counting up the feet on her fingers like some third-rate poet. I left the office no more moved than a stone that you kick down the road, and more convinced than ever that fathers — my God! what a breed!

The days that followed proved that Mother Superior hadn't spoken of my latest feat of arms to Mother Saint-Justinien. I should have been grateful to her, all the more so because gratitude is a feeling I find very pleasant to experience, not because I am better natured than some thankless people, but because I like the sharp pleasure I feel at the least kindness. That time I didn't feel a thing. It was a bad period for me and I remained as far from gratitude as from any other good sentiment.

The nuns, undoubtedly, and the curé, too, had imagined, after the threatened expulsion, after my return and the humiliation I must have felt kneeling in front of everybody, that I would be broken and at their mercy, as pliable as putty. I think the curé was the first to perceive that the plan had miscarried. I would go into his confessional with a face like a mask. I would briefly confess a few bagatelles, would listen without saying a word to all his exhortations, which grew shorter and shorter, and would walk away with a stiff gait. By the end of February all attempt at spiritual direction ceased. Confessor and confessed held each other in a mutual coldness.

Very soon, too, Mother Saint-Justinien stopped talking to me about religious vocation. In fact, she stopped talking to me altogether. And yet they kept me. I think there must have been a great difference of opinion about me in the community. Since I had been reinstated as soloist, I was often alone with Mother Sainte-Aimée. One day when I was complaining about Mother Saint-Justinien, she said:

"It's not easy, you know. Often parents send us children who they themselves have made hard-hearted, and the instructions they leave us for handling them aren't designed to soften them. But it's impossible to make Mother Saint-Justinien understand that."

We had several conversations along these lines, conversations that always ended with encouragement to be patient.

"Soon all that will be far behind you. You'll get married, and I should be very much surprised if you didn't know how to choose wisely."

"Mother Saint-Justinien would like me to be a nun."

Mother Sainte-Aimée burst out laughing and with a little gesture that was very irreverent, tapped her forehead with her finger.

* * *

Towards the end of the year it became the thing to exchange visits at night. We would tell each other about our love affairs — always the same old stories mulled over for the hundredth time and, certainly in my case and very probably in most of the others, practically all imaginary — we exchanged candies, then we would go back to bed.

"You never come to see me," one of the girls complained to me one day. I should have been suspicious, for she was Mother Saint-Justinien's pet.

So the next night I crept into her room. I had a few leftover fruit drops that we began to chew on together. Then she started to tell me about her love life: during the Easter holidays the boy next door had kissed her. On the cheek. Noisily.

"Like that," she said. "And what about you? Is that the way Jean-Marie kisses you?"

"Oh, no!" I said in a superior tone. "Like this."

And I kissed her on the mouth. Silently. At the same time I let my hand wander over her breast. Heaven knows I would never have let any boy do such a thing. It was all part of my myth-making mania: I was loved passionately and I wanted to prove it without thinking it might be bad, without feeling one way or the other about it, neither hot nor cold, just as a kind of demonstration. We ate what was left of the candies, and I went back to bed.

The next day or soon after, I was called down to the Superior's office. My father was there waiting for me. They were nothing if not sibylline.

"You are going to leave with your father," the sister said finally.

I went and put on my coat and got into the car. I was utterly dejected, for I thought I was being fetched away, as my two other sisters had been before, because someone else was about to die.

My father kept silent for a few minutes and then told me I had been expelled, once and for all, because I had been doing things with one of my companions. I had completely forgotten the story of the kiss on the mouth, and I swore I hadn't done a thing. It was all in vain, he didn't believe me. Then, suddenly, I had a revelation, though I can hardly claim it was celestial.

"The sisters hate me," I said, "because you've never made a donation to the convent."

"A donation?"

"Yes. Nearly all the parents make donations."

"Well, that's really the limit!"

My father couldn't get over it. That explained a lot of things, he said. In short, by the time we got out of the car, he had passed over to my side. I had made my point in record time, and that's all I wanted. Otherwise, once the sport had begun, it would have been hard to stop it. In due course I had to put up with a few sermons, but they were nearly always interrupted by the memory of those donations.

"Donations! That's the limit!"

My poor father was licked. Luckily for me, my betrayer apparently hadn't mentioned our respective boyfriends. I suppose to protect herself from having to talk about the boy next door, she decided to keep quiet about Jean-Marie. It's a sure bet my father wouldn't have got over that in a hurry either.

*   *   *

So after ten years as a boarder, I had finally finished with the nuns. I hadn't completed my final year (nobody studies after May anyway) and I was leaving without what we pompously called "a parchment." I wouldn't have got one anyway, because you had to pay to get it, and for this very reason my father had already forbidden me, several months before, to register for the final examinations. And what would I have done with a diploma? Work? Thank heaven my father's daughters would never need to work. Neither feel the need nor have the right to. He would raise the roof if we asked him for a pair of silk stockings, but as soon as we mentioned wanting to get a job, he would suddenly discover he was rich. Besides, only bad fathers let their daughters expose themselves to the perils of an office.

"Do you realize," this good father used to say, "those girls work all day long there surrounded by men? How do you expect them to come out of that without being dishonoured?"

I think he was sincere. He really believed that working girls have every reason in the world to find themselves pregnant after the first two weeks. Unless they are very ugly. Ugliness is the shield of virtue, he often used to say.

Custom required, when he spoke to us about dishonoured girls, which he did endlessly, that we all look agog, for it was easy to guess that though he wanted to see us quake at the threat of dishonour, he preferred us to be alarmed without knowing what it was all about. Poor man! His role was a difficult one. There was never a tyrant more ill-equipped to exercise his tyranny. All he had was his strength and his anger. Not a trace of intuition, finesse or cunning. As soon as he tried a bit of strategy, we could see him coming a mile off. Even when he grilled each member of the family individually, we could always guess without consulting each other the right answer to make up a common front. So he rarely caught us out. But it wasn't really necessary for him to catch us. To be certain in his own mind was enough, after that he moved straight into action. Without delay.

The right to buffet and cuff was a right he had acquired in giving us life.

"Me, I'm the one you owe your life to — and you, you're the one who owes her life to me — "

To owe someone something when it's impossible to be grateful is rather painful, but when it's your own life you owe it's really rotten. When I had learned enough to understand exactly what I owed my life to, how I had come to be me, a human being, with my own existence to lead and my own death to die at the other end, when I saw that all the horror that had been imposed on me came as the consequence of a moment of pleasure taken from a poor, sick, frightened woman, reduced to the state of an object, used and kicked aside afterwards, when I understood that I was nothing more than the result of an act committed without love, borne with horror and religion on one side and performed with hatred on the other, why, I treated myself to some good fits of cold fury. Search as I might,

I couldn't make any sense out of it. My fate and that of my brothers and sisters seemed worse than bestial. I couldn't see how it was that we had been condemned from the start to be hated, and yet that we had come to be made just the same.

The horror of his equation confounded me and when, on top of that, my father claimed my gratitude because a little joyless shiver of his had landed me here, I choked with anger. How was I ever able to love later, and find the pleasures of the flesh sweet? It's a mystery. Or was it perhaps from hearing my father repeat so often that love was stupid and the flesh abject? Maybe the spirit of contradiction saved me from frigidity as from so many other misfortunes.

*   *   *

During the following summer, my eldest sister got a new boyfriend — the first had evaporated during our annual claustration. He would arrive in his car as soon as my father left on a trip. By this time we would also have alerted Uncle Eugène and Aunt Berthe who would arrive in theirs. Sometimes my uncle would bring some of his friends, and that meant that a third or fourth car would be parked outside the front door. If ever Jupiter had showed up — but there must be a patron saint for child martyrs, for that never happened. Before dinner, those who wanted to would play a few sets of tennis. (I never could; I used to run away hiding my face when the ball came at me.) We ate late. We danced. Our guests stayed on and on, sometimes until two in the morning. How wonderful! Going up to bed we would sigh:

"Oh, if only we had a father like everyone else! In a big house like this we could give terrific parties."

It is only fair to say that from time to time my father would try his hand at playing the jolly father. But it was written in the cards from way back that he couldn't do anything with moderation and ease.

Take the tennis court. He had given it to us because he realized that our boredom was becoming truly dangerous. But — with him there were always buts — as soon as the court was finished it immediately became evident that we would get more vexation than pleasure from it. As usual. First of all we had to play when he wanted us to.

"It's time to play tennis."

Sick or sound, reluctant or exhausted, everyone had to get into the act. He would settle himself near the court and do a running commentary on the game.

"You play like an idiot. I've never seen a girl so awkward. My God! How stupid you look!"

In no time he had worked himself up into a real anger, and after a few rallies he would send everyone packing back to the house.

Then it was a billiard table he had installed right in the middle of the living room, pushing all the furniture back to the walls which, though fortunately it only lasted one season, was a great nuisance when he was away and we wanted to have guests. The very first night he flew into a towering rage because not one of us could make sensational caroms.

Before that it had been mah-jong. I don't know how to play mahjong; none of us ever learned the game for want of his letting someone into the house who might have taught us. But I have been forced to spend hours on end seated before those mysterious tiles that we pushed around any old way, while reading and rereading those incomprehensible and interminable instructions which came with the box and seemed expressly designed to cast us into darkest confusion. While all that bored us utterly, my father found in it the thing he liked best in the world: a stimulus for anger.

"I do everything in my power to amuse you," he would shout, "but you're such dolts you can't learn any game."

It was true. Because he was there, his presence stifled our understanding.

Sometimes he got it into his head to show us what he could do. Then it really turned into a farce. In billiards he tore the cloth on his first shot, which earned us a distribution of slaps all around: one of us had made him jump by starting to talk, another had hindered his movements, a third cast his shadow on the ball. In tennis he would throw his racket at us the first time he hit a foul: we had served him a bad ball. Only once did he try to play cards with us: Lady Luck didn't give him any trumps, and he threw the pack in our faces. For my father was never wrong.

He would rather have died than admit to the least error. If he was too obviously in the wrong, he took weeks to prove that he had been in the right, finding new arguments that seemed conclusive to him, yet going on and on to better and better ones. You might have thought to hear him that we had hotly disputed his point of view, which hardly ever happened.

I remember one incident about egg shells that threatened the whole family with extinction, my father from apoplexy, the rest of us in the usual way. It was a Sunday morning in springtime. We were busy getting lunch ready. Suddenly my father, who had gone out for a stroll in the orchard, came rushing back to the house at a sprint, shouting and waving his arms.

"Crossing the stream, I saw some eggs you had thrown away. Have you started to throw out eggs now?"

"They must be shells."

At that thrust, we thought he would go mad with rage on the spot.

"That's it, that's it, tell me I'm wrong, tell me I didn't know what I was seeing, tell me . . . et cetera."

He didn't seem able to stop. After hitting out at everyone within reach, he went out to get the incriminating eggs. We watched him from behind the curtains. Of course they were empty shells. He turned purple and threw them down violently, then crushed them with his foot, trampled them and stamped them into the ground as if he wanted to kick his way right through to the Antipodes. Then he strode off into the orchard and didn't come back until lunch time.

"There's no reason to believe you didn't throw out those eggs," he said suddenly, a few days later. "They could have been emptied by some animal."

"Sure, the same one that carefully put all the shells one inside another," Dine whispered to me.

"At any rate, don't get too smug too soon," my father continued. "There's not a single instance of your lying to me in this house that I haven't found out about. One day I'll know the truth, as I always do."

Pure illusion, if ever there was one. After such incidents, we had a hard time keeping our faces straight until his back was turned. But nothing made us laugh more than the story about the mice. I have already mentioned how sold my father was on the theories of certain American quacks. One in particular contributed royally to making our life miserable. He wrote complete books, the dog! He published magazines, diet sheets, God knows what, pell-mell, one after the other. My father read them all with a credulous eye. The trouble was that this charlatan wasn't satisfied to limit himself to dietary recommendations. He also gave psychological advice. His adepts' children and their education was one of his chief preoccupations and, like all those people who make a god out of muscle, he had very original views on the female of the species. Girls, he wrote, are hysterical from birth. Their feeble brains are easily abused by various fantasies (to be expected, since child bearing is the only thing women are good for, and children aren't born through the head), and they are inclined to see things that don't exist. For example, they sometimes think they see mice running around where there aren't any, and even cats. So if your daughter cries out, "Look, a mouse!" she needs medical attention.

Now it so happened that we had mice every fall. They were cute little field mice who took advantage of the fact that the cellar windows were always closed up too late, and crept into the basement as soon as the weather turned cold. Once they had explored the cellar, they climbed up to the first floor along the pipes.

"Look, a mouse!" my sister Dine said one October night.

"Hysteria!" my father yelled. "I am not surprised, I always thought you were all half crazy, and that's proof . . . blah-blah-blah."

Then he went back to his paper. Dine got up quietly, went and got a trap, baited it and set it down noiselessly. Thirty seconds later she had a mouse, then a second and a third. In five minutes she had caught a whole family, five or six little corpses lined up beside the radiator. We were tickled pink. It was a bumper year. There were rarely more than one or two.

"What are those noises I hear — clack, clack?" asked my father.

"It's the mousetrap."

My father jumped to his feet.

"In spite of what I just said, you went and set a trap, just another example of your habitual insolence."

By the end of this remark he had drawn abreast of the corpses. He jabbed at them furiously with his foot.

"Pick those up. Hysteria! A bunch of hysterical girls!"

The only thing that saved us from being accused of having materialized the little beasts ourselves was undoubtedly my father's own uncertainty as to the powers of hysteria. Thank heaven we lived in an enlightened age. (I thanked it every day of my childhood.) God knows how many poor witches were burned for much less in the bonfires of the Inquisition. I can well imagine my father in some darker age leading us piously to the stake, our pockets full of mice, his friend, the curé Galerneau, at his side. Hosanna!

To reinforce the image he had of himself — always right, never wrong — my father was endowed with a memory that, at best, one could call selective. Take the mouse story, for example; he only remembered the beginning — up to and including Dine's exclamation, "Look, a mouse." It would have been easier to forget it altogether, but in that case he would have had to resign himself to giving up the words "hysterical girls" which he used constantly, and those are words that are very sweet to certain masculine mouths.

One year it was a rat that took up his winter quarters with us. On a Sunday when Dine was finishing cleaning up the kitchen, she saw the creature — not too big, those field rats have nothing in common with the repulsive monsters that breed in the city — scuttle away behind the stove. Very quietly she closed one of the kitchen doors, and was just about to close the other when my father burst in.

"What are you trying to do, lock yourself up in the kitchen?"

"Sh," my sister said, as low as she could. "There's a rat."

"What? A rat!" shouted my father, upsetting tables and chairs, as a result of which the frightened enemy ran out of his hiding place and began to tear around every which way.

My father grabbed a broom, broke a window and the electric light bulb on the way, then, losing his footing, cracked his skull on the edge of the sink. In the meantime, using another broom, my sister had killed the rat. After all that, my father collapsed on the first chair handy and while we dressed his wound, told us what had happened.

First Dine had come running out of the kitchen screaming as though she had just seen the devil. "A rat! A rat!" In reply to my father's calm questioning, she had sobbingly described an enormous beast. Then he had gone very gently into the kitchen, but she had jostled him so that he hadn't been able to avoid breaking the window and the light bulb. Not a week had gone by before he was the rat-slayer himself. Hindered as he had been by that poor ninny, it was no mean feat.

Another time it was my sister Marguerite's turn to be declared the feeble-minded member of the family. Our dining room was lit by a chandelier suspended by three chains. "That chandelier is crooked," my father grumbled one evening when he was looking all over the house for some motive to devour us. And the next thing, there he was clambering up on the table, unfastening the chains, hooking them up again and, like a great bunch of boobies, we all stood around watching him, as though we didn't know it was better to keep one's distance when he was fooling around with breakable objects.

When the porcelain globe slipped out of his hands, first it hit the table without breaking, then bounced up like a rubber ball as high as Marguerite's chest, and finally shattered on the floor. Poor Margot! Who had ever palmed off such a dumb daughter on my father, a perfect idiot, a real mental case, and so on and so forth, not to mention the price of the chandelier which we heard a lot about too.

During our Sunday drives we were forbidden to talk, as I have already said. O.K. But we were triply forbidden to point out any obstacle that seemed to have escaped my father's attention. The least "Oh!" drew sharp rebukes.

"Do you think I'm blind? Insolent cocksure young imbecile!"

So we sat there as still as possible, even during the closest shaves. And God knows there were enough of them, for prudence and attentiveness weren't exactly part of the parental makeup. Often, if the obstacle was a moving one, the person who was moving it got it out of the road in time. If the obstacle was stationary, a post or a fence, we frequently crashed into it.

For the most part, it was Benoît who got it in the neck.

"Why didn't you warn me? I was counting on you. Wasn't it understood that you were always to watch out on the right? Haven't I told you a thousand times to keep your eyes open?"

"Look out! There's a bicycle."

"So what? Do you think I am blind? Cocksure young imbecile!"

I've seen it happen three times on the same drive. After that, you'd just as soon not know anything about heredity.

*   *   *

My father was never able to understand that at a certain age a child ceased being a child. We could be fifteen, eighteen, twenty, he always kept on treating us as though we were four-year-olds. The age of reason wasn't for us.

Since I haven't any children and have never had occasion to pass over to the parents' camp, I have kept a very sharp memory of one thing in particular: when a child is right, it is useless trying to persuade him that he's wrong. It is also useless to try to make him believe that you are acting for the best according to your lights — he sees through that little farce very quickly. If, on top of that, you prevent him from answering back, from explaining why he thinks he's right, well, in that case, just let me say that the child's feelings are so unflattering that it's better not to comment on them. A child doesn't just hunger after tenderness, caresses and presents, but justice. And how hungry I've been!

At the root of my father's injustice lay a profound ignorance of a child's mental development. It wasn't because there was any shortage of them, but because he hadn't watched them grow up with interest and love. For instance, he could very well accuse us of having pencilled on the wall, even though we were ten or twelve and the scribbling was at the height of a child of three, mentally as well as physically. Furthermore, since we were no sooner accused than punished, the possibility of being found innocent absolutely never entered into it. A punished child remains guilty. What's done is done, and the father of the family — maybe not other ones, but mine at any rate — is infallible by divine right. If we were too patently innocent, his bad humour knew no bounds.

"And above all don't go thinking you're the victim of some injustice or other. God willed you to be punished for some other foolishness I didn't know about."

He would march off with an angry stride, then turn back.

"I just mentioned some other foolishness I might not have found out about. But don't start thinking there's much that escapes me. You should know by now I always find out the truth in the end, and I don't think you could name a single fault you've committed without my learning about it."

After I left the convent I was forbidden to write any letters to anyone without first asking his permission.

"You've disobeyed me again," he said one morning, pulling me over into a corner. "I had forbidden you to write letters without showing them to me."

"I didn't write any letters."

"Don't lie. I found your rough copy."

And he waved a scrap of paper on which my sister Thérèse, who was still just a baby, had told some little convent friend how she played with her dolls, et cetera. The writing and the spelling were equally clumsy.

"It's Thérèse who wrote that."

My father folded his arms in a Vercingetorixian[3] gesture.

"Why don't you say straight out that I'm a fool? Thérèse? At her age? We'll soon see about that."

Summoned to the stand, Thérèse was forced to admit that she had authored the document. With that, my father suddenly believed he had fathered a genius, and in his astonishment he completely forgot about me.

Later on, if he ever referred to an event that had taken place when we were twelve or thirteen, he would always say, "You were much too young at the time, you couldn't remember that." This was due, I think (and it was perfectly understandable), to the hope that we had forgotten a great deal.

Tyranny, of course, works much better on children than on adults. As the years sped by, he grew afraid of having to sacrifice a single scrap of his tyranny. That's why he refused to see that we had outgrown our childhood. He would have liked to control our least thoughts. Indeed, he thought he could. The certificate he had been awarded by Professor L. A. Harraden, Hypnotist, testified to that. It said that the recipient had faithfully studied and completed the course in Modern Hypnotism and was now a perfect hypnotist, thoroughly qualified to practise the art. You should have seen the way my father looked us in the eye when he wanted to make us own up to something! This Professor Harraden — who described himself on the certificate as "the greatest hypnotist in the world" was undoubtedly a nut, and possibly the most obscure hypnotist in the world into the bargain; for to my knowledge not a single one of us, despite the blue paternal stare, ever yielded up anything but the first lie on the tip of his tongue. The push-button lie. We had to be past masters of that art, since we might be interrogated at any minute on any subject under the sun.

"What are you humming? Why are you humming that? Where did you learn that tune? Don't lie."

"What are you thinking about? And don't tell me you don't know. Don't lie."

"You smiled. Were you thinking about something dirty? Don't lie."

We had the answers down pat. It was a tune we had heard played in church last Sunday. I was just thinking about mending some socks for him. I was smiling to think of that awfully funny story he had told us one day about the time he lived on Anticosti Island. If he could be pushed on to the safe path of this period in his life, you could be sure to be left in peace for a good long while. You didn't even have to listen. We had heard those anecdotes a thousand times, and we all knew the moral you were supposed to draw from them: that it was he who was the wisest, strongest, bravest, purest, smartest and most humble of all.

"I don't know," he would say, squirming a little, "whether it's that I've got more common sense — or judgment, or memory, or goodness or understanding — than others, but if the truth must be known . . . et cetera, et cetera."

Poor father! He was really the only child among us, and — when I had passed the age of adolescent intolerance — to hear him rave on so made me feel something — it wasn't tenderness, you don't feel tenderness for someone who is a stranger to you, but indulgence perhaps — of the same kind one feels towards some young scamp in the street who tries to show off to the passersby.

The business about the socks was pretty good, too. He was never happy unless the whole household was busy working for him. If I was sewing a button on my blouse, he would begin to fidget, then to grumble:

"I see you are sewing on a button. What about my buttons? I'll bet it's donkey's years since you've looked them over."

It would never do, however, to fix our buttons on a Sunday. That wasn't allowed. On the other hand, we spent a good half of every Sunday doing little jobs for him — shining his shoes, pressing his suits, shortening this, lengthening that. He must have thought that since we were working on a saint's things, heaven didn't just turn a blind eye on it, oh no, but actually rejoiced. Hosanna!

If it was one of his days of high anger, he would feverishly hunt through all his clothes to find something that wasn't in perfect shape. That was hard to find, for we knew the price there was to pay for the slightest neglect. Well, never mind! He would cut holes in his socks. Through the open door, we could sometimes see him, reflected in a couple of mirrors, painstakingly occupied at this modest task.

At table it was the same story. Everyone had to wait on him. As the girls grew up, it became impossible for them to get a hot serving.

Although we made meals that were copious and elaborate — this had become easier because over the years he had started to forget about centenarian foods — no matter what trouble we took, he always found something missing.

"I'd rather have had peas with this."

Dine would leave the table to quickly heat up a can of peas.

"What about some ketchup?"

Françoise would get up.

"Or, no, make that hot relish."

I would get up.

"I'd like my bread toasted."

Marguerite would get up.

"This meal wasn't enough for me. Fry me some eggs."

Since Dine wasn't back yet, Françoise would get up again. Although the kitchen was huge we kept bumping into each other.

His appetite was limitless. Despite the four or five courses he tucked away, he always had room for a couple of fried eggs. Since he continuously told us that liars like us turned into thieves and assassins, that the person who steals an egg today will steal an ox tomorrow, we used to whisper to each other, splitting our sides laughing:

"The person who eats an egg today will eat an ox tomorrow."

With this diet, he had a world of trouble keeping his weight down to two hundred and thirty pounds, which was enormous enough. Then Lent would come along. Naive as always, he would use this occasion to try to cheat heaven. He would start on a diet to lose weight and call it penance. He thought that if he waited until Lent to start reducing they'd be taken in up there, and would tot it up in the column of mortifications. Incapable of moderation in anything, he would starve himself for forty days. The most immediate result of this fast was that it made him acutely jealous of us for all the things we allowed ourselves to eat in front of him. Even the plainest dishes seemed awfully tempting to him.

"Well! Carrots *à la poulette*. You never make them when I'm eating."

"But we had them on Shrove Tuesday."

"Anyway, you don't make them often. But it's the same thing every year. As soon as I start my Lent, you bring out all your best recipes . . . blah-blah-blah."

Not only was his bad humour aggravated — in certain circumstances even the worst can be worsened — but his health also suffered. The year he decided to eat nothing but lettuce for forty days, he suffered from some kind of complication of malnutrition which left red splotches all over his skin. He finally went to show this to the doctor, but he was careful not to say anything about his diet. Somewhat perplexed, all the doctor could think of was to give him a Wasserman test, which turned out negative, as you can well imagine. Sure that we were completely ignorant of such matters (but my sister's boyfriend was a medical student and told us all about it), he had left the results of the test lying out on his desk. Which was just one other occasion when we nearly died laughing.

So each year we saw the holy season of Lent approach in fear and trembling. In the end we had the inspiration to suggest to him that such privations, while they didn't exactly make him seem older — it wouldn't have been wise to say that — at least made him seem less young, and he decided to cut out the penance. All the same, for seven or eight years, besides the habitual rhythms that ruled our lives, we also had those seasons of mortification and of feasting.

* * *

Indeed, our hours, days, months and seasons followed a kind of pendulum motion: office hours, and the hours before and after; working days, and holidays; the season of trips, and the other, the bad one. When the pendulum was at its low point, we waited for it to swing up again. We were infinitely patient about it. It reached the lowest point on winter Sundays when the trips were a long way off and holidays were numerous. Those days we couldn't even catch our breath.

First there was the perpetual cold. Even after we had oil heating put in we still froze, for he was the one who set the thermostat (and when he became old and shivery we would be so hot in that house we could hardly stand it). To keep us from thinking we were cold he had hung a thermometer in the kitchen, just over the stove and on a bulge in the wall where the hot water pipes passed. Nobody dared tell him that we weren't taken in and that we were cold anyway, which he would have found, had he known it, sheer effrontery.

Hurrah for tomorrow!

Monday morning, before he left for the office, he would put the key to the radio in his pocket and turn the thermostat down as low as it would go. From behind the curtains we would watch him leave. As soon as the car started we would open the radio with a match and turn up the thermostat. It was relative liberty.

The time came to change the radio. It was years now since such secretive sets had been manufactured, and I think that even then it was just our bad luck to happen on a very rare species, for I never meet anyone who remembers those lockable models. My father was irritated by all these changes.

"That means," he said to the salesman, "if there's no key, anyone can play it."

The salesman looked at him, completely blank.

"Well — yes — "

On reflection, I don't know why we had the set at all. We weren't supposed to play it when my father wasn't there, and when he was he turned it off as soon as he heard anyone sing or pronounce the word "love." Lucienne Boyer was in her heyday then, which is as good as saying that the radio was condemned to silence. When I reveal that, for his own personal use, my father had transformed the words of the Barcarolle in *The Tales of Hoffman* from "Lovely night, Oh night of love," into "Lovely night with stars above," it's easy to guess what a cold reception Lucienne Boyer and Damia got. So what. I listened to them as soon as he went out.

Few people can have been wilder than I was about the popular French songs that reached our shores about 1930. Before that, there was scarcely anything to sing in French — apart from the few exceptions that crossed the Atlantic heaven knows how — only bad translations of American songs. Then, all of a sudden, there was a sort of invasion. It came with the first French talkies, I think. Quebeckers, who in these two domains were Americanized to the marrow — much more than they are now, you have no idea — were bowled over. The women were in ecstasies. The men, who saw that these models would be hard to imitate, were more reticent, and decided, for the most part, that the French singers and actors had a finicky style. Personally, having no particular taste for the big, bold style, I liked them immediately. I spent hours at the radio listening to La Palma, Pizella, Jean Clément, Florelle, and Henri Garat, followed a little later on, about 1935, by Lys Gauty, Jean Tranchant, Guy Berry, all names that were wiped away by the war. I knew all their songs by heart, and I sometimes surprise myself chirping a melody that has come up from some substratum of my memory — with words like —

A tea-time tango
With thirty-six Negroes. . . .

or

I know nothing about you
Yes, but you
Know nothing about me, too. . . .

They're a bit silly, but memory can't choose. I also remember very well the first French films. *The Three Masks* starring François Rozet, then *A Hole in the Wall* with Louise Lagrange, *A Night on the Town* with Arletty, Meg Lemonnier and Garat, *Secretary* with Marie Glory, and films by Marcelle Chantal, Albert Préjean, Colette Darfeuil, and Gina Manès. Nearly all those movies had a theme song, and in those days an actor had to know how to sing.

I was used to American songs, turned out like sausages (as far as that goes nothing has changed, and the first thing Anglo-Saxons do when they take one of our songs is to blur all their brilliance), so I was thrilled at the first record I heard — by the interpretation, by the importance the singers gave to the text, by their intonation. Needless to say, I didn't enjoy paternal approval of this new taste. As for the movies, let's not even mention them. I was thirty when I first hinted to my father that I sometimes went to the pictures. By that stage I hadn't given him any account of my activities for a long time, but there was still a little terror lurking around in the corners.

All this disapproval was directed against love. He would have liked us to know nothing of love. Neither the word, nor the thing, which was disgusting, of course, but above and beyond all, ridiculous. Yet the fact remained that a woman is obliged to love her husband.

"A woman who doesn't love her husband — "

Followed by a string of curses. The question of a husband's love for his wife was never raised. It was also out of the question that a girl might love a boy before their marriage was imminent. On top of that, where love was acceptable, it had to be the kind that could be translated as submission, subjection and servitude, not as ardour. All his contradictory speeches stemmed, I think, from a variety of feelings equally contradictory, feelings that my father refused to formulate, because to do so he would have had to use a forbidden vocabulary. *Primo*: to make love is really only permissible for men.

Secundo: women can only make love out of duty and obligation but, despite that, a woman one has "had" is a diminished creature. *Tertio:* a woman who has had a lover is a slut, but the lover isn't guilty, because he has been led into temptation by the said slut. *Quarto:* all women are disposed to become sluts. *Quinto:* a man, even a paragon of virtue, is plunged into an abyss of desire by the mere appearance of a breast. *Sexto:* an honest woman hasn't got the right to experience temptation. *Septimo:* a woman is obliged to love her husband, no matter what sort, and hasn't the right to refuse him. *Octavo:* because of all these physical interdictions, one can hardly trust love as a feeling. This being established, it's no joke to be the father of five daughters, and not one of them talking about going into the convent.

*   *   *

I had my first beau in the month of September, the year I was sixteen. He was an architecture student and he was twenty-four, which I found very flattering. It was really the only quality I was ready to grant the poor boy. I can see now that I hated him, just as I hated all my beaux until maturity came to me — late, very late indeed. Man the enemy. Who can, if he wishes, use his strength to reduce a woman to slavery, beat her, prevent her from doing what she wants. I kept watching him out of the corner of my eye, humourlessly, without indulgence. Yet he was gentle, good and far from stupid. That didn't prevent me from ditching him the first chance he gave me. Ah, no! I wasn't going to be treated the way Mother had been, not me!

Above all, I reproached him with liking women with long hair. I couldn't stand men who liked women with long hair. I could have killed them. For me long hair was a symbol of slavery. My father, need I say, held that a woman was bound to wear an enormous chignon, not because it was becoming but because her condition as a woman demanded it. I must admit that even today when a friend confides in me that she would really like to cut her hair but that her husband . . . et cetera, anger makes my ears burn. "In your place, do you know what I'd do? I'd shave my head!"

Such attitudes didn't prevent me from dreaming endlessly of marriage, for I didn't see any other way of escape. But all these matrimonial dreams were bathed in intolerance, all my speculations were stamped with inflexibility. I wouldn't let anyone push me around. I wouldn't put up with any abuse. I wouldn't be slave to anyone. As far as slavery goes, I think I was right. But there was something more dangerous than that. Deep inside me there was an unacknowledged and quite wicked plan to make any husband that came my way pay for the whole race, and if I had married young I'd have done as I intended. As luck would have it, I married at thirty-one. It wasn't a year too late.

One morning that fall my aunt, my father's sister, telephoned us. My eldest sister had been seen in a restaurant accompanied by a boy. My sister had a choice: either she told my father herself that she had a suitor, or my aunt would spill the beans. Something had to be done. Dine began by telephoning the poor boy and she laid her cards on the table: he would have to carry on the courtship in my father's presence, or it was all over.

"O.K. I'll come Sunday."

But first a water-tight scenario had to be worked out. There was no question of admitting that this had been going on for six months. Louis would have to be a friend of the brother of an old convent friend, and Dine would have met all this gang, friend, brother and brother's friend, on her way back from the parlour one Thursday. It had to be a chance encounter like this, because we weren't allowed to see anyone. Strangely enough, my aunt fell in with the scenario. There are more things in heaven and earth. . . .

It was a feverish afternoon. The dinner! It must be a good one! We spent the whole time on it. At last my father arrived. At table, nobody took second helpings of dishes that seemed to please him most. Then, when he went to sit in the living room to read his paper, Dine went in:

"I'd like to speak to you — there's a boy who would like to come to see me and who telephoned to say — "

"A boy? Where did you meet him?"

"On my way back from the parlour. He's the friend of the brother of one of my convent classmates. I was just walking along and they were going by in a car. She recognized me — "

"This girl was in the car with a boy? My poor child, these people seem quite suspicious to me."

"But their parents were there, too."

This last detail wasn't in the script, but our heads were full of details you could add at the last moment.

In short, the schoolmate's brother's friend was accepted. The rest of the week was spent in paternal counselling of all sorts. First, ask this boy at once if his intentions were honourable. Then, forbid him entry to the house if he had the nerve to show up when my father was absent. After twenty-four hours it was: "Since you're going to get married . . ." and general advice on the holy state of matrimony, on obedience to one's husband, on the Christian upbringing of children and on the obligation to breast feed them as long as possible so the husband could satisfy his needs (it wasn't said that way) without having a wife who was always pregnant. That was, incidentally, the system my father had imposed on Mother. Otherwise I would be telling the story of fourteen child martyrs instead of seven. Dine listened to all this with a goggle-eyed expression, as if she already had all Louis' future children hanging at her breasts.

Sunday night after dinner, the suitor arrived, pale as a ghost. Dine introduced him. First to my father, then to us, the children.

"How do you do, sir."

As if we had never seen him, and with the timid air of young damsels who had never looked closely at a boy before, Françoise, André and I — the others were at the convent — sat down at a table and pretended to play cards. Dine and Louis sat at opposite ends of the sofa and my father pulled up an armchair right under their noses. The interrogation began. Louis stammered as much as is humanly possible.

"Perhaps we could play cards with the others," my sister said after half an hour of this.

"With pleasure, Miss Dine."

Louis came three times. Not once more. After which, my sister never heard of him again. Since she didn't love him, that was a relief for everyone.

"That boy just wanted a little fun, that's obvious. He soon saw that he'd come to the wrong address," my father concluded.

As far as fun was concerned, it was certainly advisable to look elsewhere. In the future, despite my aunt's prying, we waited until the marriage was settled before we introduced our conquests to my father. Fiancés are endowed with the special grace of fortitude. Otherwise we were better off with our usual winter evenings, alone with our sewing and the silent telephone.

* * *

The only amusement we could count on all year round was reading. There were two kinds: secret and approved. The latter consisted mostly of *The Annals of Good Saint Anne* and various parish bulletins sent to us by my father's sister. The prevailing spirit of these pamphlets was enough to discourage any mortal from continued existence, or any woman from being a woman. They featured an "Advice to the Lovelorn" column that had more to do with the lorn than the loved. Always the same old thing: "I love a young man who loves me too and wants to marry me, but I have been asked in marriage by a widower with seven children who is twenty years older than I am. . . ." Or, "I have twelve children, I am very sick, and my doctor tells me I will die if I have another pregnancy. . . ." These predicaments always solicited the same kind of response: "Marry the widower, it is God's will. Fulfill your conjugal duties, God will see to the rest." We used to read these things together, my sisters and I.

"Sounds like a gay future for us!"

The thought of the millions of women who had bowed to this frightful fate for centuries, and would for centuries to come, made me boil with rage. I couldn't see why those idiotic women would take the trouble to write to the *Annals* just for the confirmation of a death sentence they had been labouring under so long already. Were there really that many people who believed in the truth of such a crippling system?

To console myself, as often as I could slip out from my father's surveillance I would turn to the other reading. The secret kind. These books were lent to us by friends, or their brothers or their cousins. There were all sorts, and I think people often passed on books that they hadn't read a word of, for in this fashion I got to read some pretty weird things. It didn't matter, it was all wonderful, it was all great stuff. To me, Guy de Chantepleure, Mauriac, Zénaïde Fleuriot, Dekobra, Victor Marguerite and Delly[4] were all one. They were people who made books, and all I wanted was to read. The poor little virgin who wound up marrying her rich cousin after foiling the heartless heir by a show of virtue, moved me just as much as the mistress who passed her earnings on to her true love — as long as both stories were in books. I must have been at least twenty-five before I began to put some order into my reading. Which is none too soon. For that matter, I had to reach that age to be able to think a little straight, all by myself. And even then! When I admit that at twenty-five I was fascist and anti-Semitic — and that's not an easy thing to confess, for racism is certainly the most loathsome infirmity of all forms of human ugliness — when I admit that, it's no wonder it was still a year later before I could begin to put two ideas together. As foolish as it may seem, it wasn't until the fall of France that I began to get over my political extravagances.

There were quite a few of us who hadn't the least idea where we were going. To the right, to the left, any old way. Even the right way would have been pure whim with us, since we couldn't have known what we were doing there. Sheeplike, we always believed the last person to speak. Reading Gide was enough to bring a swing to the left, reading Maurras to the right, and the reader's family and friends swung with him. Unless prompted by the spirit of contradiction. Indeed, it's quite frequent here to owe one's political convictions to an urge to contradict someone else's. I've seen it happen at first hand. My paternal grandfather, and his whole family with him, were Conservatives. After a monumental dispute with him, my father turned Liberal, and it was the most ridiculous thing imaginable to see this man, who was of the extreme-extreme-right, vote Liberal, just because his father was Conservative and they had had a fight. Oh yes, they made up afterwards, but my father remained Liberal, because he never went back on a decision.

As for us, true children of our father, we were fervent Liberals like him. Not by conviction. We didn't ask who was right and who was wrong — we hadn't been brought up to entertain such niceties — but we had no wish to do as he had done and change parties simply not to belong to his. The one thing that seemed clear to us was this: the Liberals were in power, they employed my father because he was a Liberal, and a Conservative victory would probably have obliged my father to change his job. Would he have found another like the one he had, one that took him every summer from one end of the province to the other? It didn't seem likely. That was all we needed to be thoroughly steeped in Liberalism. But thought had nothing to do with it.

Thought! Poor me! It wasn't just in politics that my inability to think made me suffer. It was in everything. Shortly after I left the convent, I perceived that I knew nothing, that I wasn't aware of anything, that I couldn't have named a great writer later than Victor Hugo, that I didn't know what was going on in the world, that I didn't know how to go about finding out or how to discover who was Victor Hugo's successor. I was a product of the most flagrant mediocrity, and I wasn't even blissfully ignorant of the fact, which was really bad luck, because that kind of bliss is quite widespread amongst my fellows.

A commonplace incident revealed the state of my silliness and ignorance to me. One day when I was having lunch in a restaurant in Quebec, two men were talking at the next table. I heard them well enough, but I didn't understand what they were saying. I knew the words they were using, but I couldn't grasp the subject of their conversation. Sometimes they would mention a writer and titles of his works; titles and names were equally unknown to me. Don't misunderstand me. The two men weren't showing off what they knew. They were simply talking, unaware that I was listening to them.

A few weeks later, I spent a good while in Garneau's bookstore leafing through one of the books my neighbours at the restaurant had mentioned. What I read was like a secret code. And yet those two men had understood. Why them and not me? Quite obviously because they had been given keys that had been denied me.

After all, what had I learned from ten sad years of study with the nuns, who thought of nothing else but to make us obey, obey, obey, to "break in our characters," — and God knows they were broken to bits — to make us servile, pious, resigned and prudish? Nothing.

I knew nothing, and I can't see how it could have been otherwise. What a system! In those ten years I hadn't met a single person — except Mother Bon-Conseil, but I was so little then — to explain to me that learning was a delightful thing. By nature I liked to learn, but I ended up thinking of it as a punishment connected with the crime of being a child — a dreadful crime because I had to pay for it in so many other ways.

No one had ever told me that learning can be loved with a life-long love, and that what I was getting was just a meagre start. On the contrary, I was taught nothing, and this nothing was all I had a right to. This nothing was to be the sum total of my intellectual baggage right up to the gates of eternity. Eternity — that was the root of the problem. I wasn't supposed to exist except face to face with God — except in terms of the human-divine relation — other people just didn't exist. Headed straight for eternity, face to face with God, no one else around, a little object in transit, I really didn't need to know anything, all I needed was to be a regular little bigot.

I don't believe I'm particularly vain, and if I say that I'm only an average sort of person, I think I am being perfectly sincere. What maddens me is not even to have been able to explore this modest averageness to its depths.

Often I hear men complain that they, too, never encountered anything but mediocrity in their schooling, and I haven't, alas! any reason to doubt them. But what about us girls then? At least it was accepted that boys should learn enough to earn their living. We girls, we only had to gain heaven, and for that the less one knows the better.

At this time no women went to university and the first bold creature to force her way through the gates of one of our faculties set the whole of Quebec talking. Was that the place for a young girl? And what a responsibility for the parents who let their child run wild in an environment so little in keeping with the feminine vocation! And what must the bold thing's classmates think of her? And what about the female brain, how would it react to this unaccustomed treatment? This was the kind of question one half of the town kept asking the other half. The answers were divided, except on one point where everyone agreed: marriage just wasn't possible for such a girl. Never, never, never, would any man on Quebec soil wish to marry this bluestocking.

"And why not, if you please?" I would ask the boys who came to see us, most of whom were at university.

The only reply I got was a shrugging of shoulders, "Come on, now!" or sometimes ready-made opinions on the place of women in the structure of the universe.

All this, when it was a matter of the first girl student in medicine, branched out into questions of morality, propriety and modesty. How could one speak of syphilis, for example, in front of a girl? And how could one utter the words, penis and testicles? And what about prepuce? And epididymis! Wouldn't it be best to excuse the student from these courses? But by the same token shouldn't she be excused from courses where the professor would have to speak to the boys, in front of her, about intimate feminine matters? Wouldn't it be frightfully humiliating for the poor girl to attend lectures where the phenomenon of menstruation was explained, for example?

"My dear! I hadn't thought of that. It's impossible. Absolutely im-possible."

Impossible. We had no right to knowledge, either general or specialized. But yearly maternities, sleepless nights and dreary days, nursing children, washing, cooking, finished off with eclampsia or puerperal fever — no objection to that. Feminine vocation.

I liked to work with my hands. I had nothing against it. I considered that a woman should know how to make a neat darn, to cut out and sew a tailored suit, to beat up a mayonnaise and turn out a *ballot-tine*, repaint a wall, plant a rosebush, change a tire and build a house; yes, why not if need be. But so many men could do such things and they weren't denied the right to think for all that. Why? Why?

I had lots of time to ask why, and painful whys at that, but that was precisely the most irritating thing of all. Why all this mediocrity? And why hadn't I had the right to choose something else? And why couldn't I put my hands on the tools or the skeleton key necessary to open the door of that damned prison? I would have had to meet people who could have helped me. I would have had to be ready, in all simplicity, to admit my ignorance and ask questions. And in the end, sloth takes hold of you when there is too much to do and all alone.

In the meantime, I continued to read *The Annals of Good Saint Anne* and the novels people lent me. It's a great crime not to put a well-organized library at the disposition of a child who likes to read. In this matter more than in any other, time lost is irrevocably lost. The balance built up by a healthy hierarchy in reading can't be duplicated. To read *Anne of Green Gables* at twenty-five, and *Forever Amber* at sixteen, is just as bad as it is disconcerting. The passion for books, like any other passion, will feed on substitutes when it lacks real nourishment. The drunkard who has trouble keeping supplied drinks hair lotion. I consumed an extraordinary quantity of hair lotion.

Usually all these books found a home under our mattresses. It wasn't very original. A well-known hiding place. And yet my father never got the idea of looking there. Our beds were a mass of bumps and hollows, for the stock of books hidden there was often considerable, but my father's attention was never drawn to these irregularities. He must have thought that all our mattresses were sadly in need of replacement, and that the best thing to do was not to notice them.

When it was a book we could keep for quite a while, I would sometimes reread it two or three times in a row. I am often surprised to find I have a such a clear memory of the plots of certain second-rate novels which, when all is said and done, is really just so much old lumber in the brain. But I am not surprised for long. Each time it turned out to be a book that in those days I read, reread and re-reread. And to think that now I can't find the time to reread as much as I'd like to.

*   *   *

We had lots of other things to hide: lipstick, cigarettes, clan clothes and, soon, love letters. Extreme caution was the rule, for my father might burst into our rooms at any time without knocking. At night, if he heard a noise outside, he would go around looking out of all the windows, coming in, banging the doors, turning on the lights, waking the whole house up. Because *he* was awake, wasn't he?

In summer, it was mainly the fear of apple thieves that sent him flying out of his bed. We had enough apple trees to keep a barracks in apples — barrels and barrels of them rotted in our cellar every year — but the thought of being done out of a single russet would drive my father mad with rage. The orchard was surrounded by a high fence. But this wasn't much of an obstacle for the neighbourhood scamps. So, urged on by what he felt to be a strict obligation not to lose a single apple, my father got up one morning possessed with a brilliant idea. That day he didn't go to the office. He gulped down his breakfast and sped off to the village, coming back shortly afterwards with everything necessary to confound the thieves. Around the orchard he installed some kind of system which I couldn't describe, but which terminated, at any rate, in an automobile horn. The loudest he had been able to dig up. From then on, you couldn't touch the fence, not even with the tip of your little finger, without a noise like the wrath of God going off. Then, his eyes sparkling with impatience, he waited for night to come. We only knew the half of it.

Along about midnight, the warning horn woke us all out of our first sleep. O.K. That was to be expected. What wasn't, was the two shots that followed. My father was firing at the thieves.

"That madman's ready to kill people for two wormy apples," a voice cried out.

I must confess that our apples were wormy. My father, who was very active when it came to setting traps, was much more sluggish when it came to spraying trees. Since the last farmer had left us, our trees hadn't been treated to the smallest measure of Bordeaux mixture. The codling moths had found in our garden the earthly paradise from which one is never banished. The same thing could hardly be said for the apple thieves. However, the horn wasn't heard again all summer long. That was too bad, in one sense. So much work for just one alarm. I imagine my father must have been disappointed, for sowing terror was his chief pleasure. He wanted to keep the thieves away from his apple trees, yes. But away from the fence so nicely rigged up? No. Just the same, the gun remained in the paternal bedroom until all the apples had been harvested.

Spraying trees, however, would have been one of the rare jobs my father could have done without causing more harm than good. He liked outdoor work. His surplus strength was put to good use there — to our great relief. As the years went by, we could see the effects of his taste for rural pleasures, and of his strength, in what he chose to call embellishments to the property. Though a trifle on the wild side, nature was nonetheless very lovely around our place. The house was situated between the cliff and the river, and I can now appreciate how beautiful it was. But at the time I was deprived of that pleasure, too, like so many others. In my eyes it was just the surroundings to my prison, and it hadn't occurred to me to think them beautiful. The river was just dirty water that, from time to time, overflowed the banks, flowed around the house, filled the cellar and made us even more isolated. The cliff was just a wall that separated us from the rest of the world. It took me years to rediscover a real love of nature.

When my father undertook his embellishments, it was a catastrophe, as usual. One or two hundred magnificent trees were cut down, "to open up the view." The beach was denuded of willows, and the escarpment, where a marvellous collection of trees and flowers grew — elms, oaks, maples, hazels, wild roses, trilliums and anemones — was scraped bare. There also was a graceful stream that cascaded down the side of the cliff and then passed quite close to the house. It was filled in and replaced by drainage pipes and a bit of canal. The view was certainly opened up.

But those were major operations that were dictated by sudden moods. The usual procedure, in the evening after office hours, was for my father to go out and hoe the flower beds — dressed commonly in his newest suit, and the palest too, for like many big men, he had a passion for summer suits that were almost white. There he would exercise a marvellous and irrepressible sort of gift for leaving the weeds and pulling up the good plants, often young seedlings we had been transplanting all day long. Then, his work finished, he would come back to the house, vigorously wiping his hands on his pale pants, a gesture that we must studiously avoid noticing. The least glance might have been interpreted as a reproach, which in turn would have triggered the mechanism of the source of all our troubles. Of our one trouble, I mean, for though its origins might be infinite, the result was always the same. The next day he would come down in a fresh suit, yesterday's trousers over his arm.

"It's practically nothing. Just a touch with a damp cloth should fix it."

With the tone one takes to explain that you can't make an omelette without breaking eggs. And let someone else clean up the shells! Sometimes the three of us would spend the whole day at it. Then he would go off to work, but not without first casting a satisfied glance at his flower beds. The weeds were burgeoning!

*　*　*

Things were burgeoning under the parental roof, too. And my father was getting worried. His five daughters now ranged from eleven to twenty-three. Was he going to be left with all that on his hands? But to let us do what was necessary to find ourselves husbands — that is, go where there was some risk of meeting boys — that was out of the question. All things considered, it would be much easier to push us towards the nunnery. The day he got that idea he attacked head-on:

"You never speak to me about your vocation," he said to my sister, Dine. "Don't you realize that if the good Lord doesn't send you a husband, it's because he's set you aside for the religious life?"

Poor Dine turned green. Once my father had got wind of God's projects, it wouldn't be easy to explain that she had other plans in mind. From then on the private interviews between them multiplied rapidly. Dine would promise nothing, and my father would leave his study edgier every time.

"I've consulted my spiritual director [we never had one, any of us; for all we had to say any old confessor would do] and he doesn't agree. He says I haven't got the vocation."

The day Dine had that stroke of genius, my father was stopped cold. But when he tried to begin over again with my sister Françoise, I took alarm. Soon it would be my turn, and it was scarcely possible to use the same argument for the third time running. But at this moment fate stepped in, on our side. One of our convent friends was going to join the Carmelites. Before leaving she came to see us and, incidentally, spoke of the dowry — a modest sum, a few hundred dollars — that her parents had to pay. Although we were forbidden visitors, we decided to mention this one.

"One of our school friends came to see us today. She's going into the Carmelites."

"Ah? Her parents must be delighted!"

"In a way, yes. But they have a big family, and the dowry — "

"What do you mean, the dowry?"

"Well, you know, the dowry. Ten thousand dollars."

"What? Why that's sheer madness! And what if the parents are poor?"

"They pay by instalments, so much every month. But they have to be really poor, because inquiries are made."

From that day on God changed his plans for us. My father decided to marry us off. One of the men working under him was a young engineer, still a bachelor. He invited him to lunch one Sunday.

About half-past twelve we saw him get out of his car, a regular colossus, as tall as that, and as broad as that, and what hands! what feet! what shoulders! You know, the ideal son-in-law! Though the reason for inviting him had not been divulged, one look at this edifice was enough to advise us. The giant was destined for one of us, preferably the eldest, as the custom goes.

After the introductions, my father led Hector off to the living room and we returned to the kitchen to put the finishing touches to the meal, whose main dish was a large baked ham. My father, whose taste buds were a little blasé, liked his ham with plenty of strong mustard. Dijon mustard was too mild for him. We made up our own with mustard-powder, great quantities of pepper and really sharp vinegar.

"Do you think he puts his knife in his mouth?"

"I wonder if he likes mustard?"

We nearly died laughing. The meal began. We had purposely complicated the table setting, and there was so much silverware around each plate that it would have taken a master cutler to find his way around in it. A perspiring Hector wore himself out surreptitiously changing forks whenever he found himself in error. Then came the ham.

"Do you care for mustard?" asked my sister, as sweet as an angel.

"Only if it's not too strong."

"No, no. It's quite mild."

Hector reached for the mustard pot and, like the good country boy he was, spread a thick layer over his sliced ham. Even before he had taken his first mouthful, the diabolical exhalations that rose from his plate set his eyes watering. From then on it was mainly scraping off his ham that kept him surreptitiously occupied. Meanwhile, my father, who had never for a moment lost sight of the purpose of this meal, kept on praising our talents without ever noticing the problems his potential son-in-law was wrestling with.

"My daughter are all first-rate cooks, real *cordons bleus.*"

Hector wept assent. In mustard cookery we were second to none.

"They make their own clothes."

We were quite put off by this flood of compliments, which were unaccustomed to say the least. Through his tears, Hector studied our "chapels" and managed to utter a few flattering grunts.

When lunch was over the two men went off together. Originally the house had been without a fireplace, and my father had just realized a long-standing dream by having one put in. It was so new it hadn't been tried out yet. Hector was to have the honour of the first fire. No sooner was the match struck than billowing clouds of smoke invaded the room. His eyes still moist from his confrontation with the mustard, our suitor began to weep anew.

"The worst will soon be over," my father assured him. "Just wait till the draught takes."

We left them to seek refuge in our rooms, the doors closed and the windows open. From there we could hear my father fencing with the tongs, but the fire smoked as much as ever. It should be said that the fireplace remained unusable. My father refused to believe that it was a job for a specialist and had had it built by a man who often came around to do odd carpentry work. Not only did it never give out any heat, it drew off the heat from the radiators. It was never very popular with us girls.

About four o'clock we heard Hector's voice coming up from the front hall.

"Our guest is leaving," my father shouted out.

The three of us came down to say good-bye. Our poor intended looked like a man suffering from acute conjunctivitis. We never saw him again. My father let the subject drop. For several weeks, apparently, he nursed the hope of placing one of his daughters. Months went by. About half a year later, Hector presented his fiancée to him. A young giantess who weighed in at a couple of hundred pounds. That won us some scathing remarks.

"With all your fads about staying thin — as I've told you a hundred times — you'll never get married. That boy is no fool. He meets a nice big healthy girl and he marries her."

The one thing he never suspected was that despite our great desire to leave what we called among ourselves "the dungeon of perpetual virginity," not one of us would have left on the arm of a young man chosen by my father.

Nine months later, Hector's pregnant wife died of eclampsia.

"And yet she looked the picture of health," my father commented.

"Ah yes! That's what happens to fat women," one of us said wickedly.

He caught the intention on the wing.

"At any rate she didn't die an old maid!"

That, at least, was a great consolation.

Though he wanted to marry us off, he always refused us the right to look at boys. Every morning he went to mass, on foot, and we had to accompany him, each in turn. If we inadvertently chanced to glance at the driver of some car, we could expect to be called fallen women all the way there and all the way back. If no automobilist went by — we went to mass in every kind of weather and I remember going when it was thirty-five degrees below zero, a temperature not fit for a car to be out in — he would seek, and find, other symptoms of our rapidly approaching perdition. In winter it didn't matter, for the countryside was deserted, but in summer it was painful. I can still see myself going along beside him while he shouted out, at the top of his lungs, "whore" and all its synonyms because, coming back unexpectedly the night before, he had caught me with bare legs. It was hot. All the houses had their windows open — the neighbourhood had grown populous since the road had gone in — one after another, summer visitors, hearing these shouts in the distance, appeared at their front doors to watch us go by.

"I'll end up sending you to the reformatory!"

The women hurried in and came out again accompanied by the rest of the family. Head hanging, I passed before the wondering gaze of the populace. Something like glory!

I shouldn't have let myself be caught with bare legs. I deserved to have my silk stockings washed in public. It was just too bad. It was worse to have to take this kind of tongue-lashing when we weren't directly involved. It occasionally happened that our only crime was to belong to the same sex as some guilty party we didn't even know. By not acting the way my father expected women to act, any female was likely to get us into the worst kind of trouble. The wife of my father's Minister got us into a jam that lasted for months.

Even though my father shunned every kind of meeting like the plague, sometimes he couldn't avoid them. One summer he had to go to an engineers' convention. He was giving a paper. As is customary in that kind of gathering, the delegates talked all day and had fun at night. There was a ball. That year fashion had dictated evening gowns with no backs, or hardly any. Of all the women present, the Minister's wife's reverse side exhibited the most plunging backline.

"A disgusting spectacle. Skin all over the place. Street walkers don't show so much. But women aren't happy unless they're showing off their skin. If I gave you your own way, you wouldn't hesitate a second to wear those devilish dresses. I know all about you. Leading men into temptation, stirring up bad thoughts, evil passions, that's your favourite pastime. You're all the same . . . blah-blah-blah."

He used to maintain that the least square centimetre of bare skin, or hint of skin beneath material that was a little sheer, would throw a man into agonies of excitement, that the vaguest suspicion of the existence of a breast, or even of a knee, would set off a series of uncontrollable erections. If we hadn't got into the excellent habit of never listening to him, we might have been led to believe that a wave of impotency had swept over all our little boyfriends, for we never met anyone quite so lecherous.

"A dress open right down to here," he bellowed, putting his hand almost on his rump. "Right to here!"

For all the horrified faces we put on, for all the disapproval we displayed, and for all our treacherous disavowal of our own sex, we didn't escape a thing. What my father hadn't dared say to the Minister's wife, we got an earful of. He got so worked up that he came close to believing he had seen us in backless dresses, too. And he might have. For there were dresses he didn't know about hanging at the back of our clothes closets.

* * *

We had scarcely got over this scandal when another broke out. One day when he had some urgent business to settle with one of his engineers, my father decided to go and discuss it on the spot and to take my brother André along with him. It was a Sunday, the offices were closed, and he was invited to the engineer's house. At first everything went all right. But after a while André noticed the paternal brow beginning to cloud up and then my father began to speak of leaving, although he had already agreed to stay to dinner. Without knowing why, André saw that he was being constantly watched by my father's pale blue eyes which were growing paler by the minute. A sure sign of anger. Not knowing what kind of expression to put on, André stared fixedly straight in front of him.

Suddenly my father got up as only he knew how to do it when he was furious, that is, with a violence which imperilled the chair he had just left and everything within reach. The farewells were brief. My brother followed him out in perfect docility.

"If I'd known the kind of people we were going to get mixed up with, I'd have left you at home. And all the more so if I'd known what an ass you were going to make of yourself."

André couldn't understand. He didn't say a word, waiting for the explanation to come. It was delayed. My father lost himself in various imprecations and in general observations on morality, on the inroads evil makes on the soul through the eye, on the dangers inherent in leaving one's home and associating with other human beings, for perversion is everywhere nowadays.

"Instead of turning your eyes away from that nude, you couldn't keep them off it. You were hypnotized by that picture, and you made sure you sat down right across from it. Do you realize that you are now in a state of mortal sin? That if we had an accident on the road you would go straight to hell? You took communion this morning and this afternoon you sit there gobbling up all that nudity. I've done all I could to protect you from the spectacle of immoral pictures, et cetera."

The best part of the story was that André hadn't even seen the nude. When we were with my father, we were so preoccupied with watching ourselves that we never noticed anything that was going on around us. This particular scandal absorbed us for several months. Whenever he came into the house, my father would cast a disgusted and scornful glance at his son, as if saying to himself, "It's really something to have to live with such pollution." Poor André couldn't cleanse himself of his disgrace. As soon as his attention seemed to wander:

"Still thinking of that filth? But, by God, you'll go mad!"

Which might have happened.

It was true that every provision was taken to spare us the spectacle of immoral images. My father subscribed to the *National Geographic Magazine*, which from time to time carried photographs of naked aborigines. He received it at his office and only brought it back to the house after he had meticulously scribbled out everything that might have given us food for thought. Which is to say, that he left nothing visible but the heads, hands and feet. He might have simply torn out the page. That would have deprived him of the pleasure of bearing down on us, roaring:

"One of you tried to scrape off the ink I blackened out these photographs with. Who was it?"

How to explain that we weren't ready to risk torture to get a glimpse of the scribbled-out sausage-like breasts of some African or Australian bushwoman? How to make him understand that it was he himself, in an excess of zeal, who had scratched through the paper?

As for the pictures that graced our walls, there was no chance they would lead us into temptation. They were all by my father's own hand. The resurrection of Christ, the sick child healed by

Christ, Christ crowned with thorns. When I was still too young to have a sense of humour, these pictures filled me with shame. Not that they were particularly ugly when compared to what one finds elsewhere. It was all this parading of piety I found so humiliating.

"I did these myself," my father would say naively to the vicar on his parochial visit — the only official visit we were sure of having once a year.

The vicar would protest admiringly, especially if he was the one who never knew how to leave and was accordingly always short on conversation.

My father's attitude towards painting might seem mysterious. It was only revealing. He was interested in no other painting than his own. Other painters were a subject of complete indifference to him, and he had no wish to know about them. The sum total of pictorial art was himself. He never felt the need to visit a museum or leaf through an art album — after all, they were usually full of naked women — for he already knew all he wanted to on that subject. And yet, to hear him talk about the time when he had painted all those daubs was enough to be convinced that he had put his heart into them. How long ago exactly? It was hard to know, for, eager to pass as an ex-child-prodigy, every once in a while he would take them all down and set back the dates that appeared at the bottom of the canvases. As a result, "I wasn't twenty-five years old," little by little became, "I wasn't fifteen."

He went back to it in his old age. And what subject did he choose? His own portrait, after a photograph that showed him already beginning to grow a little bald. In the portrait his hair crept down and nearly covered his forehead, Beatle style. What I admire is the sort of simplicity that presided over such frauds. He knew that we saw him setting the dates back, that we could compare the hairline he had given himself with the one on the photo, but it never occurred to him that we might find that funny.

Just as naively, he left the expense account sheet the Ministry provided him lying around. With a certain bitterness, we could see where he had billed the government for all kinds of little services he made us do for him for nothing. This way he drew credit on one of his paternal rights, since he had them all.

"One must never lie, either to spare someone sorrow, or even to save a life."

It was one of his numerous principles. He often repeated it. All it really meant was, "No one has the right to deceive me." Nothing more.

"Think of others!"

Which meant, "Think of me." For the greater comfort of this "me," he had mobilized morality and religion to serve him. We were supposed to spare him every inconvenience, out of a spirit of Christian charity; but to accept the same inconveniences ourselves, still in a spirit of Christian charity, if he should be the author of them.

"Do unto others as you would that they should do unto you."

He was always ready with that one — for our benefit. If it had been pointed out to him that perhaps he wouldn't have liked to be beaten, what would he have answered? That that didn't have anything to do with it, since his anger was saintly anger.

The older he got, the more he was filled with the sense of his own sanctity. As he was built solidly and his life seemed likely to last a long time yet, there came a day when impatience got the better of him. So his canonization wasn't for next week — not that he hoped it would be, for he still wanted to die at a hundred, but a saint in the family would have tickled his fancy. It was a time when young candidates for beatification were springing up all over the place: Guy de Fontgalland, Gérard Raymond. Their photographs were going around. Usually they were first communion pictures, the kind where the photographer tells you to join your hands and look at the ceiling. Our paternal grandparents had had a little girl whom they lost quite early. Little Eva. Unfortunately her first communion photograph couldn't be displayed — she had died at three.

"I wouldn't be surprised if little Eva had died in the odour of sanctity," my father began to repeat in a dreamy voice. "I can remember her well. She was a good little thing."

Soon he was talking about nothing else, and thought it necessary each time to add a word of scorn for Guy and Gérard. Impostors! After a few weeks it was quite common to hear him say: "I myself, who have a little sister among the saints . . . ." Then one day he told us he intended to advise his confessor about this. That was the end of the adventure. After that confession we never heard any more about the little saint.

*   *   *

My father's confessions must have been really something! Never wrong, always right, and the angels not fit to be my cousins. He went every two weeks and came out of the confessional with the air of a man who is to be congratulated. While he recited his three Aves penance, he kept track of the time we spent when it was our turn behind the curtain.

"You stayed quite a while at confession. What did you have on your mind?"

It didn't take much prompting after that to cut it down to a minimum. So in ten minutes the whole family was absolved. Hands joined, eyes lowered, we would leave the sacristy one after another and take our places in the church. We had to find a place in the very front pews — masses heard at the back of the church weren't worth a fig. The same applied to late services — winter and summer we always went to six o'clock mass, the only one that counted. In the long run, a Protestant wasn't any worse in my father's eyes than a Catholic who went to eleven o'clock mass in the last row.

Then came the awesome moment of communion. My father would stay in his place until he had seen his whole tribe file up to the rail, and only then would he go up himself. For us, coming back from communion was a dangerous exploit. Whatever attitude we adopted, it was never the right one.

"Can you tell me why you looked so idiotic coming back from communion?"

Ah, those paternal questions!

If one of us hadn't taken communion, as soon as we got back to the house there was a private interview in store for him, during which he would be ordered to say why he had abstained. It was an interview to avoid at any price.

In winter we went to mass in a taxi because my father could never coax a cold motor into life without stalling it completely, which would have put us in great danger of not arriving until the seven o'clock mass. If the cab was late, my father would begin to stew:

"All right! We'll start off on foot and meet it on the way."

We had to leave the house at a run and hurry along the road. After a few minutes the taxi would show up. In we'd pile. And to get headed back in the right direction, the driver would have to come all the way back and turn in front of our house, since it was the only place in the road there was enough room. We would stifle our laughter in our coat collars and the driver, who knew my father well, would wink at us when he got the chance. He was a very good-looking young fellow.

How to penetrate my father's attitude towards religion? Maybe he had such a good opinion of himself that he saw God in his own image and likeness: intolerant, impatient, incapable of putting up with the least tardiness or the least inconvenience, deaf to reason and predisposed to pommel the people in the last row.

Our reputation for piety was widespread throughout the whole county. So it was a great surprise the Sunday my father was accused from the pulpit of maintaining a brothel. His name wasn't mentioned, but "the owner of the red brick house by the little station" was him. Everyone knew that.

My father had bought this red brick house in the course of the winter. For several years, one of our convent schoolmates had lived there. She died when she was twenty-two, in the spring, exactly one year after Mother. During the funeral service for Marie-Laure, I had cried a lot, not for her — I didn't know her very well — but for Mother, who I had just lost. That seems to me to be quite a natural reaction, but the nuns made fun of me. I was crying for someone who wasn't anything to me, they said, and I was the very worst sort of actor.

Anyway, my father had bought this house along with two or three others. It was during the Depression, and you need to have lived through it to know how easy it was to be rich as long as you had a good steady salary and money in the bank. The fall in prices quadrupled the buying power of the privileged few. As evidence of the point I am trying to make, just before the crash my father had sold part of his land for forty thousand dollars cash and shortly after bought it back again, plus several other neighbouring properties, land and dwellings, for six thousand dollars.

One of these houses was rented at the time of this transaction, and my father had agreed to respect the lease. With our habit of never sticking our noses out the door after sundown, we hadn't noticed that there was a good deal of traffic there at night. Obviously there was a lot of coming and going on Sunday afternoons, too, which we could observe, but we thought the tenants just had a big family. Alas! the people we took for cousins were only clients.

"My dear brethren," said the curé, "one amongst you, whom we might have taken for a man of duty, tolerates his tenants keeping a house of ill repute where all the youth of the parish go to their perdition. You all know the place to which I refer — the red brick house near the little station. Is it from love of money that the landlord refuses to oust the proprietors of this house of ill repute? If such is the case, he is as guilty as his tenants, and it is as though he ran this brothel himself."

All eyes were focused on my father, whose ears had turned to violet. As soon as the last word of the sermon was spoken, he rose up like a fury, strode down the aisle — his raincoat floating out behind him, he walked so fast — and into the sacristy where the curé had just preceded him. The whole congregation heard a few well chosen shouts, but someone shut the heavy door almost immediately. After that, all we could make out was a sort of muffled barking. When he came back to his place, his raincoat still out like a topgallant, a loud murmur filled the church. There wasn't a person there who wasn't whispering to his neighbour. My father didn't enjoy a reputation for being good-natured, still he wasn't known as the kind of parishioner who insults the priest in his sacristy. Excitement ran high.

The impure tenants left, and the next week the curé made a statement which, with considerable good will, one might have called a retraction, though one in which his own vanity was better served than my father's honour. But despite that, my father had to be satisfied with this lukewarm apology.

Before the house was rented again in the spring, my sisters and I went to visit it. Except for a narrow passage that had been cleared from the foot of the stairs to the furnace, the cellar was full of empty bottles. There was nothing so very surprising in that, there was no reason to be encumbered with all that glass when you moved. A little notebook that had been left in the attic surprised us more. It was one of the ladies' account books:

Joseph	$2.00
Paulo	$2.00
A little dark fellow	$1.50
An American	$4.00

The melancholy rates of the thirties. Up until then, I had thought what went on in this house, and what was known under the general term "disorders," was only the illegal sale of liquor. On the other hand, I did know the word prostitution, but it had only a bookish connotation for me. So I was astonished to learn that there really were women who sold their bodies, real live women who had nothing to do with literature. I didn't dare reveal my stupefaction to my sisters — they were probably as astonished as I was — for fear of seeming to be an ass, but for months I was tormented by this discovery. So there really were men who, after they slept with a woman, asked, "How much?" paid and went off? That seemed impossible. As for the woman who got the money, I was convinced that she wept herself dry for shame. I didn't lose this last illusion until I had seen the horrible faces of the whores around the Palace Station in Quebec. You didn't have to study them long to be sure there wasn't a single tear to be got there. But I still didn't understand any better the mechanism of prostitution. On the contrary, I was more scandalized than ever. Love seemed to me, if it was free, something nobody is rich enough to pay for, but if it wasn't free, not worth a nickel — and I haven't changed my opinion about that. And it also seemed to me to be worst of all if you had to give good money to girls so horrible they wouldn't have found anyone to make love with for nothing. The world certainly wasn't a very savoury place.

* * *

That same spring we came within a hair's breadth of getting caught. My father had to make his first trip of the season by train, since the roads in the north of his district were still snowed in. So he had left his car at home. Why not use it to take a long drive with some of our friends? Saturday was spent preparing a picnic, and about ten o'clock Sunday morning we were on our way. Although we were a little nervous — taking the paternal car was a bit much, and accidents happen quickly — the party was gay. My sister's boyfriend, who was driving, had relatives in the Beauce and, since none of us was inclined to mischief, we decided to make a round of visits in that area. After dropping in on some cousins, overrun with children, who welcomed us with surprise and embarrassment, we were received with no less surprise and embarrassment by an ancient relative who lived in an old people's home.

"I never have more than three visitors in the whole year," she kept on saying, "and here you are, six all at once."

She couldn't get over it, and to hide her emotion she kept offering us fruit drops. Her bewildered little eyes were topped by two pieces of adhesive tape to hold her paralyzed eyelids open. When the time came to go, she had grown perfectly at home with us and her eyes filled with tears to see us leave.

We headed back on the road to Quebec. Quite happy. Visiting some children and an old lady was quite enough excitement for us.

Just as we were on the point of reaching the house, we saw André who rushed out in front of the car.

"Papa is back. He's in the house."

Warned by some presentiment, my brother had telephoned late that afternoon. As soon as he recognized my father's voice, he had hung up. Then he had come to wait for us at the side of the road.

I don't remember if we screamed, or wept, went pale or red. All I remember is that it was one of those numerous times in my childhood when I would rather have died than face what lay ahead. I only remember the horrible feeling of crumbling away inside, fear and the humiliation that goes along with it. The humiliation of being afraid is the hardest thing of all to forgive.

André had already decided what we should do. We, the three girls, should continue home on foot and pretend that we had spent a couple of hours with some old school friends whom we had met on our way to visit the two little ones at the convent. André would drive the three boys home and bring the car back late that night. Then he counted on disappearing for a few weeks. That is, he would take the blame for the whole escapade himself.

We were used to these sacrifices for the common good. Because we really loved each other. That was why, for example, we had each in turn, for several years, taken the blame for little scrapes Benoît got into — a window broken here, or a cup there. Because my father had conceived a strong hatred for this child and felt himself obliged to punish him even if he came to acknowledge his fault himself, whereas we big girls only ran the risk of a long sermon if, with contrite faces and tear-filled eyes, we would throw ourselves down before my father as soon as he came in, sighing, "I broke a light bulb."

"In recognition of your frankness," he would say to his lying daughter, "I won't punish you as you deserve."

There was no question of debating André's sacrifice. It was the only solution. If our escapade had been discovered, the next day all three of us would have been on our way to reform school. After due consideration, the authorities of these schools probably wouldn't have taken in charge three young virgins who had spent their Sunday with children and old ladies, but it was just as well not to tempt fate. In 1930, in Quebec, all such institutions were administered by nuns, so one had to look out!

Meanwhile, we were walking towards the house as quickly as we could, considering the state of our shaking knees. We nursed the hope that André had dialed the wrong number and had mistaken the voice at the other end for my father's. A minimal hope. We had to abandon it as soon as we opened the door. The air was foul with the smoke of all the cigars my father had smoked waiting for us. He was sitting in the living room in the dark, and didn't stir when he heard us come in. That way, he hoped to overhear some revealing remarks.

"Goodness, how late it is!" said Françoise in a trumpet-like voice. "Let's hurry up and say our prayers and get to bed."

These pious words must have disappointed my father's hopes of hearing anything worthwhile, for he turned out immediately.

"Where have you been? Where is André? Where is the car? Was André here when you left?"

The questions came like bursts of machine gun fire. The answers too. It dragged on and on. Our knees were still trembling, but our voices were firm.

Since my father used his car mainly for his work, it was half paid for by the Ministry. None of us had thought of that. After about an hour, with no sign of André yet, my father telephoned to the Deputy Minister to advise him, "My son has stolen the automobile," and to ask if he shouldn't call the police immediately. There were two telephones in the house, which enabled us to hear this conversation. The Deputy Minister seemed very shocked at my father's suggestion.

"All the same, you are not going to compromise your son's future for something that doesn't amount to a hill of beans yet? It isn't even nine o'clock. If he took the car for the evening, he'll be back around midnight, I suppose."

It was my father's turn to be scandalized.

"I don't know how that man brings up his children. He tells me it's only nine o'clock and André may not be back until midnight. . . ."

When evening prayers were over at last, we were given permission to go to bed. Françoise and I shared the big northwest bedroom. As soon as we started to whisper, my father burst in.

"I heard you whispering. What were you talking about?"

The uselessness of these inquiries had never been proven as far as my father was concerned. In twenty years he had never got an honest answer, but he continued to ask questions; for even though he held us all to be liars, he was convinced that we couldn't go on abusing him very long. Nature, which doesn't give all offensive and defensive devices to the same animal, to prevent the other species from disappearing, has made tyrants vain. That's why the race of the tyrannized has been able to survive and to propagate until our own times.

Stretched out in our beds, neither of us could get to sleep. Though God knows how tired we were. And bruised too, it goes without saying.

About two o'clock we heard the crunch of tires on the gravel, then André's footsteps going away. We were quaking for fear that he would be caught, for my father had already been up two or three times to ask us questions that had just occurred to him:

"What did you have to eat for lunch?"

We had had our picnic, of course, and the Sunday roast was still uncooked in the refrigerator.

"Steak," we answered in chorus.

My father:

"And why not the roast?"

The chorus:

"There was a power failure until noon."

For that matter, these supplementary interrogations went on all night. The next morning, while my father was at mass, Dine telephoned, despite the early hour, to her friend Annette to inform her that "we were at your place yesterday." Annette was in on the whole family story and was always ready to help us.

It was my father's sister who took charge of the telephone part of the investigation. But the enemy camp really didn't stand a chance. Whereas our batteries were already in place by Monday morning, they didn't think to check out our alibis till Wednesday. We had time not only to invent them and spread the word, but even to polish them up. Try as they might to make us confess that this memorable Sunday had had dire effects on our virtue, lack of proof forced them to drop their charges.

* * *

André came back after a couple of weeks. He had spent this time with a friend, Jean, who drove him back and waited in the car outside the front door to see what the result of the interview would be. For the first time, my father was obliged to compromise with one of his children. It was summer, the windows were wide open, the least yelp could be heard by the strapping youth waiting outside in his car. In addition, my father seemed a little confused by this turn of events. What next! Despite the sequestered life he had forced on us, he was obliged to see that his daughters did have some friends, and that his son even had a very devoted pal. It was the beginning of the end. A very modest beginning. I should say right away that this progress was regularly accompanied by daily setbacks.

During the following winter our friend Marcelle, who had often come to spend the afternoon with us, found the courage to stay rather than leave before my father came back, as she usually did. I say courage, because if my father was quite conciliatory when he had a boy like Jean in front of him, he was perfectly intrepid with feeble females.

A few weeks later Marcelle invited us to spend Sunday afternoon at her house and, after interminable hesitations, my father agreed to liberate us. Before we left we had to think up some pretty smart hiding places for our things — letters, cosmetics, et cetera — for we hadn't the least doubt that he would want to compensate for his tolerance with a little curiosity.

We tried the same thing every third Sunday, then every other Sunday. Almost right away calls from our girlfriends masked other invitations. Instead of going to see them we would go to the movies with our boyfriends.

The year before, too, we had been able to sneak away for a few hours on Sunday, but only one Sunday a month. My father had started again to attend the services of the Tertiary Order of Saint Francis which he had neglected for some time. He took us with him because he cherished the hope of seeing all three of us join the Tertiary Order. The ceremonies took place in the little church in the rue des Franciscains. Our beaux waited for us on the street corner, we went into the church at the back, and when we saw my father dressed in his brown robe come out of the sacristy and sit down at the front, we would slip out and join them. We didn't have a thing to worry about. The brown robe was our guarantee of security. You can scarcely chase your daughters through the streets dressed in a cassock. The only trouble was this hope of his that we, too, would end up wearing Franciscan brown.

"If you turn up in cassocks, it's all over with us," our boyfriends said, for we had told them of our father's dreams for us.

Once again it was my eldest sister — I am thinking of the business about religious vocations — who had to bear the brunt of the first attack. Day and night she heard about nothing else than the Tertiary Order. My father even went so far as to insinuate that she might find there the young man whom God had destined for her. A false promise! We had had an eyeful of the young men who used to go there. As a general rule — and I mean very general — they tended to be pretty washed-out, and the Franciscan outfit didn't suit them badly at all. If, after having done so little for us already, that was what God had in store for us —

This time again, Dine used the pretext of her confessor's advice.

"I spoke to my director of conscience about it. He says I have an overscrupulous soul. I am too punctilious to get involved in a congregation, in works of charity and so on — He says I should use my leisure time to get out and amuse myself, to see people. He claims it's the only way to get over my scrupulosity."

Astonished and admiring — though overscrupulousness is considered a defect elsewhere, it has always been well regarded in Quebec — my father stared at Dine in complete silence. Françoise and I, our teeth clenched for fear of breaking out into laughter, stared at her too. Looking like a perfect booby, her hands clasped and her eyes lowered, Dine played the part of a village bigot.

Little by little my father came back to his senses. There were things in this revelation that didn't seem to please him.

"To see people? — to see people? That's a funny kind of remedy."

By great good fortune he didn't often figure things out in terms of two plus two make four. When Dine asked his permission to go and spend three days in a retreat house, she was granted it right off. He had forgotten her spiritual director's recommendations. The truth of the matter was quite different — my sister had been invited to a ball!

The week before this event was spent sewing. It was the first time I had worked on an evening gown. I was all of a tizzy. It had to be made so that it could be shortened and used again, for our secret economies didn't permit us dresses that were only worn once.

At last Friday came, and Dine left, supposedly for the retreat house. In fact she went straight to Uncle Eugène and Aunt Berthe's where she spent a memorable weekend which gave us things to talk about for months afterwards: he said, and I said, and he replied, and it's then that . . . all winter long!

The other side of the coin was that she had to give an account of all the sermons preached during the retreat. That was really something! But on the same order, something happened to my brother André that was a lot tougher. Reading in the newspaper that pious young men went to Sainte-Anne-de-Beaupré on foot, and that these pilgrimages took place at night, gave him "ideas." When told about the pilgrimages, my father proved enthusiastic. To be able to combine walking and piety like this, fell in exactly with all his predilections. At seven o'clock Saturday night, André left, sped on with paternal blessings. He came back about noon the next day. This went on for a good part of the summer.

One Saturday morning, my father got up feeling frisky.

"I've decided to go along with you to Sainte-Anne's. Of course, I'm not in condition like you, but I think I can keep up, and twenty-five miles doesn't frighten me."

André couldn't say so much himself. The poor boy came back next day with bloody feet and drooping wings, and all the more exhausted because he had had to pretend not to be, for hours on end.

$$* \quad * \quad *$$

Little by little, thanks to obstinacy, courage, imagination, and fraternal solidarity, our life was becoming less intolerable. It was now common for us to obtain permission — not always without difficulty, but difficulties were our stock in trade — to go to Marcelle's or Aline's or Annette's. If one of us happened to be out when my father came back from a trip, there were no longer life-and-death clashes. Of course this required imagination. We were up to it. You had to swear there was no "boy business" involved. We swore. Yes, truly, our life was becoming less intolerable. It was around this time that my father's family chose to find us a stepmother. Just when we were beginning to breathe a little easier.

Here I pause for a word with the reader. It is extremely unliterary, I know, but I can hear what you are thinking from here, Dear Reader, and I can't resist making room for a bit of dialogue.

"You're not going to throw in a stepmother on top of all the rest?"

"You will have to excuse me, Dear Reader, I don't wonder that at times you must think I'm laying it on a bit thick, but I can't help it. Truth is sometimes . . . et cetera. Yes, as a matter of fact, I am going to throw in a stepmother."

"A real stepmother? That's all you needed!"

"A real one. We did need one desperately."

My father was supposed never to remarry. He had promised heaven that, as I told you. And then, suddenly, all the women in his family, sisters, cousins, et cetera, got it into their heads to find him a wife. I do believe that among all their nasty reasons there was one nice one — a stepmother would help us to find husbands. A relative of my father's knew a nurse who would fill the bill and who, it just happened, had three sons. There are people like that who see things with great simplicity: a girl, a boy; a girl, a boy; a girl, a boy; that makes three marriages. My father's sister was immediately convinced that the finger of Providence was pointed in that direction. The possibility that the young people might not please each other was excluded. Even then, my father's relative had known the matrimonial candidate for years, so the fact that they could have thrust this foolish, ignorant, wicked stepmother on us remains one of those enigmas I have never been able to solve.

Their first encounter was arranged for a Wednesday at five. My father came back about seven to announce his marriage. After taking tea with the women of the family and the lady in question, he had driven the latter home and asked her to marry him. She accepted. Just like that. It was November the seventeenth; the wedding would take place the twenty-ninth, a Monday.

We weren't presented to her, Dine, Françoise and I, until Saturday, the twenty-seventh. The others were at school and weren't to meet their stepmother until the Christmas holidays, a month later — they didn't know what they were missing.

"She's a pretty woman," my aunt had said. "Lovely brown eyes."

There wasn't anything impossible in that, for she was only forty-nine and, as we were well disposed to her, we immediately imagined her handsome, pleasantly plump, just enough to be well rounded and graceful, large eyes with dark eyelids, her hair heavy and well dyed, her voice harmonious — in short, a lush autumnal fruit. For my part, I imagined her as I should want to be myself, and I still don't like people who don't age well.

What we saw enter the house was a kind of Buddha with cascading chins. The lovely brown eyes were mighty small, and no trace of thought enlivened them. The mouth was shapeless and looked more like a bad scar — and a scar that opens from time to time is abominable. Behind this, two cheap dentures clattered loosely and noisily. The body was like a cone standing on its point: the shoulders were massive, the breasts enormous, the waist bigger than the hips. The remainder dwindled down: thin hips, skinny legs. This precarious structure rested on a pair of uncommonly deformed feet. But the worst thing, I come back to it, was the chins. They were enhanced by long vertical wrinkles, and they trembled ceaselessly. We were speechless.

We pushed her towards the living room where she sat on the very edge of a chair — out of respect for her corset, a powerful housing with as many whalebones as the sands of the sea — placed one hand on top of the other over her left breast and said, in an excessively vulgar voice:

"It's a big house!"

"What were you doing when I called to tell you we were coming?" my father asked.

"We were making cakes."

"Cakes! What kind of cakes?"

He grinned widely and incessantly. He licked his chops like a greedy boy. He made coy faces. We hadn't ever seen that before, and we gaped at him incredulously. So that we forgot to talk.

"It's a big house!"

"What kind of cakes?"

All during the visit that was the main gist of their conversation. Every time a new silence threatened, one of the two would pitch in with the house or the cakes.

After half an hour they left.

"She's pretty ugly — "

"But she seems to be a nice person — "

"Did you see the bridegroom? A lambkin."

"A chick."

To tell the truth, he looked so touchingly harmless it was pitiful to see. On the telephone he didn't speak, he cheeped, and in a voice so soft and thin that she was forever asking him to repeat. However, her apparent deafness didn't seem to bother my father. One defect more or less —

Though there may be something very unpleasant in a man choosing a woman on the strength of looks alone, it must be said that the man who picks them too awful isn't any more excusable. It looks as if he were thinking: "For my purposes it's quite sufficient." In the case of people who have known each other for a long time and who can justly appreciate other qualities of mind or heart, maybe it's different, but in this case —

* * *

At last Monday, the day of the wedding, arrived. The elements were opposed. The day before, just after lunch, snow began to fall so heavily that my father judged it wisest to go and sleep in town for fear of being snowed in the next day. The ceremony took place at nine. Because of the storm it was impossible for us to attend. The first train through after the tracks had been cleared got us to Quebec just in time for the wedding lunch at my father's sister's.

From having to wade through snowbanks in which we had sunk up to our waists, we arrived with skirts, stockings and shoes wringing wet. I don't remember how my sisters were dressed — in "chapels" for sure — but I remember I was wearing a wretched claret-coloured dress, an old castoff of that very aunt's, as it happened. This dear woman, out of kindness I have no doubt, gave us the dresses that she didn't wear any longer. As soon as we got them, in her mind they turned new again. If only we had been able to do them over. But my aunt wouldn't hear of it. She retained the right to have a say in how we used them. We had to wear them as they were, badly cut and badly sewn, especially the sleeves, which were so sloppily mounted that in no time the cloth split at the back seams. Which gave us a chance to throw them out.

"You don't sew too badly," she used to say sometimes. "You get that from me."

Happily for our vanity, we ourselves claimed to hold this talent from Grandmother. Claimed silently, that is. In short, my claret dress took all morning to dry. The wide pleated skirt had plenty of time to blister and waffle and turn up at the edges. While I dried out in my chair, I noticed one of my new stepbrothers staring at my feet. I was keeping them crossed so the sole of my shoe showed. The lack of sole. To block the hole I had put in a piece of rubber, a nice bright red piece. The boy must have been quite puzzled, for my father had just built up a grand reputation for generosity in the family. He had offered his penniless bride a fine trousseau: dresses, coats, furs and all the little things that go with the big ones. She had accepted gladly, and it was a good thing too, because these handsome gestures were not likely to be repeated often. My young stepbrother probably took me for a sloppy girl who didn't care if she went around in rags. I did have another pair of shoes, but I couldn't wear them in front of my father who forbade us, as I have said, to wear high heels.

The newlyweds left for New York on the half-past-one train. On a two-week trip. We had never had such a holiday. It should be said that we had had to push pretty hard to get my father to take the plunge. At the start of the engagement he was determined not to budge.

"What's that? No honeymoon? The poor woman has been working without a break for so many years, a little rest wouldn't do her any harm. And you, too, you never go anywhere except on business — "

As you can imagine, kind wishes swelled our hearts. For my own part, I practically had tears in my eyes.

"You really deserve it, both of you — "

By temperament, my father wasn't one to forego any advantages he justly deserved. Thanks to that, we were able to enjoy two weeks of peace. The last for a long time.

Without cutting down on our usual number of outings and little dinner parties, we sent out invitations for a really grand reception as soon as the date for the marriage was fixed.

My father always got a great many presents at Christmas. Road contractors making up to him. Those who knew him well sent him cigars, those who didn't, whisky or champagne. By cases of half a dozen bottles each, usually. These would lie around in the cellar for a while, until finally my father would get around to disposing of them. At the time I'm talking of we had two cases of champagne and a case of whisky. Since the future promised to be uncertain, we had decided to shoot the works and help ourselves to these. It was a somewhat perilous plan, but at the time I had a boyfriend who claimed he could rig things up to make it look as though the bottles had exploded all by themselves, which really might have happened, he said, if someone had had the bad judgment not to lay them down on their sides. All you had to do, he said, was to uncork the bottle very carefully and, once it was empty, break it, after replacing the cork and its wire guard. In practice, we discovered that our little friend's know-how was illusory, and that when a bottle of champagne had been relieved of its cork it's useless to try to put it in again. So what! We had invited our friends to a champagne party, and technical problems could wait until tomorrow.

I was really disappointed by my first glass. Once again I had let myself be taken in by literature. I had thought, from associating with the characters of Maurice Dekobra, that one couldn't drink champagne without experiencing a pleasure that was almost too great to bear. I was even more disappointed — though I had been advised, thanks to literature again, about the merits of *brut* and *extra-dry* — to find, as it seemed to me, that it was drier than need be. I was still at an age when to be good, everything had to be sweet. And it was Pommery 1926. I'd gladly take a little glass of that today.

To make things look genuine, it was decided, with regret, not to drink it all. We left several bottles as proof of good faith. In the morning, after disguising our theft as an accident by a few hammer blows, we carried the debris off to the stream. As for the whisky, which we had already tasted at less sumptuous receptions — I had been disappointed in that too — it was easier to recork. Our procedure here was to make extractions and replace them with tea.

* * *

The honeymooners returned on the date scheduled. On pretext of wanting to prepare a homecoming lunch, we had persuaded them to telephone us the day before they got back. They arrived about one. We welcomed our stepmother with open arms. Good will oozed out at every pore.

She had a funny look on her face, the stepmother. Later she confessed to us that the honeymoon had been somewhat painful. From the second day on, my father had indulged in interminable scenes of jealousy.

"That man was looking at you. Who is he? Is he one of your lovers who's followed you down here?"

After that, any man loitering around alone in the hotel lobby was suspected of being a jilted lover who had travelled from Quebec to New York in the hopes of finding the unfaithful one and of being able to contemplate her from a distance. Hoards of lovers. That might have been flattering — especially since the poor creature had manifestly passed the age a good many years ago when a man, and in this case several men, would jump on a train to follow her on her honeymoon. But my father didn't have the knack of the flattering reproach, and his wife was soon reduced to crossing the lobby at a dead run. So she brought back with her certain doubts as to her marital future.

The lunch was ready. The whole family sat down. On occasions like this, good humour is the order of the day. So we were all good humoured, but the tone was artificial and it was hard to keep up.

"I'm waiting for your report," said my father as soon as he had unfolded his napkin. "Did anything unusual happen?"

It was too good a chance to miss.

"No — Oh, yes — You know those bottles in the cellar, some kind of cider — "

"The champagne?"

"Yes, the champagne cider — "

"Not champagne cider," my father cut in, exasperated — our ignorance made him almost ashamed — "just champagne, or champagne wine."

"All right. Well, nearly all the bottles are broken. It's as if they'd exploded. The stuff was running all over."

"Were they lying down?"

"No, no, no! They were all standing straight up, over in a corner."

"But they should be kept lying down."

"Ah?"

"Maybe that's the reason — too bad! I'll take what's left, and the case of whisky, over to the party the people at the Ministry are giving for me. It's a good chance to get rid of the filthy stuff."

We heard from friends that the Scotch served at this reception was judged insipid and ineffective. And yet the colour was good.

We had juggled our way through that one nicely, and the luncheon continued.

"The cutlets are delicious," said the stepmother.

"I hope you won't get into the habit of buying veal at this time of year," my father remarked. "It's the season when it's most expensive, and after all I've just spent it's time to start making economies."

After this thoughtful observation, general embarrassment settled in, and the meal ended in almost total silence.

The first days, seven or eight in all, our stepmother was very friendly. Then everything went sour over money. She was so afraid that our father would give us a single cent, that it made her sick. She cried all day the first time one of us got enough to buy a pair of stockings.

"What are you crying for?"

"I've just had a letter from my daughter. I haven't seen her for so long — "

It was always Françoise and I who went to get the mail at the post office, so we knew there hadn't been any letter from her daughter, but since the same "pigeon post," as we called it, seemed to operate each time we received a half-dollar from my father, it didn't take us long to recognize the source of the salt water. The fear of seeing us with a little pocket money lasted until her death. When she was in her last week, she still kept her purse under her pillow and struggled up out of partial unconsciousness to pay the tradesmen, who had to be brought to her bedside and to whom she would go so far as to say, "Pay yourself," rather than let my young sisters touch her cash. A few weeks after Christmas — our annual present had been upped, we now received five dollars — we each noticed, one after another, that some of our money was missing. Then it was our handkerchiefs, gloves and rosaries that disappeared. When my sisters began to get their trousseaux ready, they had to go three times a week and retrieve their pillow cases and table napkins from this person's bureau drawers. Whenever she noticed that the things she had stolen had been taken back, the pigeon post passed again. Before spring had come, open war had been declared between us.

About this time, our paternal grandmother became gravely ill.

To tell the truth, I must confess that I never experienced any tender feelings towards this grandmother. Then as now, and as always, it wasn't, and isn't, her face that the word "Grandmother" evokes for me. I transferred to her part of the animosity her son inspired in me. I was convinced that she was responsible, by weakness, or ineptitude, for part of our misfortunes and that the only reason my father's violence was so devastating was because no one had checked it at the source. Then, too, I didn't know her very well. I had almost always seen her in my father's company, that is, in an atmosphere of silence, uneasiness and boredom. I never had a chance to learn what she was really like. My cousins liked her, and not without reason, I think. But then, for them everything was quite different. They were happy. That changes everything. They went to her house whenever they liked, each deciding for himself, alone; whereas we never went except as a delegation, as the Pumpkin Family, we used to say. My cousins didn't live under the same system of arbitrary edicts and it wasn't felt necessary to uphold a paternal tyranny on their behalf, whereas we couldn't do a single forbidden thing without being denounced — if we were caught. That's what's called upholding authority. As if children were so stupid they didn't know the difference between authority and justice. As if we had a respect for authority that must be carefully preserved.

When we met our cousins at our grandmother's, we looked like some strange kin from the other end of the earth, mumbling and outlandish. That didn't humiliate us. It was a precious façade, our mask, and it was too useful to sacrifice in the name of vanity. It was common knowledge that we didn't know anyone, that we never saw anyone, that we never went anywhere. So where would we have learned any of the social graces? And how could we have explained away the ones we could have shown if we'd wanted to? It was always a little annoying to be compared unfavourably to our cousins who were so intelligent and self-reliant, but it was the price we had to pay for our all-too-relative liberty. And who would have believed to look at us that we could receive guests graciously, hold a conversation, drink champagne and dance the fox trot. Even though in moments of rage my father used to call us "fallen women" for no reason at all, he must have thought, to see us looking such simpletons, that we couldn't fall very far.

"You're just like a band of wild Indians," my aunt used to say.

It was true. We would lower our eyes and blush while our civilized cousins collected compliments. For all that, they were very nice to us, and we might have been friends if my father had permitted it, but there wasn't a hope of that. Our grandmother's illness gave rise to several gatherings which might have brought us closer together, but fate took all that trouble for nothing.

Ordinarily, these encounters took place at night. Towards one in the morning we would be advised that the patient had taken a turn for the worse. My father would come up and shake us out of our sleep. Every time, he pulled out all the dramatic stops. He was really good at this. He used such a tragic vocabulary you would have thought that his young mother was quite unexpectedly in some dreadful danger. Now aged eighty-seven, she had been ill for a long time and had only managed to stay alive over the past five years by putting up a prodigious fight. We would have to get dressed in two minutes and all jump into the car which my father would drive off like a madman.

This sometimes happened three or four nights in a row. Terribly groggy and desperately short of sleep, we were still supposed to appear grief-stricken. I kept thinking of Grandmother who had died without having seen us a single time in three years, and I fumed with rage. I thought of Mother, too, and of the parental decree issued when we went to look at her for the last time: "I don't want to see a single one of you crying." That didn't help me put on a grief-stricken expression now. The situations were just too grotesquely disproportionate.

In ten minutes, when it normally took twenty, we would arrive at my grandmother's house. All eight of us — my brother André was working in Montreal that summer — piled into the vestibule. When my uncle, my father's brother, was there with his wife and children, that made eighteen people in the house, if you counted the regular inhabitants and excluded our grandmother.

"We'll say the rosary," my father would decree.

There was no question of the whole tribe crowding into the sick room, but we still had to be supervised. That's why our recitation took place as we tramped up and down the passageway outside our grandmother's room. I don't know what the poor woman thought of all this, but I hope on my deathbed I will be spared having eighteen rosary-reciters in the neighbourhood, and ambulating ones at that. This woman had nothing of the sinner about her, and during the last five years she had lived in a diminished state totally incompatible with even the consciousness of sin. What change in her eternal destiny did my father hope to bring about by our noisy prayers? None. But he wouldn't for the world have missed such a good opportunity of acting out his tragic role. At dawn, the noble father and his rosary chorus returned to their dungeon.

"No sense in going back to bed. We'll have breakfast right now."

Chilled, dull-witted, somnambulant, we could hardly wait for my father to leave for work. As soon as the door closed behind him, the stepmother would burst out sobbing.

"If I'd known the number of beads you say in this family, I'd never have married. And all these sleepless nights — how long is this going to go on?"

Her observations fell on a simulation of outraged silence. We went to bed. About nine, the telephone would waken us: a medical bulletin from grandmother's house. The stepmother would burst into tears again.

"If I'd only known! Can't even get any sleep!"

"If I'd only known" became for a while her most frequent remark because, a short time after her marriage, she learned that a widower she had had designs on had just died. And he was even younger than my father. But fate sometimes played such tricks — and she would carry on, philosophizing shamelessly on her bad luck.

Our grandmother died at the beginning of July. In my memory this event is quite confused. For me it's the time that Dine was almost burned alive, and everything else is wiped out by that frightful memory.

Why did my father have a gasoline water heater put in instead of an electric one like everybody else? For reasons of economy assuredly, for the use of such an apparatus didn't represent any other advantage, either real or imaginary, as the one about its economy was. It was difficult and dangerous to operate. My father was careful never to touch it himself. I wished to heaven that the stepmother had done likewise. But she was the queen of meddlers.

It happened the day of the funeral. We girls were alone in the house. Dine went down to the cellar to light the water heater,

Thérèse following her. In the general confusion no one remembered that it had been used twice the day before and that it had been our stepmother who had lit it the last time. And who had turned it off. We had told her a hundred times that there were two taps to close, one for the air, the other for the gasoline. She had only closed the first one. The tank had emptied onto the floor, but the cellar was too dark to see that. Dine didn't notice the smell either, the whole cellar always stank of gasoline. She struck a match. One of the last drops remaining in the tank caught fire, fell to the ground and turned the whole place into a sheet of flame.

Françoise, Margot and I were on the verandah when Thérèse came tearing out. I'll never forget her horrified face, all covered with red splotches. She had only followed Dine to the top of the stairs, and now she rushed out at us shouting:

"Dine's on fire!"

Without really understanding yet, we ran to the cellar door. Thick black smoke poured out.

"Dine! Dine!"

No answer. Then we all got the same idea at once — to try to reach her through the cellar windows. But that year my father hadn't got around to having them opened; the heavy winter shutters were still nailed over them. Then Dine was going to die down in that cellar. I felt that suddenly, like something that had already happened, like something nothing could stop. I instantly had a vision of the future without her, a sort of black hole, and I was submerged by a feeling of horror and despair, the like of which I have rarely experienced in my life. We were racing back inside the house when we saw her coming out the kitchen door. She was still running but she stopped short. She couldn't answer our shouts of joy. She couldn't get her breath back, and each attempt to breathe made an awful noise, a kind of strangled rasping. Our joy gave way to stupor, and we all began to cry.

What a frightful sight! From head to toe, she was black with soot. Strands of hair, burned away by the fire but still held in her chignon, hung down all around her head. Her clothes were in rags, but since her dress was made of a closely woven cotton, luckily it hadn't caught fire; it was just scorched and torn.

All the soot prevented us from seeing if Dine was badly burned, but what we did see was the hand she held out, the hand she had had to seize a burning beam with to get past some obstacle or other. From the base of the fingers the skin was peeled back right to the wrist, where it made a heavy fold that could only be described by the word "cooked."

"We have to put the fire out," she gasped.

In the house it was almost impossible to breathe. Margot, armed with a chair, broke one of the big windows in the study. Then she went to help Françoise and Thérèse who were busy putting out the fire. And very capably, too, because they saved the house and won the praise of the firemen who arrived half an hour later. Meanwhile I helped Dine up to her room, got her into bed, and covered her up.

"I'm going to call the doctor before I tell my father, because he's likely to want to take care of you himself."

"You'll be scolded," she replied.

For once I didn't care a hang. I remember that on the telephone, in my excitement, I shouted like a maniac and the doctor's wife could hardly understand me. The next ten minutes were endless. Dine was suffering more and more and couldn't help crying out in her pain. At last the doctor arrived. While I was waiting I had cut off her clothes and her stockings which showed the extent of the burns — her legs, her forearms, and her face.

"As far as the face is concerned, it's not too serious," the doctor said right away. "They're just superficial burns."

With this good news, and the fire out, we could think about telephoning my father. The funeral was over and he was at his sister's, along with his brother who was, as I have said, an eye, ear, nose and throat specialist. We might need him. My father let out a few well articulated yells over the phone, then crowded everyone into his car and came over.

By the time they all arrived — our cousins came too — we had already begun to wash off the thick layer of greasy soot that covered the walls and the floors. We knew this would be the thing my father would consider the most urgent. This tragedy gave him yet another opportunity to show himself at his best. As soon as my uncle and cousins had left, he took me to task for having cut off Dine's clothes.

"Why would you ever cut things that weren't burnt? I can't understand you."

That was mutual. He also blamed me for telephoning the doctor on my own. But that was nothing to what followed.

As the hours passed, Dine suffered more and more from thirst. In the state she was in — hands bandaged, lips swollen — she certainly couldn't drink without help. I spent the first night with her. When I was settling down for the second, my father came into the room like a lion.

"What's all this about spending the night together? Do you think I'm blind? I know what's behind all this."

"Dine is thirsty all the time."

My father called his wife.

"Give her a bell. When she's thirsty she can ring and you can bring her something to drink."

The stepmother guaranteed she was a light sleeper, went off to bed and woke up next morning fresh as a daisy. Dine had rung and rung, in vain — the other bedrooms were too far away for us to hear the little bell — and she had had to spend the night alone with her thirst. When we got up, we found her feverish and demoralized. I felt my anger turn to homicidal madness. This suspicion of us, the circumstances surrounding it and their consequences, my father's and stepmother's indifference to Dine's horrible suffering, their joint stupidity and cruelty — all that really passed the limit.

A child's heart stubbornly clings to its illusions. (I was almost an adult, so I use the world "child" to suggest the relationship between a father and his offspring.) Between catastrophes he doesn't ask any better than to forget just how far human wickedness can go. He is quite willing to believe that he has gone to the limit in suffering and that this time things won't go as badly as they did the last. He persuades himself that the other's heart must soften in time, and that the time of softening is perhaps already here. And when he runs into the same old rock he is hurt anew, and each time more grievously. I had seen plenty of horrors in our house, and yet this new one took me by surprise.

Our stepmother had been a nurse — not certified, she didn't have the cerebral equipment for diplomas — and the doctor thought he could trust her with changing the bandages once a day. Instead of unbandaging and immediately rebandaging each burn in turn, she uncovered everything, the face, the two arms, the two legs. Then she would stand at the foot of the bed studying the wounds in a learned manner, taking her time, clucking her interest, while Dine, lying there between the open door and the open window, writhed in pain from the effect of the air on the raw flesh.

"Quickly. Do it quickly."

But accustomed to the sick and their childish babblings, the stepmother didn't even answer.

The burns to Dine's face healed quickly and didn't leave any scars. It wasn't the same for her arms and legs. Dine spent six weeks in bed and her case was aggravated after a few days by a long series of boils. At last she was able to get up. After which the doctor sent in his bill. My father flew into a fury.

"Do you see what you've cost me? Without counting all the other expenses: your clothes, the window in my study [all of which had been amply covered by the insurance], your scatterbrained carelessness — "

"If there's any scatterbrained carelessness in it," said Dine, in a trembling voice, "I'm not the one to blame, she is."

Astounded at her own boldness, she pointed a finger as shaky as the voice, at the stepmother, who began, as she always did in embarrassing situations, to cluck like a hen whose chicks are being molested. For the moment, my father didn't find anything to reply to Dine, who took advantage of this to add:

"I'll have scars all my life, and she's the one I'll owe that to. She's the one who left the tap open."

My father finally got his breath back. His reply was ineffable:

"Even if it's true, it's not very charitable to reproach her with it."

It was Dine's turn to be taken aback. She couldn't reply. During the whole conversation, I was at once so satisfied and so terrified that I didn't know what to do with my facial muscles. I felt them twitching every which way, pulled here and there by incompatible emotions.

After these events we were at daggers drawn with our stepmother. Personally, I couldn't even look at her without thinking of the role she had played in this business and the complete absence of any feeling of regret on her part. Up until then there hadn't been, on one side or the other, anything more than little tiffs which mutual fear had prevented from swelling into something bigger. Afterwards, there were to be terrible fights. It was my brother Benoît who always took the prize in such cases. He had a talent for flying into spectacular rages. The wings of his nose would turn green, his eyes would pop out of their sockets, and the veins in his neck would stand out like cords. I can still see him bearing down on our stepmother, who would back up until the wall stopped her; which didn't stop Benoît, for he would come on, and on, until they were finally nose to nose. Since neither of them would deign to lower their eyes, that made them both look horribly cross-eyed.

"I'll kill you," Benoît would shout. "I'll kill you."

The stepmother didn't have the gift of the lethal reply. She only produced a little onomatopoeia. The onlookers choked with laughter at this squinting match, which had the effect of calming Benoît on the spot while multiplying the stepmother's fury a hundredfold.

My father didn't know anything about these battles. If he had, it would have reassured him. He was extremely jealous of Benoît. A short time after his marriage some evil genie had put into his hands a book by his favourite charlatan — and you can imagine what significance that gave the omen — in which remarried widowers were put on guard, in no uncertain terms, against sons born of a previous marriage. "Nearly always," wrote Know-It-All, "such fathers are cuckolded by their sons." The revelation fell upon fertile ground. The poor man read this pirate's story one night before going to bed. If he was suspicious on retiring, he awoke the next morning dead certain. Unlike other men, for whom the night brings good counsel, he always woke up further astray than ever.

That morning it was my turn to accompany him to mass. He didn't open his mouth, either going or coming back. Then he sat down at the breakfast table, still silent, his face twisted, his eyes pale. Nobody breathed.

"Would you like some sugar?" the stepmother suddenly asked Benoît.

My father violently shoved his plate away, leapt to his feet, and barked out several commands which lifted the stepmother from her chair and carried her swiftly into the conjugal bedroom.

We looked at each other completely mystified. Upstairs the din was lively and sustained. Doors slammed, shrieks broke out. As hard as we listened, we couldn't make out much, because both of them were shouting at once. At last the stepmother stopped and started to cry which enabled us to hear the closing paternal imprecations:

"I'll kill you both," he bellowed.

At this — she told us after my father had gone to work — he went to the clothes closet and took out the double-barrelled shotgun previously intended for apple thieves. As for Benoît, he wasn't molested. My father must have thought it was better not to add any fuel to ideas that might come of their own accord. He settled for black looks cast his son's way, which could be interpreted to fit any crime.

After my father left, the poor woman began to sob in a pitiful manner, and went on for hours. Search as she might, she couldn't understand what had got into him.

"Just because I said 'Would you like some sugar'? What kind of proof is that? I've married a madman."

It was Dine who, remembering the story about the mice, got the idea of taking a look at what my father had been reading the night before. At the bookmark, of course, she found the key passage. My father had innocently underlined it. It read approximately as follows: "If you have grown-up sons, it is better not to remarry, for all you do is provide them with a mistress. If you have already remarried, keep a sharp eye out around you. Often such a slight thing as a polite phrase, at table for instance, will put you on the right track and explain a good many things, if you are keen enough to see it." You'd have to be pretty stupid to ignore that kind of a warning.

* * *

Marguerite was the one who suffered most from bad treatment at the hands of the stepmother. That was easy to explain. We big children were beyond that stage. Benoît terrified her. Thérèse still held a dangerous influence over my father. That left Margot as a subject on whom the stepmother's temperament could exercise itself at leisure. Margot kicked back. War ensued.

It was the nine years' war. Margot spent the better part of it boarding at the convent and wasn't taken out until she was twenty-one. She was sent to school beggared of everything, without a cent of pocket money, equipped with only one item of the most necessary things: one pair of stockings, one pair of panties, one towel, et cetera. She had to request permission to do a little wash every night. The time came when her dress was so darned that the sisters didn't know where to hide this pauper when there were receptions at the convent. By this time all the bigger ones had left home. The stepmother could lay it on as thick as she liked. There weren't any embarrassing witnesses.

And yet when she fell ill, who was it who looked after this horrible woman for more than a year? Marguerite. And devotedly.

It is always tempting to try to figure out what goes on in a wicked person's head. Real wickedness is quite an amazing thing. There are several categories. And there could be several methods of classification, but the simplest is to establish two varieties: intelligent wickedness, and stupid wickedness. Intelligent wickedness strikes me as being a rare thing, I have seldom encountered it, but I wouldn't wish anyone to be exposed to the latter variety. One doesn't know which end to pick the thing up by. One doesn't even know if it has ends. There it is, just like that, and one can't tell where it comes from, what its parentage is or how it comes to be there in one's path. It's just there, like some huge immobile and inexplicable monster.

"Well now! What did I do to raise that up?" one asks oneself. "I certainly can't have been acting as I should."

So one acts otherwise. Puts one's heart into it. The huge monster is still there *without knowing itself why it is.*

As I said, we had welcomed this woman pleasantly and even tenderly. That was logical. We had enough on our hands with one enemy around; we weren't going out of our way to make another.

Then too, at the beginning, we didn't have any quarrel with her. Children sometimes feel bitter towards the person who takes their mother's place in their father's heart. But our father's heart — and the place Mother held there. . . . So that as soon as she arrived we greeted her, not perhaps with open hearts — we had only seen her for two hours in all — but with open arms. The first day we spent alone with her was charming. If she had remained what she was that day, everything would have been simple. Much too simple. Like all idiots, she didn't enjoy peace. On the contrary, she set great stock in complications, gossip, secrets, their discovery and propagation, intrigues, plots, and cabals. One session of gossiping with a friend was enough to give her a new lease on life. She would come back with feverish cheeks and sparkling eyes, as if she had just been lovemaking. She was certainly in clover with our family. There was plenty of raw material there. Before you had time to blink, all her friends and all her friends' friends knew all our little secrets, our lies, our tricks, in short, the whole little show we had rigged up for my father. For such "yackers"[5] raw material is never enough and it runs out quickly. You can see where that leads. At first sight, one might think that a yacker might develop some tenderness for the person who furnishes such keen pleasure. Not at all. The gossip is always spiked with hatred directed at the person being talked about. Otherwise one couldn't say anything really evil about him.

The most disagreeable thing about this woman was her complete impermeability to pity. Nothing touched her. I told how unmoved she was by Dine's awful burns. I could even beat that. This woman had a friend who had been reduced to poverty by the Depression. She used to telephone her all the time to tell her stories about new dresses, fur coats, fabulous hats, and then invent stories about dry cleaning, "right now all my nice things are at the cleaners," whenever the friend chanced to visit her.

"Why do you do that?" I asked her one day.

"Bah! That'll teach her!"

To be poor, I suppose.

When none of my father's children remained at home except the two youngest — Margot, at last delivered from the convent, and Thérèse — she was able to give free reign to all her petty instincts. She was good at humiliating people, a talent which gives wickedness a very solid foundation. Thus every blessed evening she would cook two big steaks. One for my father and the other for herself.

"The price beef is at nowadays," she would say, "I can't buy steaks for everyone. You can eat applesauce."

Without counting the feeling of frustration one has, especially when one is young, to see others eat better at the same table, there is something profoundly humiliating in being treated in this way. When I try to imagine this scene, I am blinded by tears. This diet went on for a full year, and my father never found it unusual. A charming couple!

I won't tell everything. Some things are too stupid or too difficult to put into words. Too unbelievable, too. When she finally died after nine years, there wasn't any weeping.

"I didn't make a very good choice," my father said to Margot, after several weeks of widowhood. "She wasn't any too intelligent."

For my father to say that, a man who didn't like intellectuals — anyway, he married again six months later.

*　*　*

The year Dine was burned was also the year my father acquired his first son-in-law. Paul was still a medical student when he met Françoise. It was one of our friends, a student himself, who introduced them. After ten months of secret dating — for on this score nothing had changed, and although my father had been pushed into marriage in order to see us all safely established, we were still

compelled to secrecy as long as the suitor wasn't ready to be meta-
morphosed into a fiancé — Paul wanted to be presented to my
father. It was Easter time, he was going to get his doctor's degree
that summer. He was ready.

The scenario we had used to present Dine's boyfriend was used
over again, practically unchanged.

"I've met a boy. He is a friend of my friend Aline's brother."

As you can see, the only difference was that we now had the right
to see a few girls.

Paul was interning in a mental hospital. Naturally, some pretty
extravagant things went on there, but we had known him so long we
had heard all his stories ages ago. The first evening he came to open
his official courtship, I remember that Dine maliciously pushed him
into telling them all over again from beginning to end. Poor boy!
He was bored to tears. Since he was skeptical by nature, I don't
think he took all the stories we told him about my father very seriously. My father soon managed to set him right on that score.

The last Sunday in the university year the sisters at the hospital
decided, before the interns left, to organize a theatrical and musical
evening with the participation of patients who were not too seriously ill, many of whom had very real talents. The sisters thought
it would be a nice thing to ask Paul to bring his fiancée.

"Paul's on the telephone. The patients are giving a little concert
and the sisters have invited me to go."

Silent, incensed, my father couldn't take his eyes off his daughter.
Another blow of fate! You slave all your life to give your daughter a
sense of virtue and decency and all that, only to perceive suddenly
that she is still harbouring an old residue of licentiousness ready to
declare itself at the least provocation.

"What's that!" he roared finally. "But that boy wants to dishonour you! Did you ever take the trouble to think that if I let you
accept this invitation, that's the last you'll hear of him? That he'll

have every right to despise you? That's what he's trying to find out this very minute, whether you're marriageable or not."

"But the nuns will be there."

"They might have to leave you to look after some patient or other. It doesn't take very long to dishonour a girl. Even if nothing happened, even if you just get yourself into a situation where something bad might happen, you can't help giving this boy a very shabby idea of your virtue. He'll say to himself that if you're in the habit of running that kind of risk, someone has probably already taken advantage of it."

Paul was still waiting on the other end of the line. He must have found permission slow in coming. When he finally learned that Françoise hadn't been granted it, and why, he couldn't believe the receiver. But he was beginning to understand.

Our poor father was determined to drive into our heads that a man left alone with a woman can do only one thing: jump on her, undress her if he has the time, and if he hasn't it's all the same, and rape her. All that in less time than it takes for a nun to give a patient his medicine. That says a lot for the confidence he had in his system of claustration. It never occurred to him that we might, despite him, have some experience of solitude for two, and know that rape isn't necessary. The fact remains that it's a real disservice to girls to lead them to think that men are so ardent. They can't be anything but disappointed.

*   *   *

A few days later, Paul left the hospital. Now he had to find a village or small town where he could set up practice. At this juncture my father left on a trip. Ever since Françoise had become engaged, my father's departures were prefaced by a host of recommendations to his wife. Not to leave them alone for a second, not to let them out of her sight, et cetera. Then he left reassured. In which he was mistaken, for the stepmother didn't much like staying in the same room with Paul, whose irony frightened her. Besides, just like the rest of us, she took advantage of my father's trips to take a little air, to go and see her friends, and receive their visits. None of that was, strictly speaking, forbidden her, but it always provoked scenes and moods. So it was easier to do it in secret as we, the children, had always done.

Now finding herself at liberty, Françoise decided to accompany her fiancé on the tour of inspection he had planned. Dine was invited to chaperone. They left early in the morning and were to come back the same night. But my father must have cut his trip short, for he got back before they did. My stepmother and I had to face the music.

"Your father won't think Dine is enough as a chaperone," she whispered to me. "Tell him that Paul's aunt is with them."

O.K. I was always ready to add a little something for the sake of the common good. So off I sailed on a description of Paul's aunt, whom I had never seen in my life — hair, face, figure, clothes. As soon as the door of the conjugal bedroom had closed behind her, the stepmother speedily confessed that the aunt wasn't one of the party.

First visit of the father to his daughter:

"You lied to me. You made up that story about the aunt. Your stepmother's just admitted it."

"But she's the one who asked me to tell you that."

Second visit:

"Your stepmother assures me she didn't ask you anything of the kind. You're making your lie worse."

To that, no reply. I was disgusted. Such treachery was unheard of among us. Who were we living with!

Third, fourth and fifth visits:

"Do you realize that your sisters aren't back yet? That boy has probably led them into some evil haunt."

They got back at one in the morning. My father had fallen asleep in spite of everything. Françoise and I shared a room. I whispered to her what had happened. That didn't bother her particularly. She was soon getting married, and one hardly feels pain when the end is in sight. She went to sleep, and so did I. My father woke up about four and without waiting —

The last visit:

"My poor girl, you are dishonoured. Never again, you can be sure of that, never again will that boy even look at you. Your life is finished."

It went on for a good quarter of an hour, during which my father explained to Françoise that at dawn Paul would be out in the streets hawking the news of what had happened, making an open mockery of it, and that she, poor girl, would bear the stain to the end of her days. Did he really believe what he said, or did he just find it convenient to bring us up in the atmosphere of such threats? It's something I have never been able to disentangle.

Then my father went to Dine's room. There it was another line. Hadn't Paul picked up some other hoodlum in his car, just to keep the chaperone busy? Or better still, hadn't he dishonoured them both, one after the other? Such things had been known to happen. Once he got off on that track, there was no stopping my father's imagination. He found all sorts of muddy slopes and dizzying perspectives. At last he went back to bed, ready to take up the burden of his sermon at breakfast. We were so preoccupied shooting furious looks at our stepmother, which made her ears turn red, that we scarcely listened to him. Just before he left for the office, he fired his final sally.

"I have told you, Françoise, and I'll say it again. You can wash that boy right out of your mind. He won't ever want to see you

again. Besides, he wouldn't dare show his face to me after dishon-
ouring my two daughters."

Then he left, slamming the door. When he came back at five,
Paul was already there. My father didn't show any surprise, and
didn't breathe a word about yesterday's happenings. As if nothing
had happened. Paul, who was never short on impertinence,
explained at length the advantages and disadvantages of the villages
he had visited. My father nodded in agreement. It was mainly in
dealing with women that he was brave.

Finally Paul made his choice and left to open his office in a village somewhere on the south shore. He wrote every day. Françoise
and I would go to get the mail at the post office. Myself, I didn't get
any daily letter. There was, as a matter of fact, a young man in my
life who was a doctor too, but his letters were of a different kind.
They were weekly, secret, boring, and riddled with spelling mistakes. Which didn't stop me from waiting for them feverishly all the
same. One afternoon after reading Paul's letter, Ti-Fan looked at
me with that expression she has for grand occasions, and which is
always accompanied by large red splotches on her neck.

"It's for October 20," she said.

"What's for October 20?"

"My wedding."

I was stunned and realized all at once that I had never really
believed in this marriage. No more than in marriage for any of us.
I was witnessing a miracle. Not a dead man brought back to life, but
a real miracle, like a legless person whose legs grow on again, who
gets up and walks off. I was in seventh heaven. I, too, would get
married. I was in love with someone too, wasn't I? At least I was
convinced I was, because even at twenty I still hadn't learned to see
the difference between love and my wish to get out from under the
paternal roof. This boy wasn't good looking, he had a ridiculous
name, he didn't have any of the qualities that I admire — simplicity,

disinterestedness, generosity, love of work. What did that matter? I had decided I was in love. Even at that, any pithecanthrope who had asked for my hand in marriage would have seen my affections swing his way, and feverishly at that! I had quite forgotten, I can see, the promises I had made to Grandmother. All I looked for in boys was the quality of the conductor who shouts "All aboard." And it's because girls are pressed to marry for such silly reasons that a great many conductors wind up as station masters.

Françoise was getting married. Just to look at her, I could hear the music of the hymn to liberty. I didn't know that music isn't always the wedding march, and that one mustn't mix genres. Since a little peace seemed to me a modest wish, I counted on achieving it by a modest choice, for I didn't know that peace is a great possession that comes to you from the possession of things that are greater still. I was ready to step into the first marriage that came along. Life was to keep its promises quite differently, and far beyond what I was then asking of it.

Only a few weeks remained before the twentieth of October. Françoise began to get her trousseau ready. By great good fortune, Paul had inherited household linen and the necessary furniture to set them up, for rarely has the young bride of a well-to-do family brought so little to her husband. My father paid out the first dollars without too much asking, but at the second request he declared that he wasn't bound to pay such expenses. Marrying off his daughter cost him not quite one hundred dollars, reception included. And he complained bitterly. To hear him, it was a blow he would never recover from.

The day before the wedding, all the women of the house joined forces to prepare the wedding lunch. The stepmother's best friend came to help us with the petits fours and everything that could be got ready ahead of time. It was agreed that I would take charge of the other dishes. That was decided the moment I asked for a new hat to wear at the ceremony.

"A hat? And who'll stay at home and put the finishing touches on everything?"

The one who asked for a hat, naturally.

In short, when all the little problems connected with a wedding had been settled in the most disagreeable way imaginable, dawn finally broke on October twentieth.

When he had finished sprucing up and had put on his morning coat, my father decided to hoist the Union Jack over the house. We were nearly all married this way, under the protection of the British flag, which annoyed us a great deal, not so much for the obvious reasons, but because my father never went to raise it until he was dressed for the ceremony, with the result that we were all given away by a father who was a little creased, dusty at the edges, and, when the flag started to get old, adorned with one or two red wool threads. Not to speak of the fact that the operation was dangerous and we were afraid he might fall. Oh, no!

Once His Gracious Majesty's standard was raised, everyone left for the church. Alone in the car with Françoise, my father realized that perhaps the time had come for a "talk" with his daughter.

"Do you know what to expect?" he asked her point blank. "Have you consulted a priest?"

I haven't said yet that my sister was twenty-four years old, and I think this is the place to mention it.

"Yes, yes," she said without cracking a smile.

"And there's something else. You're marrying a boy who looks pretty frail to me. It's all your doing. If you become a widow, don't count on coming back to me with all your brats."

Charming man! That reminds me of the advice he gave me when it was my turn to marry.

"I don't know your fiancé any too well," he said. "I hope you're marrying a good man."

356 • In an Iron Glove

"Oh! the best in the world!" I replied. "Intelligent, cultivated, gay and marvellously gentle."

My father gave me a black look.

"My girl, intelligence and gentleness aren't in the least important. I am asking you if he's a good Catholic, and I don't care a rap about the rest."

So, leaving my father to his own personal cares, I went on caring about the rest for both of us.

Coming back to Françoise's marriage, there followed a dissertation on the obligation of maternal breast-feeding for every Christian woman, complete with explanations, motivations, deductions, the whole casuistry of the thing. Completely abashed, Ti-Fan found the last moments of her single state interminable.

While the two families revelled in the splendours of the religious ceremony, I busied myself in the kitchen and in laying out the buffet in the dining room. When they arrived, everything was in readiness. The reception was gloomy. Paul's sister and brothers were intimidated. They immediately perceived that we were of the monastic breed. The total absence of anything you might put in a glass proved that well enough, and those who were thirsty had to wait for the coffee.

My father's brother and his wife, who were Françoise's godfather and godmother, were the only guests on the bride's side. For, naturally, there was no question of asking Uncle Eugène and Aunt Berthe, and as for my father's sister, we hadn't been on speaking terms for almost a year. One day the poor woman had let slip an unlucky remark which concealed a veiled allusion to her brother's baldness. She should have known better that forgiveness didn't come any more easily to him than to the celebrated prophet Elisha who had so shocked me when I was small because he had thrown to the bears forty-odd kids who had called him "baldy," but without a trace of evil intent, I'm sure. This quarrel lasted fourteen years.

If I remember rightly, there were fifteen or sixteen of us at the wedding lunch, counting the bishop who had blessed the union. Fifteen people who were as silent as one. Thoroughly enervated, Françoise was on the verge of tears. Each minute that came along might bring a scene with it, and yet they all had to be lived through, each and every one. At last, after having been reduced to silence, embarrassment and boredom for so long, the moment that everyone had been waiting for arrived, and it was time for the young couple to depart. My father pronounced a few deeply felt words on the sadness and emotion a young girl feels on leaving the paternal roof, the car doors slammed and Paul drove away with the first of my father's daughters to marry.

*   *   *

"Well!" sighed Dine on the evening of the wedding day, "if someone had told me that one of us would find a husband — "

My father reacted vigorously hearing this remark, in which he detected a whiff of unpleasantness directed his way.

"Is that your way of reproaching me for not letting you run the streets?"

He wasn't in any mood to ignore such insinuations. There was something in the day's proceedings that he couldn't get over. Not only was one of his daughters alone with a man this very night, but all his other daughters knew their sister to be alone with a man. So after Françoise's departure, he prowled around like a bear in a cage and would come and peer into our faces to see if we seemed to be harbouring any lecherous thoughts. Dine's sigh was really the height of impropriety.

He went on talking, but nobody listened.

Ottawa, April 1957–July 1966

NOTES

THE LEFT CHEEK

1. In *Dictionnaire général de biographie, histoire, littérature, agriculture, commerce, industrie et des arts, sciences, moeurs, coutumes, institutions politiques et religieuses du Canada* by the Reverend Father Louis Le Jeune Volume II, p. 248, one may read:

"MARTIN (Abraham) (d. 1664), known as 'the Scot,' pilot, farmer, clerk of the *Compagnie des Marchands.*"

There follow the principal details, some certain, some hypothetical, about his life. Then the article lists his children, only the daughters, seven of them, married. No information is provided about the elder of his two sons except the date of his baptism, at Quebec in 1621. The second son became a priest and was the first curé of Sainte-Foy.

"Thus," says the account, "the name of Martin like that of Hébert, was not perpetuated by the male line but only by the Plains of Abraham."

On reflection, this state of affairs is even more catastrophic for the Héberts who don't even have an Abraham. The Reverend Father Le Jeune was a Breton. He was born at Pleyber-Christ, in the department of Finistère, in France. He died at Ottawa in 1935 [C. Martin].

2. One of a group of five hundred Canadian volunteers who joined the papal army in 1868 to defend the temporal power of the pope [P. Smart].

3. Her real name wasn't so sweet. For that matter, I have changed the names of all the bad ones because, who knows, perhaps they turned good [C. Martin].

4. Cf. French: *connerie* – goddam stupidity [P. Smart].

5. Cf. French: *cul* [P. Stratford].

6. *Caparaçonnée* [P. Stratford].

7. *Imbécillité* [P. Stratford].

8. Although Claire Martin has told us she doesn't remember this nun's real name, she has made a little joke with her choice of pseudonym: Figaro, of course, is the popular character in Beaumarchais' trilogy of plays, *Le barbier de Séville (The Barber of Seville)*, *Le mariage de Figaro (The Marriage of Figaro)*, and *La mère coupable (The Guilty Mother)*, two of which were made into operas (*The Marriage of Figaro* by Mozart and *The Barber of Seville* by Rossini) [P. Smart].

9. See Introduction, page xxi.

THE RIGHT CHEEK

1. Noël de Chamilly was the lover and the recipient of the love letters of Sister Marianna Alcoforado, which were published in France under the title "Lettres portugaises" (known in their many English editions as "Portuguese Letters"). It is generally believed today that this book was a literary fake, and that the real author of the letters was Gabriel Joseph de Lavergne, vicomte de Guilleragues (1628-1685) [P. Smart].

2. Louise-Françoise de La Baume Le Blanc, mistress of Louis XIV from 1661 to 1667, received the title of duchesse de la Vallière

after being supplanted in the king's affections by the marquise de Montespan. The duchesse retired to a Carmelite monastery in 1674 [P. Smart].

3. Vercingetorix (72–46 BCE), a leader of the Gauls, joined battle with the Roman conquerors. He was defeated by Caesar at Dijon in 52 BCE and died in prison at Rome [P. Smart].

4. All novelists, but of a range of different types. Chantepleure (pseudonym taken by Mme. Edgar Dussap) and Dekobra were primarily sentimental writers; Mauriac's novels of intrigue explored the passions and the Jansenist sense of guilt of the Catholic bourgeoisie in his native region of Bordeaux; Fleuriot wrote novels from a conservative, Catholic viewpoint, intended to edify; Marguerite was a militant writer, particularly with respect to the emancipation of women; and Delly, actually a sister and brother writing in collaboration, produced novels of adventure and love that had a wide readership among the female public [P. Smart].

5. I couldn't forgive myself if I didn't use here that wonderfully descriptive Quebec word *placoteuses* which combines the merits of connotation and onomatopoeia [C. Martin].

WORKS BY CLAIRE MARTIN

Avec ou sans amour. Montréal: Le Cercle du livre de France, 1958. (*Love Me, Love Me Not,* trans. David Lobdell. Ottawa: Oberon Press, 1987).

Doux-amer. Montréal: Le Cercle du livre de France, 1960. (*Best Man,* trans. David Lobdell. Ottawa: Oberon Press, 1983).

Quand j'aurai payé ton visage. Montréal: Le Cercle du livre de France, 1962. (*The Legacy,* trans. David Lobdell. Ottawa: Oberon Press, 1986.)

Dans un gant de fer. Part I: La joue gauche. Montréal: Le Cercle du livre de France, 1965; *Dans un gant de fer II: La joue droite.* Montréal: Le Cercle du livre de France, 1966. (*In an Iron Glove,* trans. Philip Stratford. Toronto: The Ryerson Press, 1968.)

Les morts. Montréal: Le Cercle du livre de France, 1970.

Moi, je n'étais qu'espoir. Montréal: Le Cercle du livre de France, 1972.

La petite fille lit. Ottawa: Éditions de l'Université d'Ottawa, 1973.

Toute la vie. Québec: L'instant même, 1999.

L'amour impuni. Québec: L'instant même, 2000.

La brigande. Québec: L'instant même, 2001.

Il s'appelait Thomas. Québec: L'instant même, 2003.

L'inconnu parle encore. Québec: L'instant même, 2004.

BIOGRAPHICAL NOTES

*C*LAIRE MARTIN was born on April 18, 1914, in Quebec City. She studied at the convent of the Ursuline sisters and later at that of the Congrégation de Nôtre-Dame. She began working as a secretary in 1937 but soon traded in her typewriter for a microphone, becoming a broadcaster with CKCV and later with Radio-Canada. In August 1945 she married Roland Faucher in Ottawa. In 1958 she published her first book, a prizewinning collection of short fiction. Several novels as well as her autobiography were to follow over the next decade and a half. In 1972 Claire Martin left for France with her husband. During her time there she translated works by such well-known Canadian authors as Margaret Laurence and Robertson Davies. In 1982 she returned from France to live in Quebec City, where her husband died four years later. Since 1999 she has published a collection of short stories and several novels. Claire Martin has received a number of awards for her writing, including the Prix du Cercle du livre de France, the Prix de la Province de Québec, the Prix France-Québec, the Governor General's Award, and the Médaille de l'Académie des Lettres du Québec. She became a Companion of the Order of Canada in 2001.

*P*ATRICIA SMART is the author of a critical edition of Claire Martin's autobiography *Dans un gant de fer* (Les Presses de l'Université de Montréal, 2005). A Distinguished Research Professor of French at Carleton University, Dr. Smart is the author of *Les Femmes du Refus global* (Boréal, 1998), a finalist for the 1998 Governor General's Award. Her feminist study of Quebec literature, *Écrire dans la maison du Père* (Éditions Québec/Amérique), won the Governor General's Award for 1988, and her translation of it, *Writing in the Father's House: The Emergence of the Feminine in the Quebec Literary Tradition* (University of Toronto Press 1991), was awarded the Gabrielle Roy Prize of the Association for Canadian and Quebec Literatures. She was an editor of *The Canadian Forum* from 1989 to 1998, was elected to the Royal Society of Canada in 1991, and received the Order of Canada in 2005.

*B*orn in Chatham, Ontario, in 1927, PHILIP STRATFORD studied at University of Western Ontario and did his doctorate in Comparative Literature at the Sorbonne, in Paris, where he met his wife. They shared their life between France and Canada and raised six children. He died in 1999, after having published his memoirs, *Hawthorn House*.

Winner of the Governor General's Award for Translation, Philip Stratford was one of the most knowledgeable observers and critics of the Quebec literary scene. He was one of the founding members of the Quebec Translators' Association, having translated works by André Laurendeau, Antonine Maillet, Félix Leclerc, Robert Melançon, and many other French-Canadian writers, as well as René Lévesque's *Memoirs*. He is the author of *All the Polarities*, a comparison of English- and French-Canadian fiction. Philip Stratford taught English-Canadian and French-Canadian Literature at Université de Montréal for over thirty years. He was also an accomplished Graham Greene scholar and poet.